O.C.T.

OCCULT CRIMES TASKFORCE

12-GAUGE

OCCULT CRIMES TASKFORCE

HQ STATION F-31, 022575.

WRITTEN BY DAVID ATCHISON W/ ROSARIO DAWSON
ILLUSTRATED BY TONY SHASTEEN
EDITED BY BRIAN STELFREEZE & KEVEN GARDNER
LETTERING BY MATTY RYAN
LOGO AND BOOK DESIGN BY TONY SHASTEEN

12 GAUGE COMICS
PRESIDENT KEVEN GARDNER
MANAGING EDITOR DOUG WAGNER
ART DIRECTOR BRIAN STELFREEZE
DIRECTOR OF DEVELOPMENT JASON PEARSON
CREATIVE CONSULTANT CULLY HAMNER

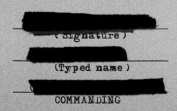

(Signature)

(Typed name)

COMMANDING

CONFIDENTIAL

OCCULT CRIMES TASKFORCE, VOL. 1
ISBN: 978-1-58240-675-6

IMAGE COMICS, INC.

® **ERIK LARSEN** - Publisher
TODD McFARLANE - President
MARC SILVESTRI - CEO
JIM VALENTINO - Vice-President

ERIC STEPHENSON - Executive Director
MARK HAVEN BRITT - Director of Marketing
THAO LE - Accounts Manager
ROSEMARY CAO - Accounting Assistant
TRACI HUI - Administrative Assistant
JOE KEATINGE - Traffic Manager
ALLEN HUI - Production Manager
JONATHAN CHAN - Production Artist
DREW GILL - Production Artist
CHRIS GIARRUSSO - Production Artist

WWW.IMAGECOMICS.COM

DEDICATION

I would like to thank Grand Mother Isabel
"Mima" Stokilo, Uncle Gustavo "Skunky
Goospapo" Vazquez, and Brother Clay
Alexander Dawson, my greatest comics
resource.

> — Rosario Dawson

I would like to thank Mom Heidi, Pop Jesse,
bros Mark and Joseph. Friends: Khalil Reid.
Derrick Baxter. Curtis Jenkins.

> — David Atchison

To Sarena, my wife and my best friend. To my
boys, Jay and Max. Without the support and
understanding of my family, this would not
have been possible.

> — Tony Shasteen

Chapter One

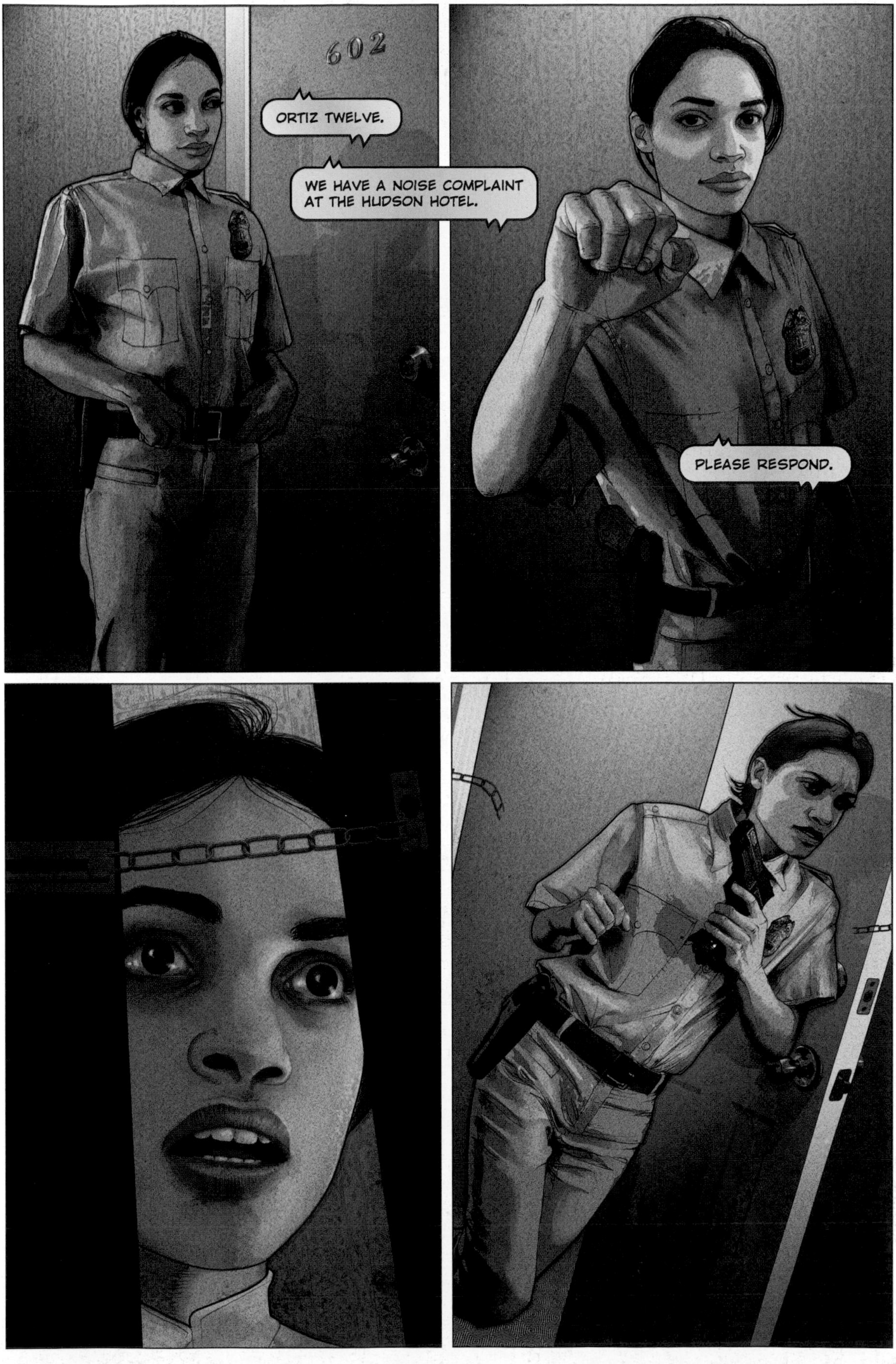
602
ORTIZ TWELVE.
WE HAVE A NOISE COMPLAINT AT THE HUDSON HOTEL.
PLEASE RESPOND.

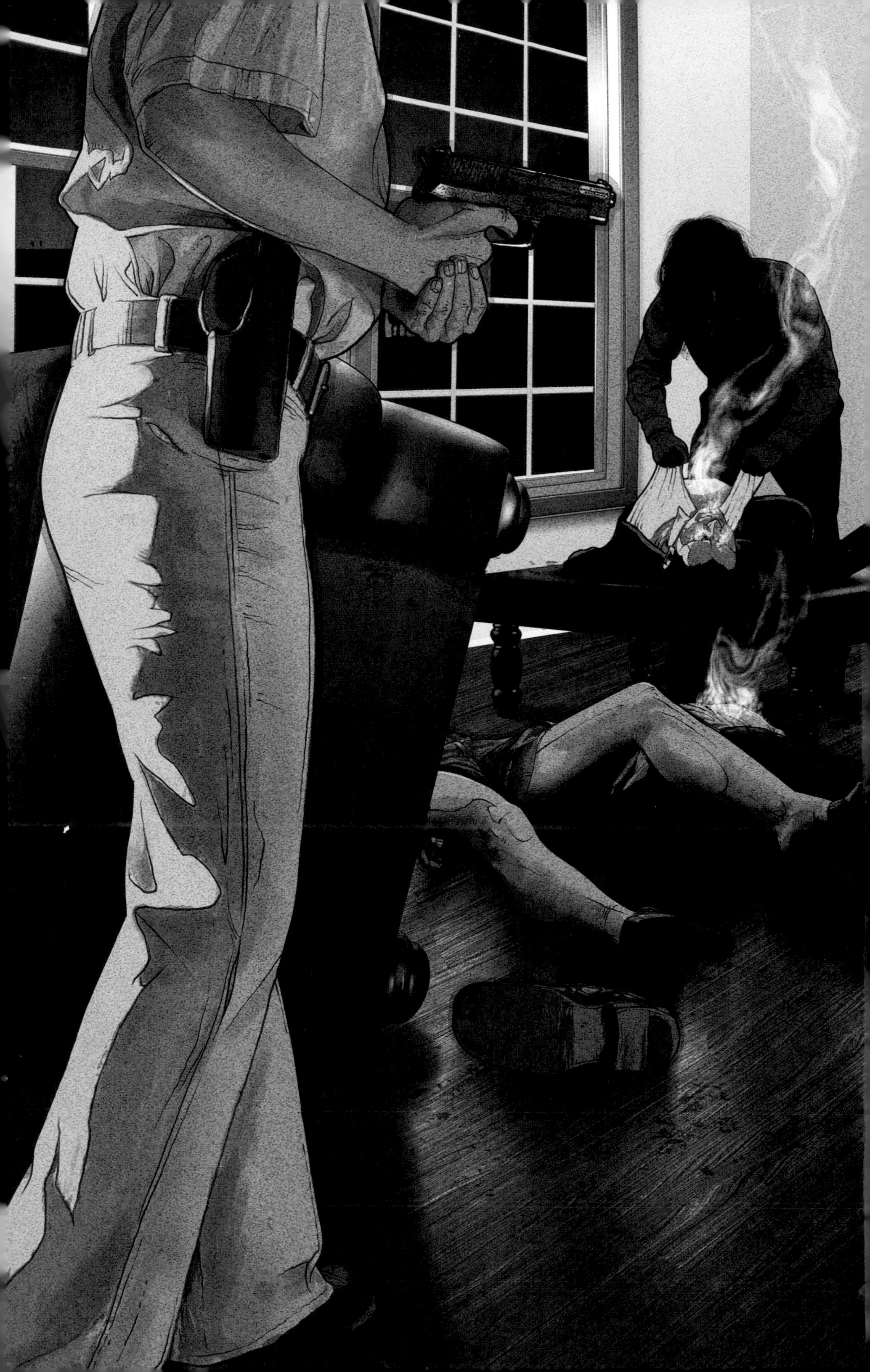

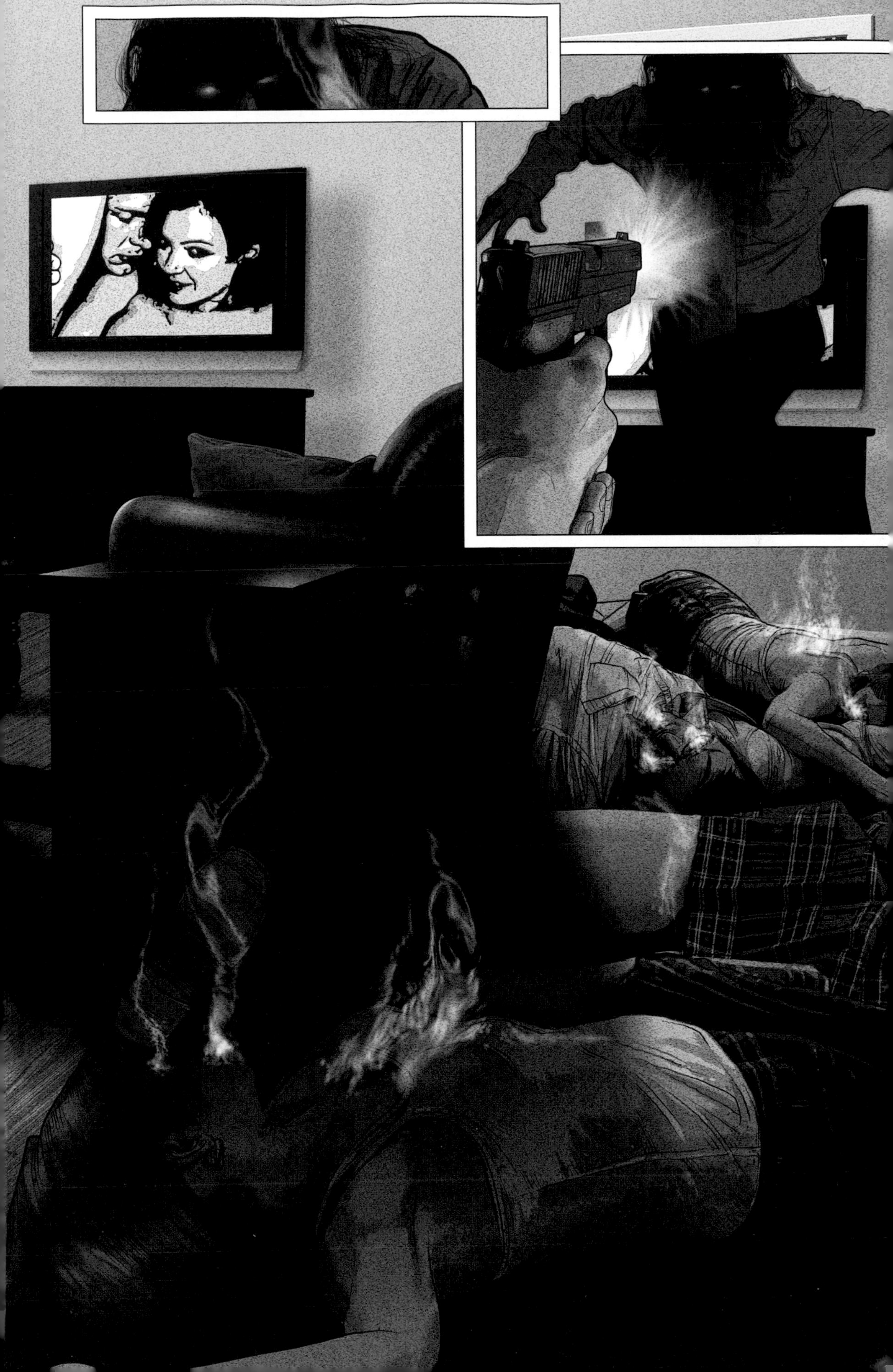

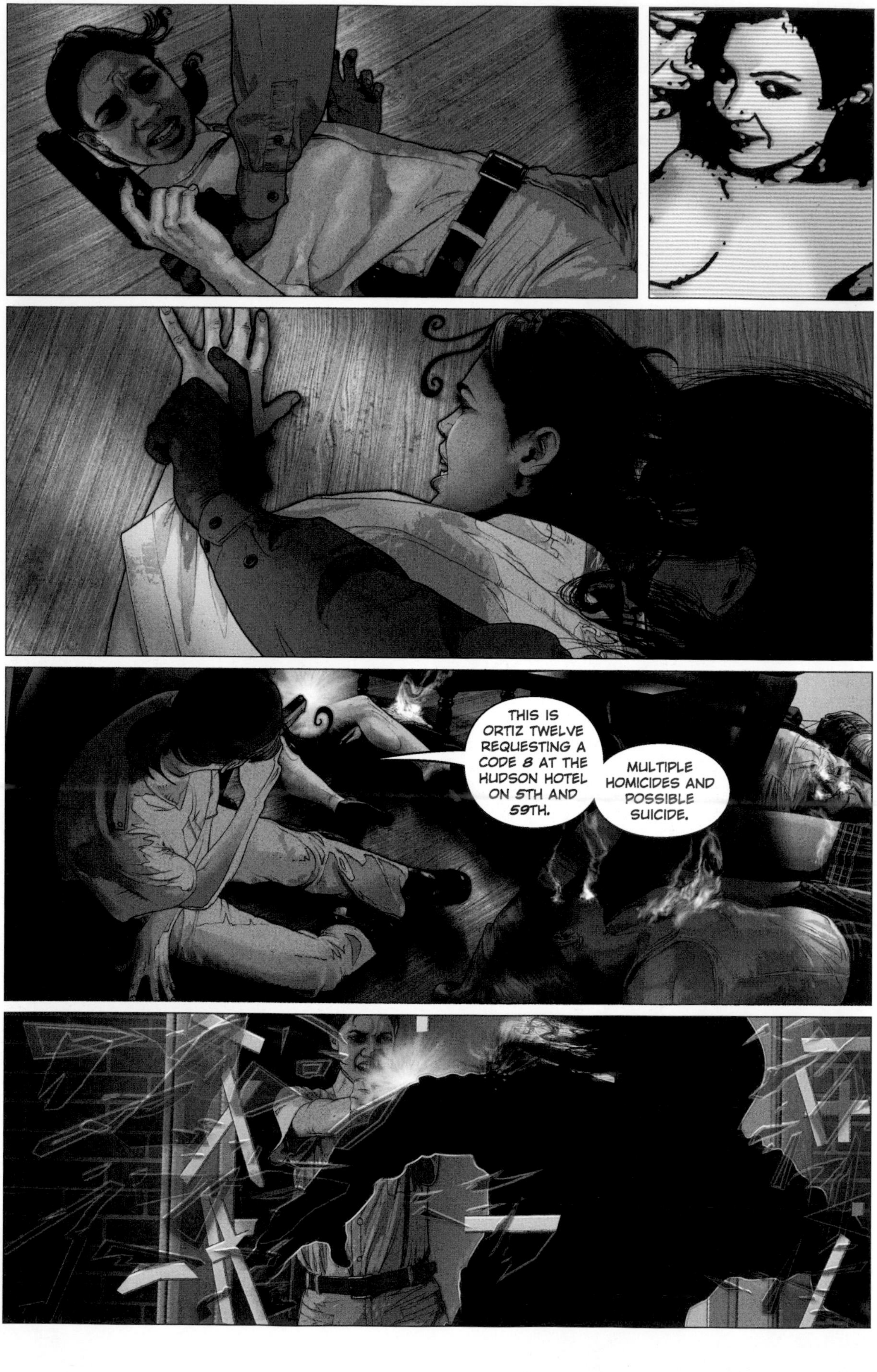
THIS IS ORTIZ TWELVE REQUESTING A CODE 8 AT THE HUDSON HOTEL ON 5TH AND 59TH.
MULTIPLE HOMICIDES AND POSSIBLE SUICIDE.

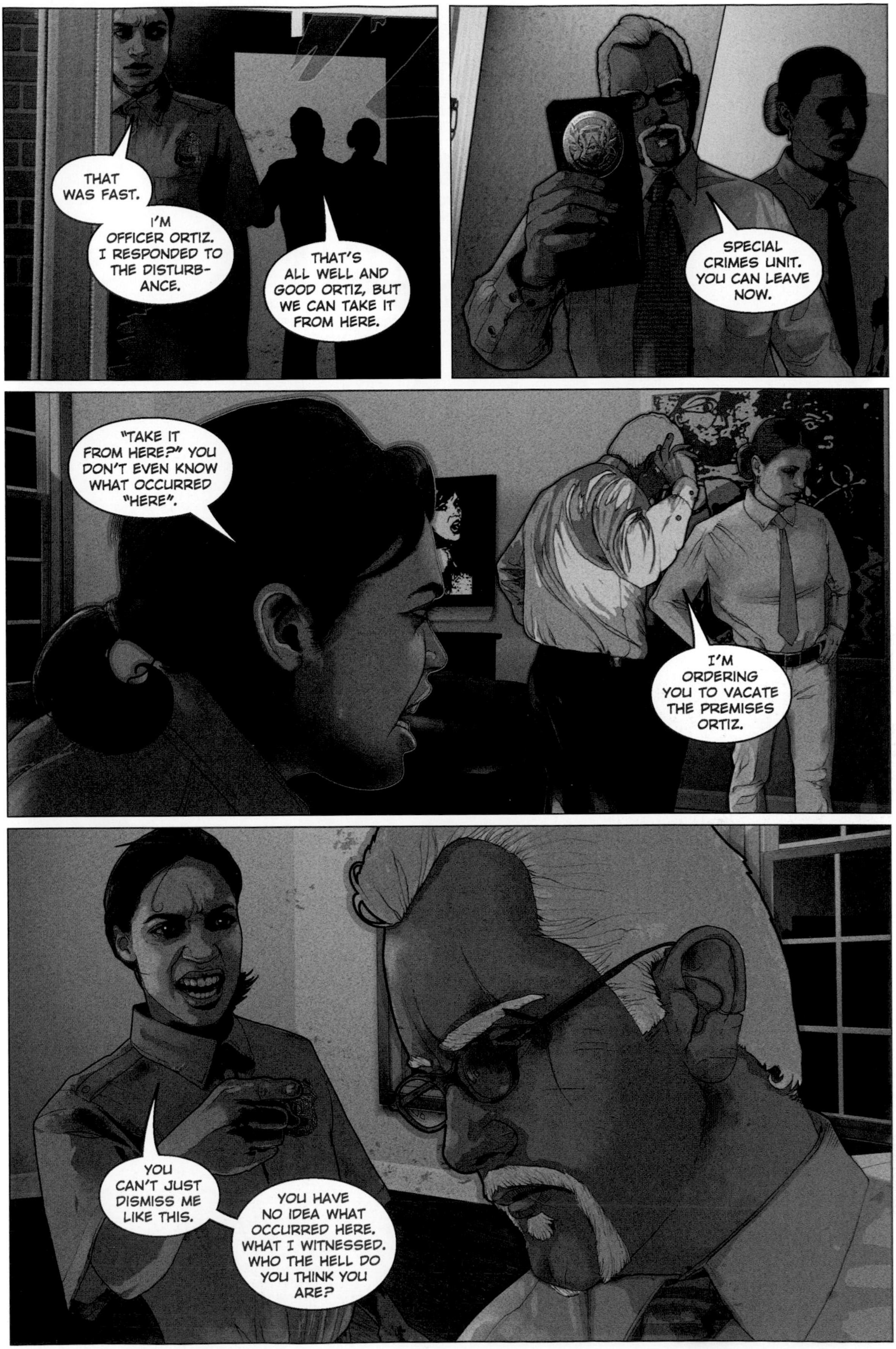
THAT WAS FAST.
I'M OFFICER ORTIZ. I RESPONDED TO THE DISTURB-ANCE.
THAT'S ALL WELL AND GOOD ORTIZ, BUT WE CAN TAKE IT FROM HERE.
SPECIAL CRIMES UNIT. YOU CAN LEAVE NOW.
"TAKE IT FROM HERE?" YOU DON'T EVEN KNOW WHAT OCCURRED "HERE".
I'M ORDERING YOU TO VACATE THE PREMISES ORTIZ.
YOU CAN'T JUST DISMISS ME LIKE THIS.
YOU HAVE NO IDEA WHAT OCCURRED HERE. WHAT I WITNESSED. WHO THE HELL DO YOU THINK YOU ARE?

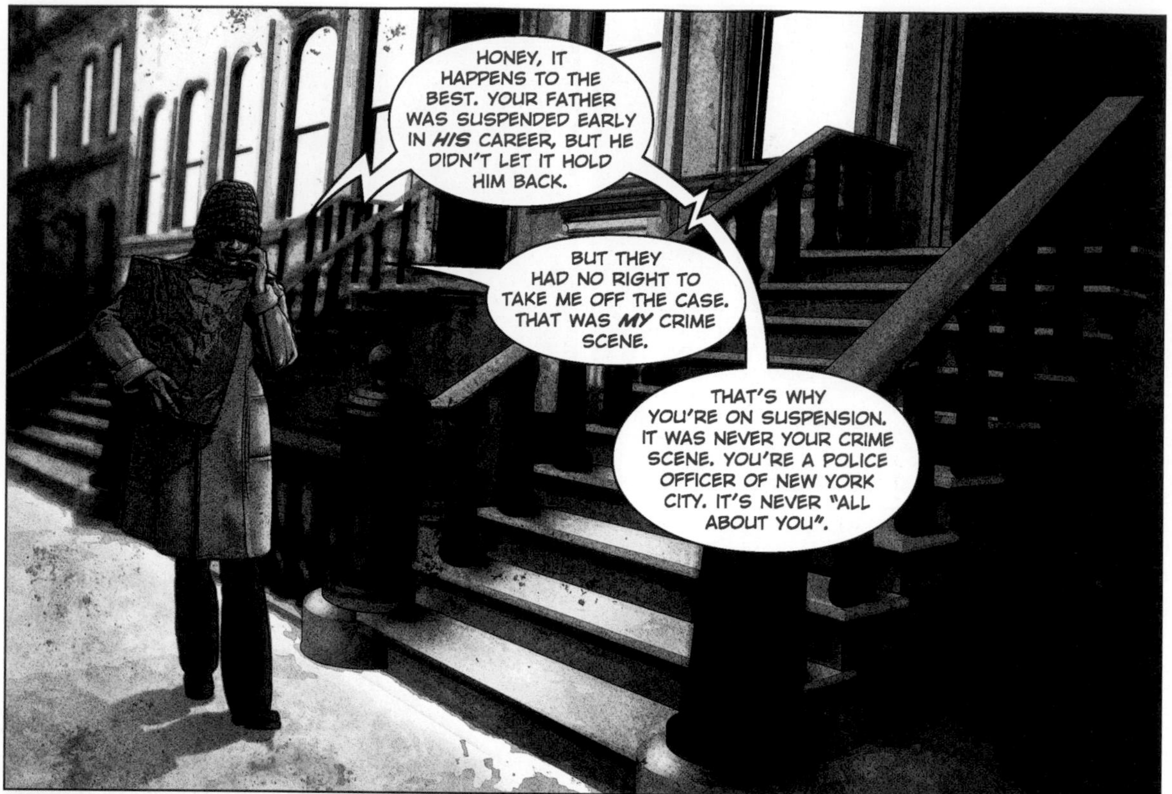
HONEY, IT HAPPENS TO THE BEST. YOUR FATHER WAS SUSPENDED EARLY IN *HIS* CAREER, BUT HE DIDN'T LET IT HOLD HIM BACK.
BUT THEY HAD NO RIGHT TO TAKE ME OFF THE CASE. THAT WAS *MY* CRIME SCENE.
THAT'S WHY YOU'RE ON SUSPENSION. IT WAS NEVER YOUR CRIME SCENE. YOU'RE A POLICE OFFICER OF NEW YORK CITY. IT'S NEVER "ALL ABOUT YOU".

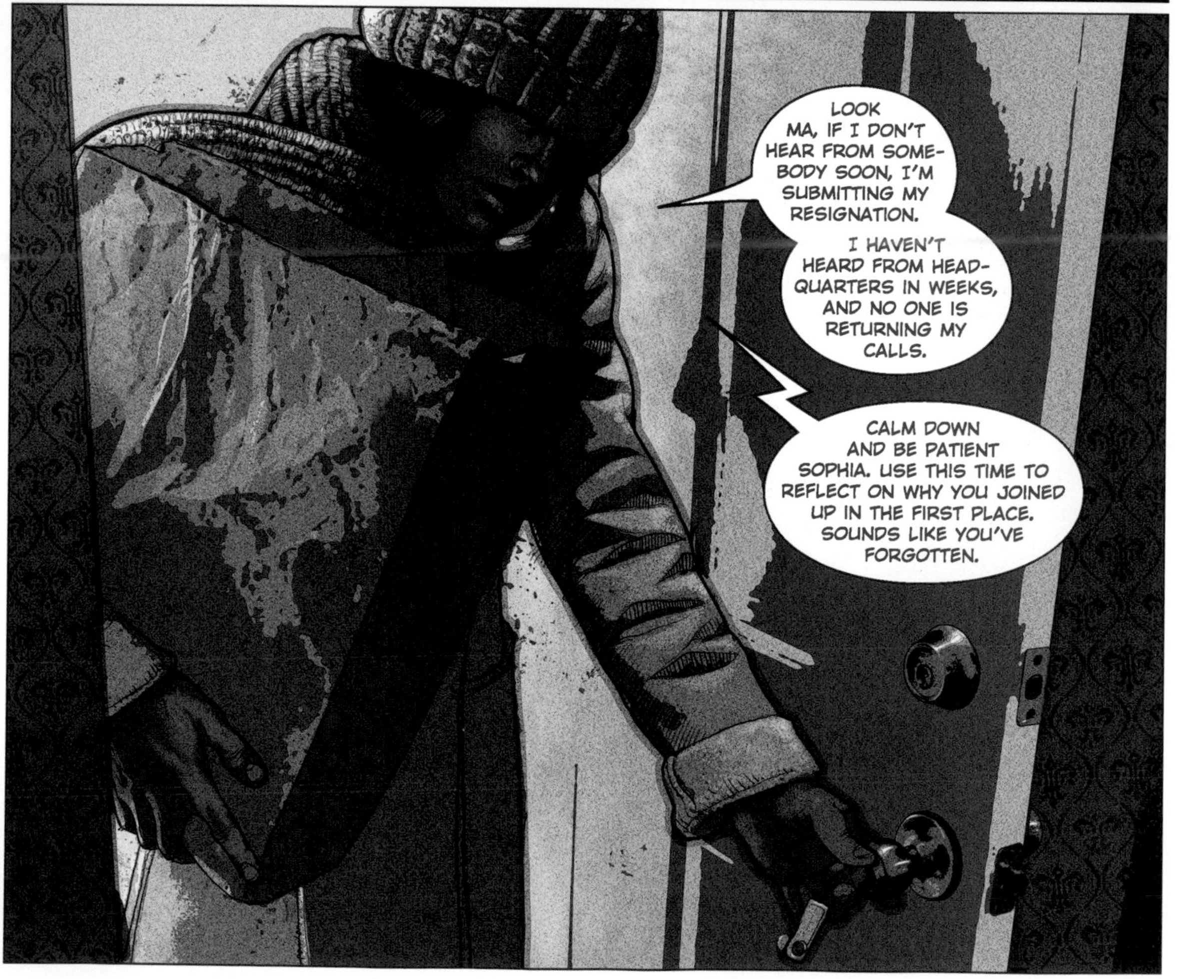
LOOK MA, IF I DON'T HEAR FROM SOME-BODY SOON, I'M SUBMITTING MY RESIGNATION.
I HAVEN'T HEARD FROM HEAD-QUARTERS IN WEEKS, AND NO ONE IS RETURNING MY CALLS.
CALM DOWN AND BE PATIENT SOPHIA. USE THIS TIME TO REFLECT ON WHY YOU JOINED UP IN THE FIRST PLACE. SOUNDS LIKE YOU'VE FORGOTTEN.

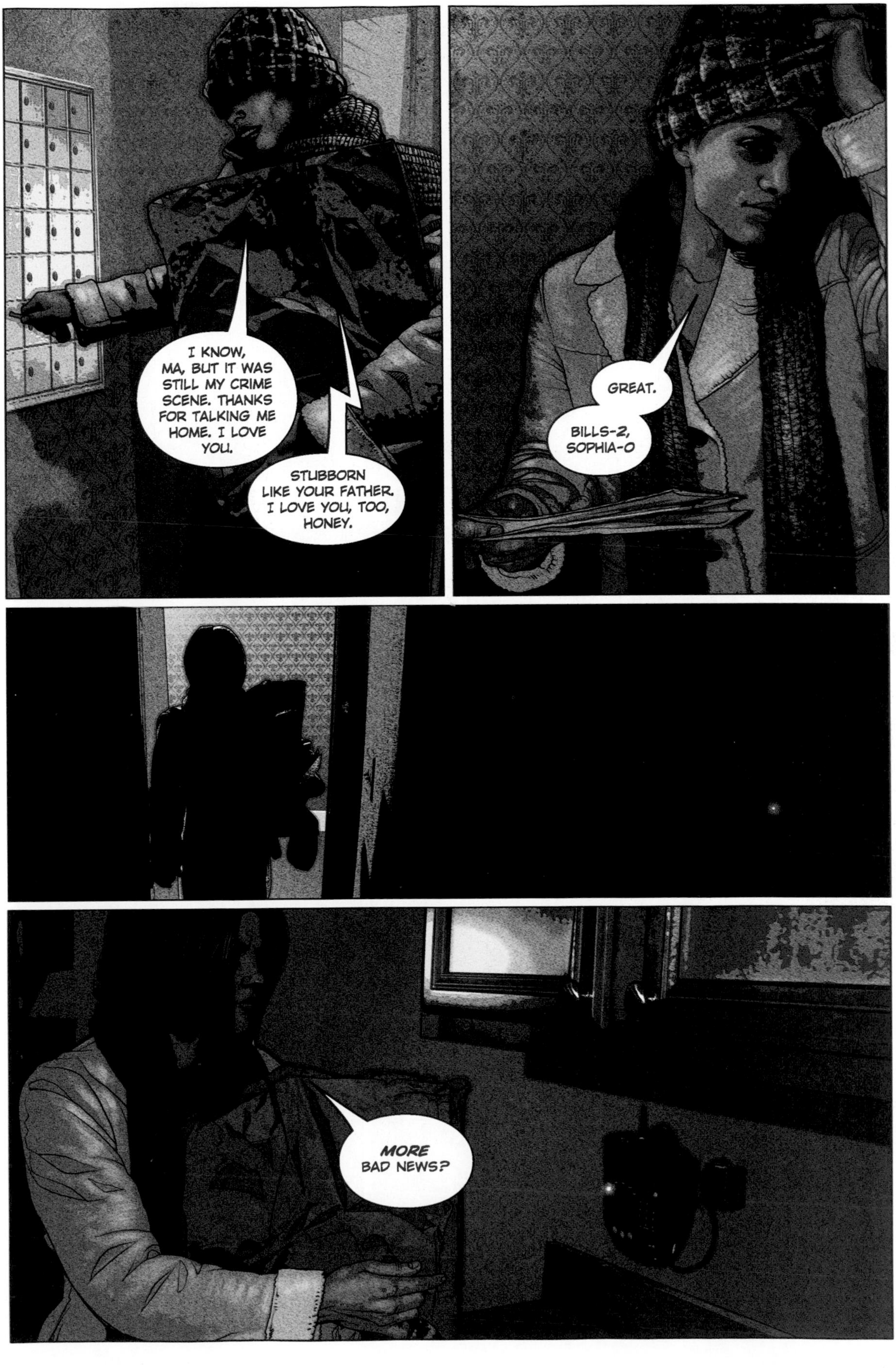
I KNOW, MA, BUT IT WAS STILL MY CRIME SCENE. THANKS FOR TALKING ME HOME. I LOVE YOU.
STUBBORN LIKE YOUR FATHER. I LOVE YOU, TOO, HONEY.
GREAT.
BILLS-2, SOPHIA-0
MORE BAD NEWS?

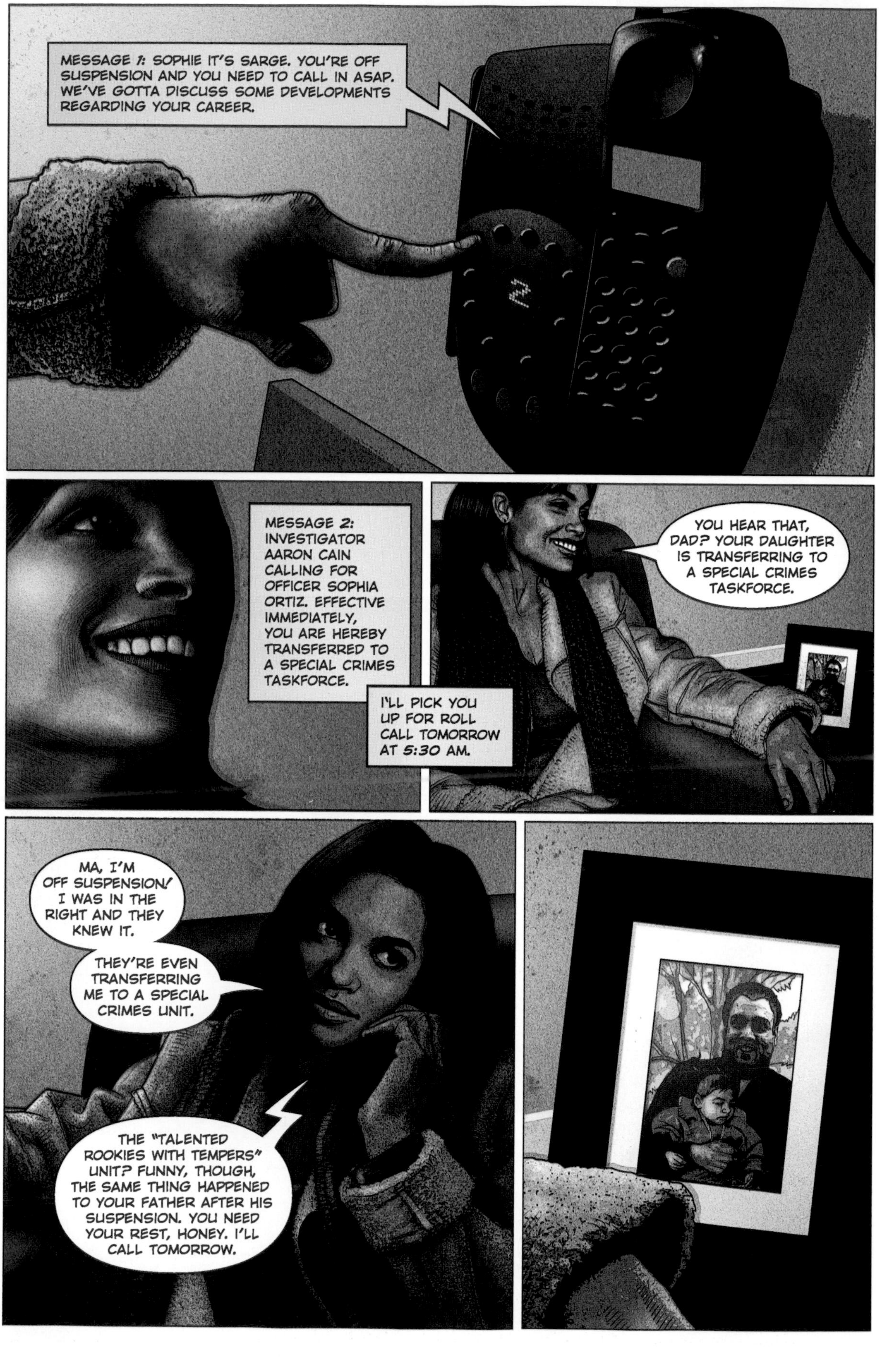
MESSAGE 1: SOPHIE IT'S SARGE. YOU'RE OFF SUSPENSION AND YOU NEED TO CALL IN ASAP. WE'VE GOTTA DISCUSS SOME DEVELOPMENTS REGARDING YOUR CAREER.
MESSAGE 2: INVESTIGATOR AARON CAIN CALLING FOR OFFICER SOPHIA ORTIZ. EFFECTIVE IMMEDIATELY, YOU ARE HEREBY TRANSFERRED TO A SPECIAL CRIMES TASKFORCE.
I'LL PICK YOU UP FOR ROLL CALL TOMORROW AT 5:30 AM.
YOU HEAR THAT, DAD? YOUR DAUGHTER IS TRANSFERRING TO A SPECIAL CRIMES TASKFORCE.
MA, I'M OFF SUSPENSION! I WAS IN THE RIGHT AND THEY KNEW IT.
THEY'RE EVEN TRANSFERRING ME TO A SPECIAL CRIMES UNIT.
THE "TALENTED ROOKIES WITH TEMPERS" UNIT? FUNNY, THOUGH, THE SAME THING HAPPENED TO YOUR FATHER AFTER HIS SUSPENSION. YOU NEED YOUR REST, HONEY. I'LL CALL TOMORROW.

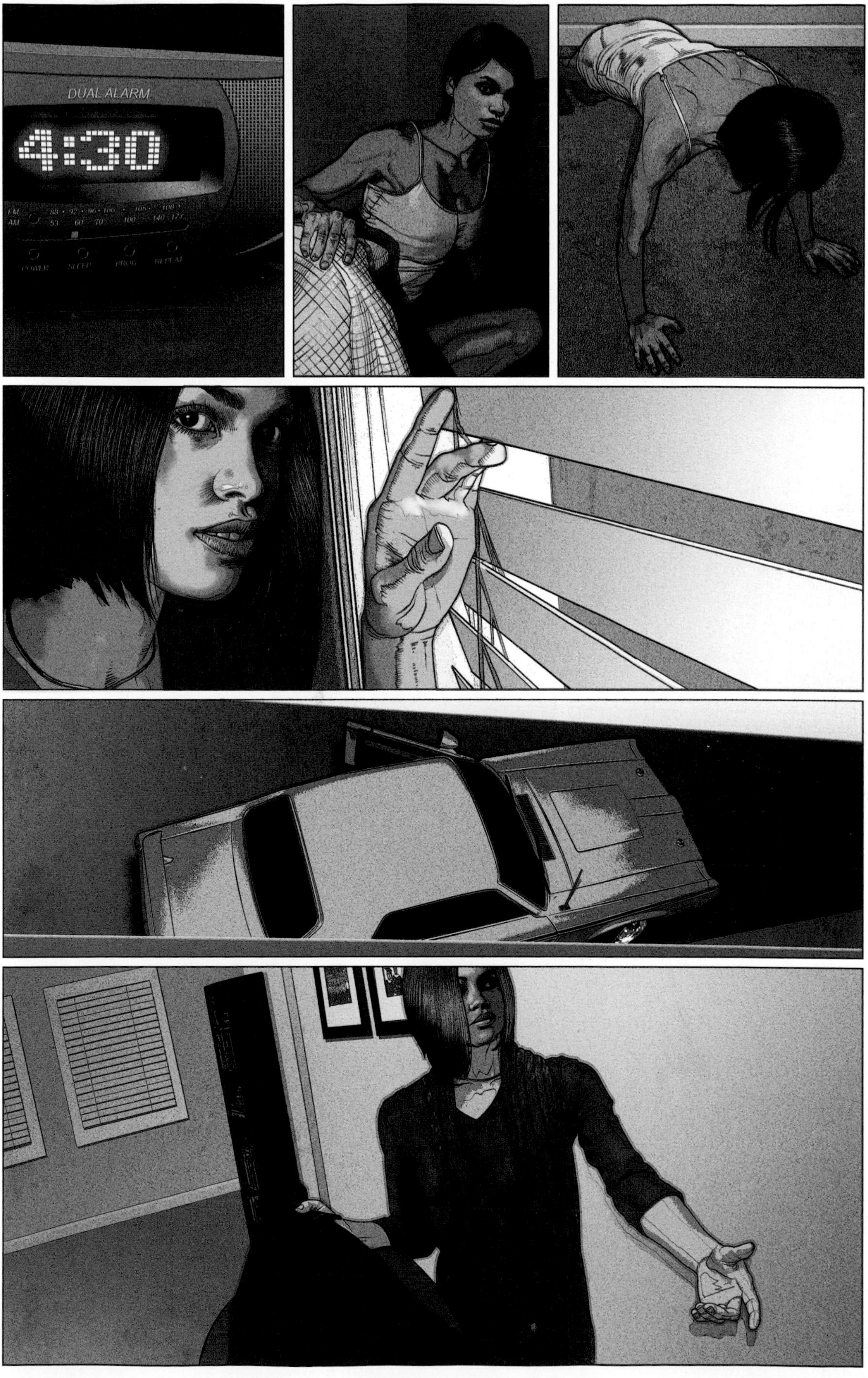
DUAL ALARM
4:30
POWER
SLEEP
PROG
REPEAT

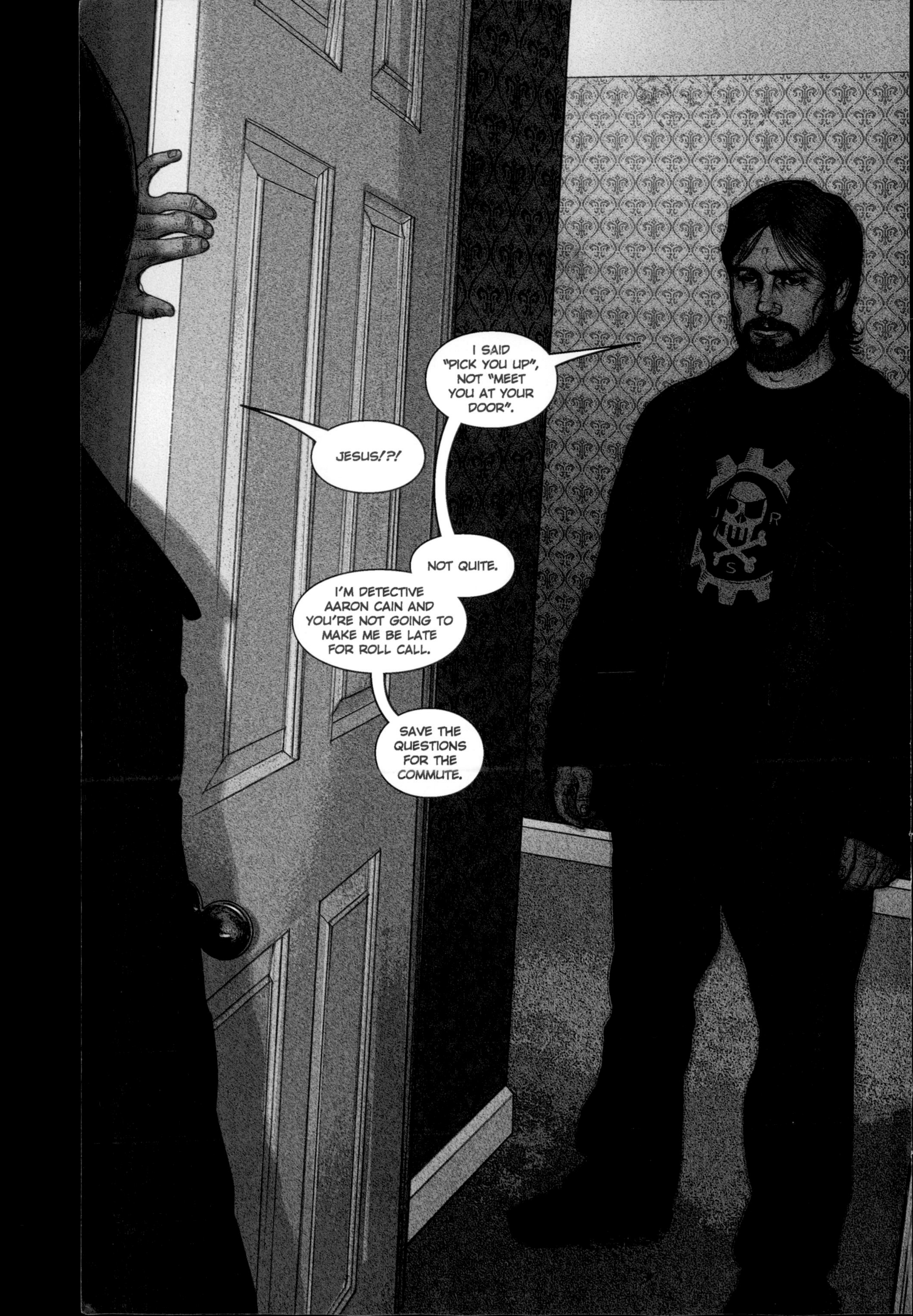
I SAID "PICK YOU UP", NOT "MEET YOU AT YOUR DOOR".
JESUS!?!
NOT QUITE.
I'M DETECTIVE AARON CAIN AND YOU'RE NOT GOING TO MAKE ME BE LATE FOR ROLL CALL.
SAVE THE QUESTIONS FOR THE COMMUTE.

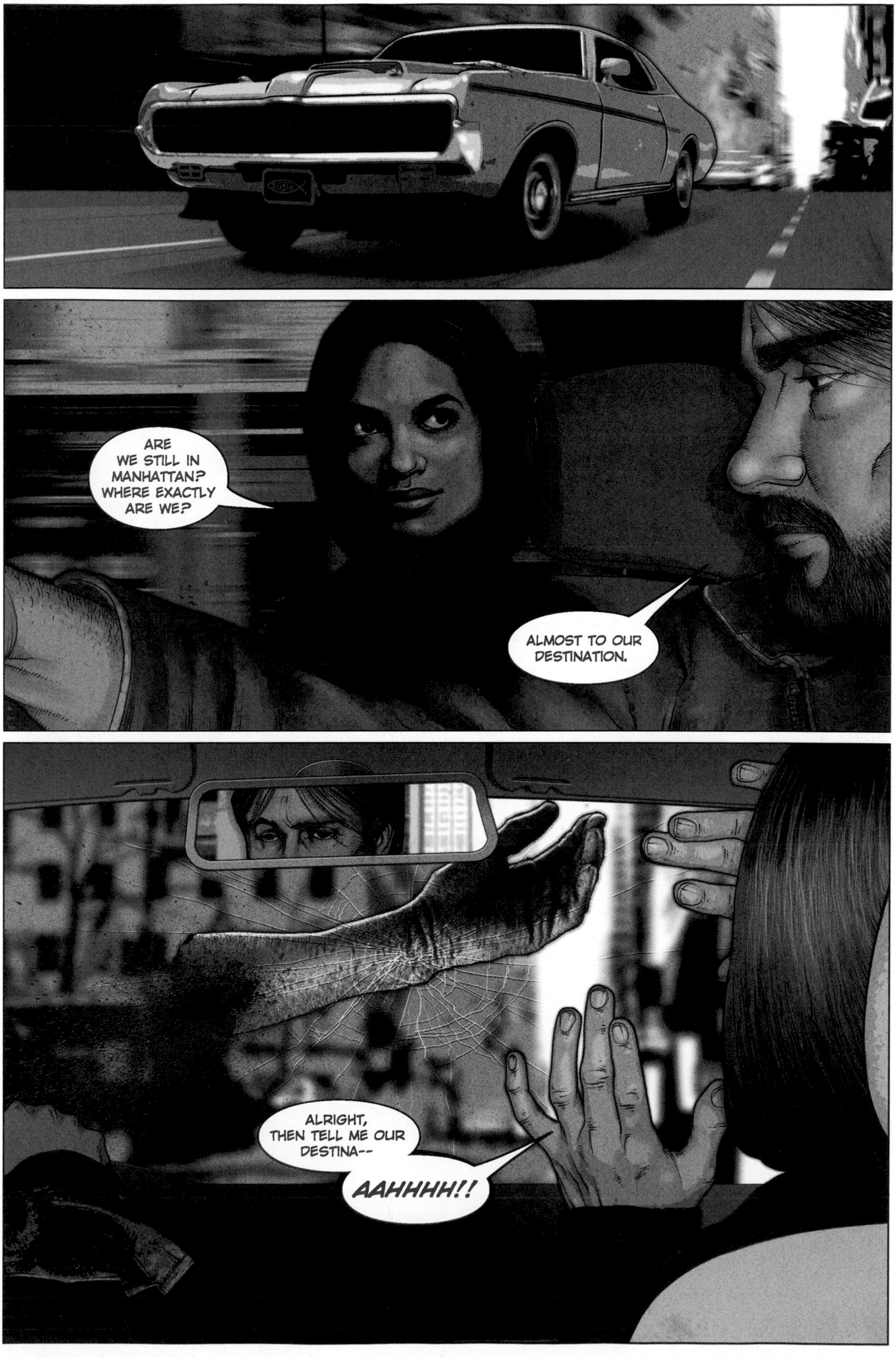

ARE WE STILL IN MANHATTAN? WHERE EXACTLY ARE WE?
ALMOST TO OUR DESTINATION.
ALRIGHT, THEN TELL ME OUR DESTINA--
AAHHHH!!

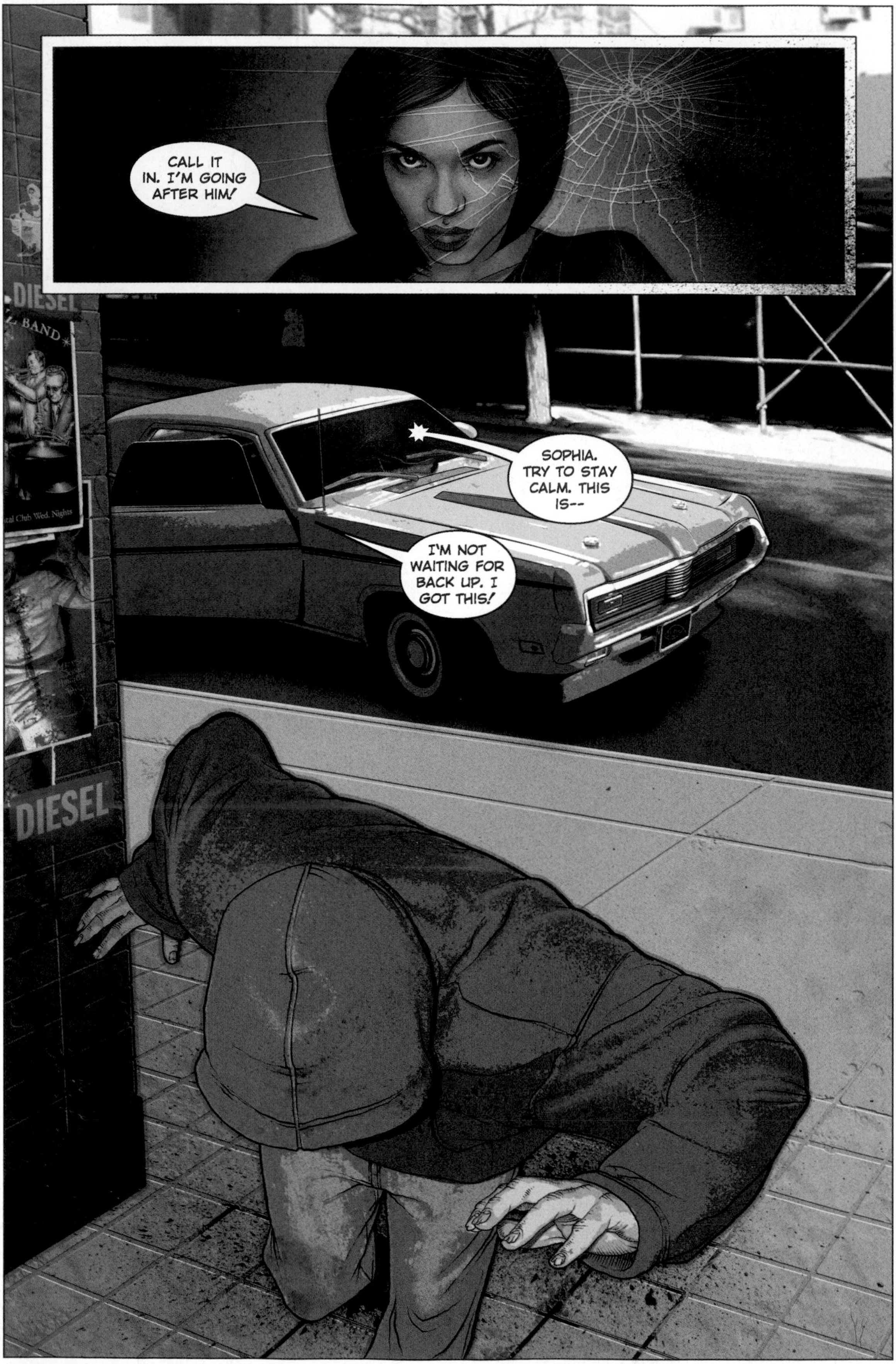
CALL IT IN. I'M GOING AFTER HIM!
SOPHIA. TRY TO STAY CALM. THIS IS--
I'M NOT WAITING FOR BACK UP. I GOT THIS!
DIESEL
DIESEL

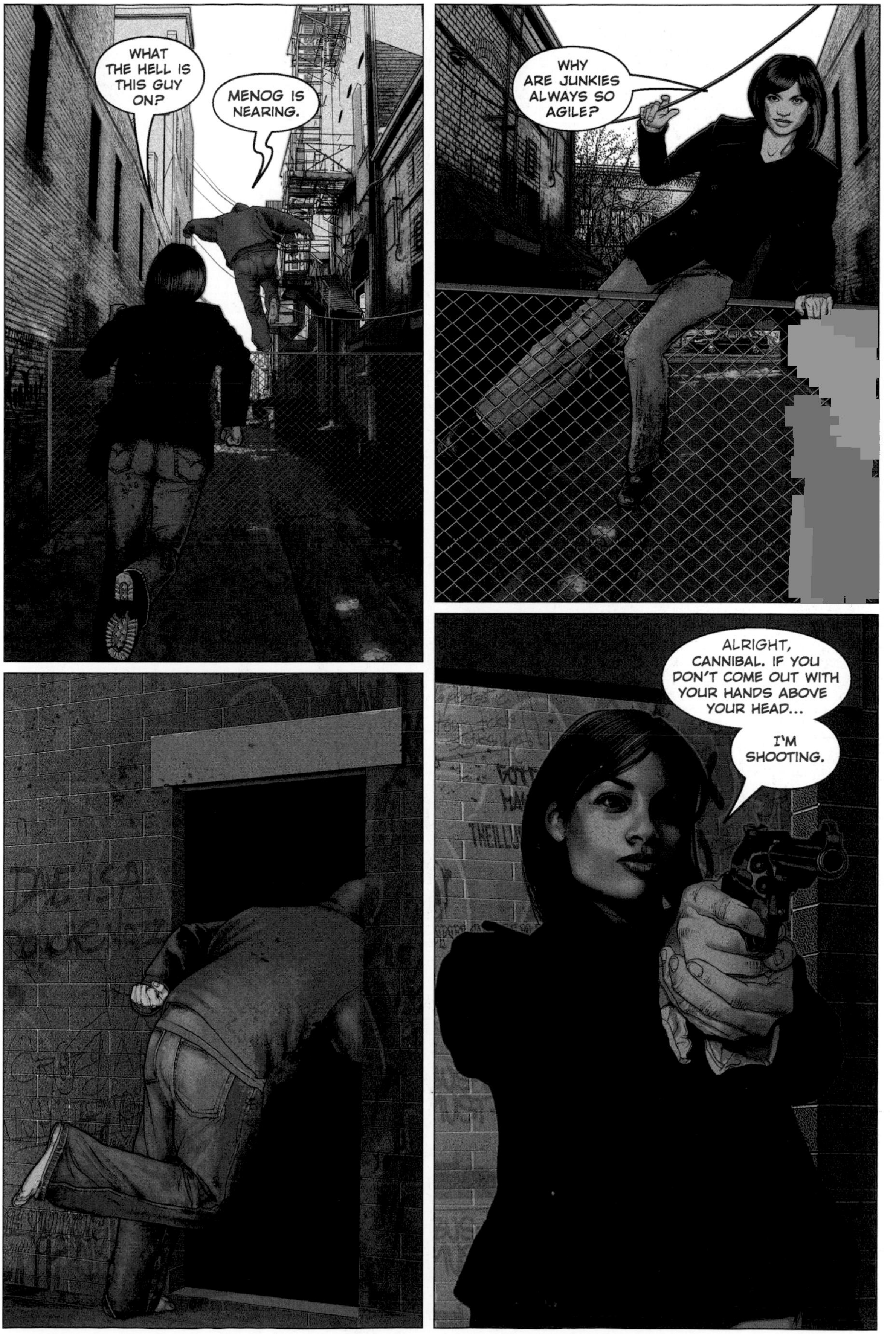
WHAT THE HELL IS THIS GUY ON?
MENOG IS NEARING.
WHY ARE JUNKIES ALWAYS SO AGILE?
ALRIGHT, CANNIBAL. IF YOU DON'T COME OUT WITH YOUR HANDS ABOVE YOUR HEAD...
I'M SHOOTING.

WHAT'S THAT SMELL?

WHERE THE HELL IS IT COMING FROM?

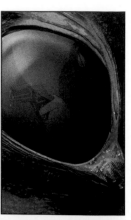

YOU MOCK A HARBINGER OF MENOG? FOR THAT YOU WILL NOT LIVE TO SEE THE MASTER'S RETURN!

BACK AWAY FROM HER!

OR YOU WON'T LIVE TO SEE MENOG, EITHER.

SOPHIA, CAN YOU HEAR ME?

O.C.T. RECOVERY

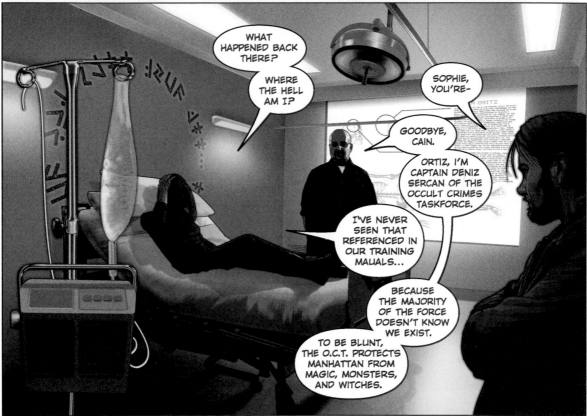

WHAT HAPPENED BACK THERE?

WHERE THE HELL AM I?

SOPHIE, YOU'RE—

GOODBYE, CAIN.

ORTIZ, I'M CAPTAIN DENIZ SERCAN OF THE OCCULT CRIMES TASKFORCE.

I'VE NEVER SEEN THAT REFERENCED IN OUR TRAINING MAUALS...

BECAUSE THE MAJORITY OF THE FORCE DOESN'T KNOW WE EXIST.

TO BE BLUNT, THE O.C.T. PROTECTS MANHATTAN FROM MAGIC, MONSTERS, AND WITCHES.

THE N.Y.P.D.'S GOT A SECRET GHOSTBUSTER CLUB? WHO PAYS FOR ALL THIS?

WHY ONLY MANHATTAN?

I DON'T HAVE TIME FOR THIS, BUT IN LIGHT OF RECENT EVENTS, I'LL CUT YOU SOME SLACK.

WE USE TAXPAYERS' DOLLARS, LIKE OTHER UNITS.

WHY MANHATTAN?

IT'S A GATEWAY TO ANOTHER REALM.

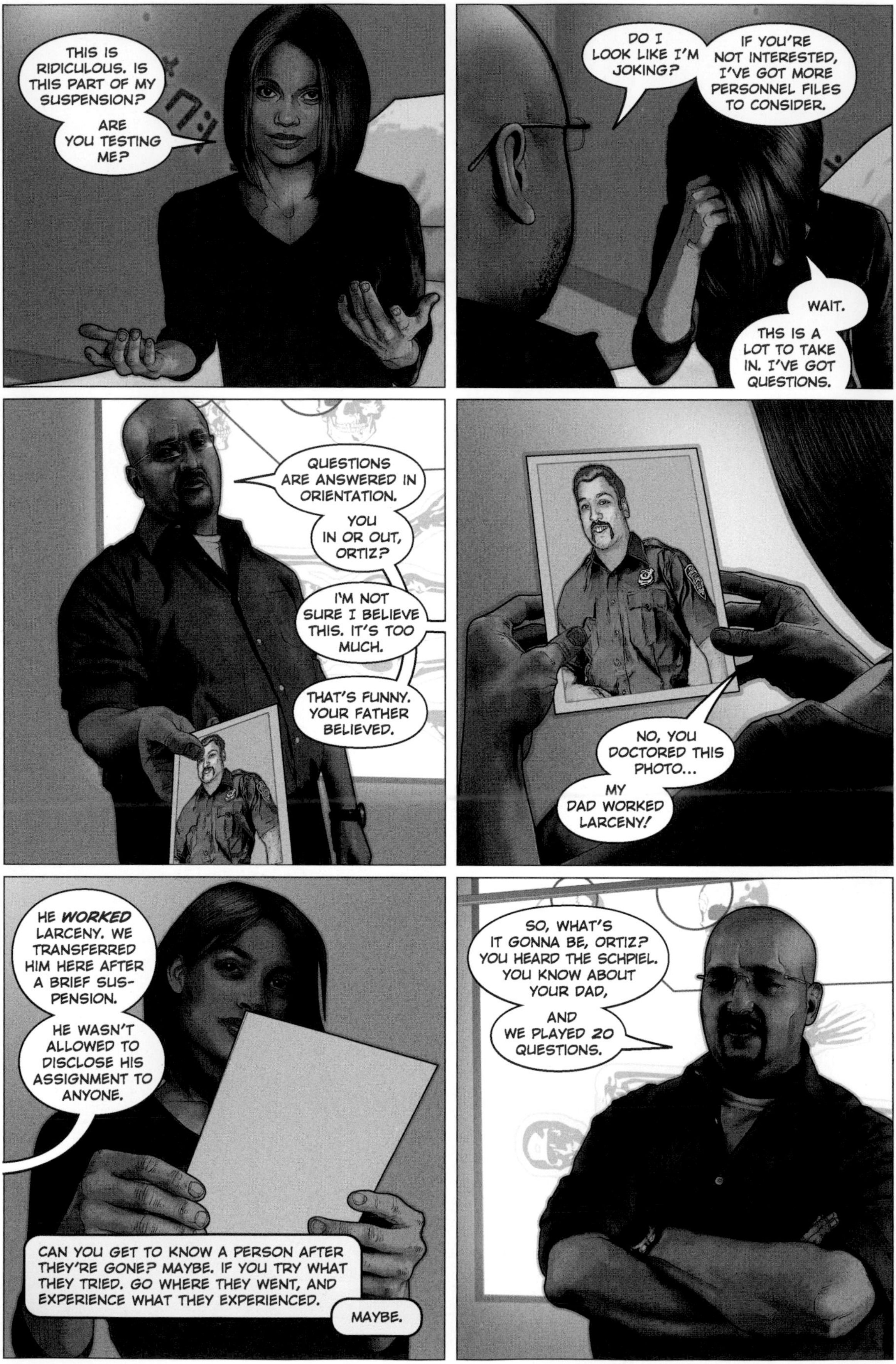
THIS IS RIDICULOUS. IS THIS PART OF MY SUSPENSION?
ARE YOU TESTING ME?
DO I LOOK LIKE I'M JOKING?
IF YOU'RE NOT INTERESTED, I'VE GOT MORE PERSONNEL FILES TO CONSIDER.
WAIT.
THS IS A LOT TO TAKE IN. I'VE GOT QUESTIONS.
QUESTIONS ARE ANSWERED IN ORIENTATION.
YOU IN OR OUT, ORTIZ?
I'M NOT SURE I BELIEVE THIS. IT'S TOO MUCH.
THAT'S FUNNY. YOUR FATHER BELIEVED.
NO, YOU DOCTORED THIS PHOTO...
MY DAD WORKED LARCENY!
HE *WORKED* LARCENY. WE TRANSFERRED HIM HERE AFTER A BRIEF SUS-PENSION.
HE WASN'T ALLOWED TO DISCLOSE HIS ASSIGNMENT TO ANYONE.
CAN YOU GET TO KNOW A PERSON AFTER THEY'RE GONE? MAYBE. IF YOU TRY WHAT THEY TRIED. GO WHERE THEY WENT, AND EXPERIENCE WHAT THEY EXPERIENCED.
MAYBE.
SO, WHAT'S IT GONNA BE, ORTIZ? YOU HEARD THE SCHPIEL. YOU KNOW ABOUT YOUR DAD,
AND WE PLAYED 20 QUESTIONS.

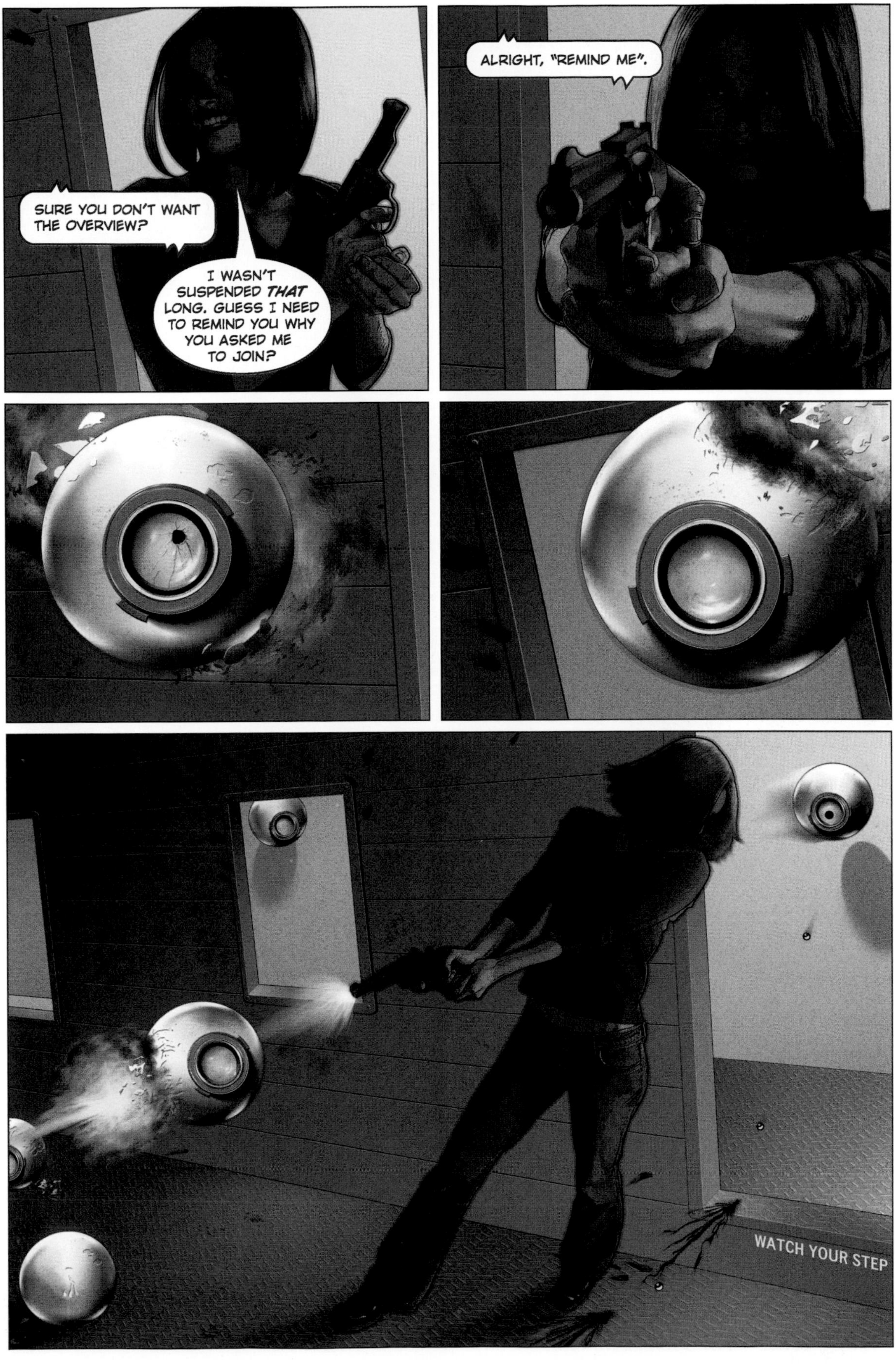
SURE YOU DON'T WANT THE OVERVIEW?
I WASN'T SUSPENDED *THAT* LONG. GUESS I NEED TO REMIND YOU WHY YOU ASKED ME TO JOIN?
ALRIGHT, "REMIND ME".
WATCH YOUR STEP

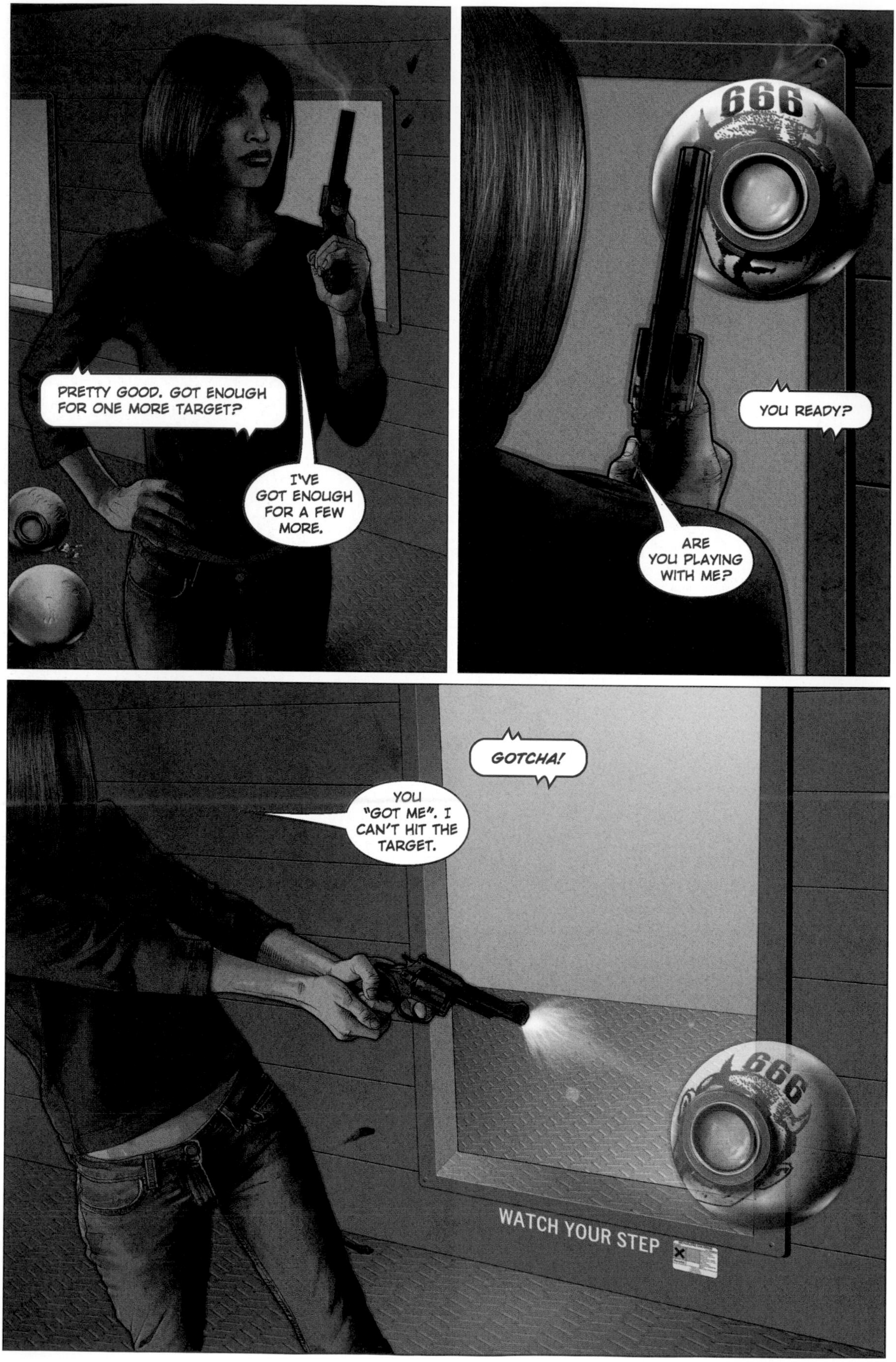
PRETTY GOOD. GOT ENOUGH FOR ONE MORE TARGET?
I'VE GOT ENOUGH FOR A FEW MORE.
YOU READY?
ARE YOU PLAYING WITH ME?
GOTCHA!
YOU "GOT ME". I CAN'T HIT THE TARGET.
666
WATCH YOUR STEP

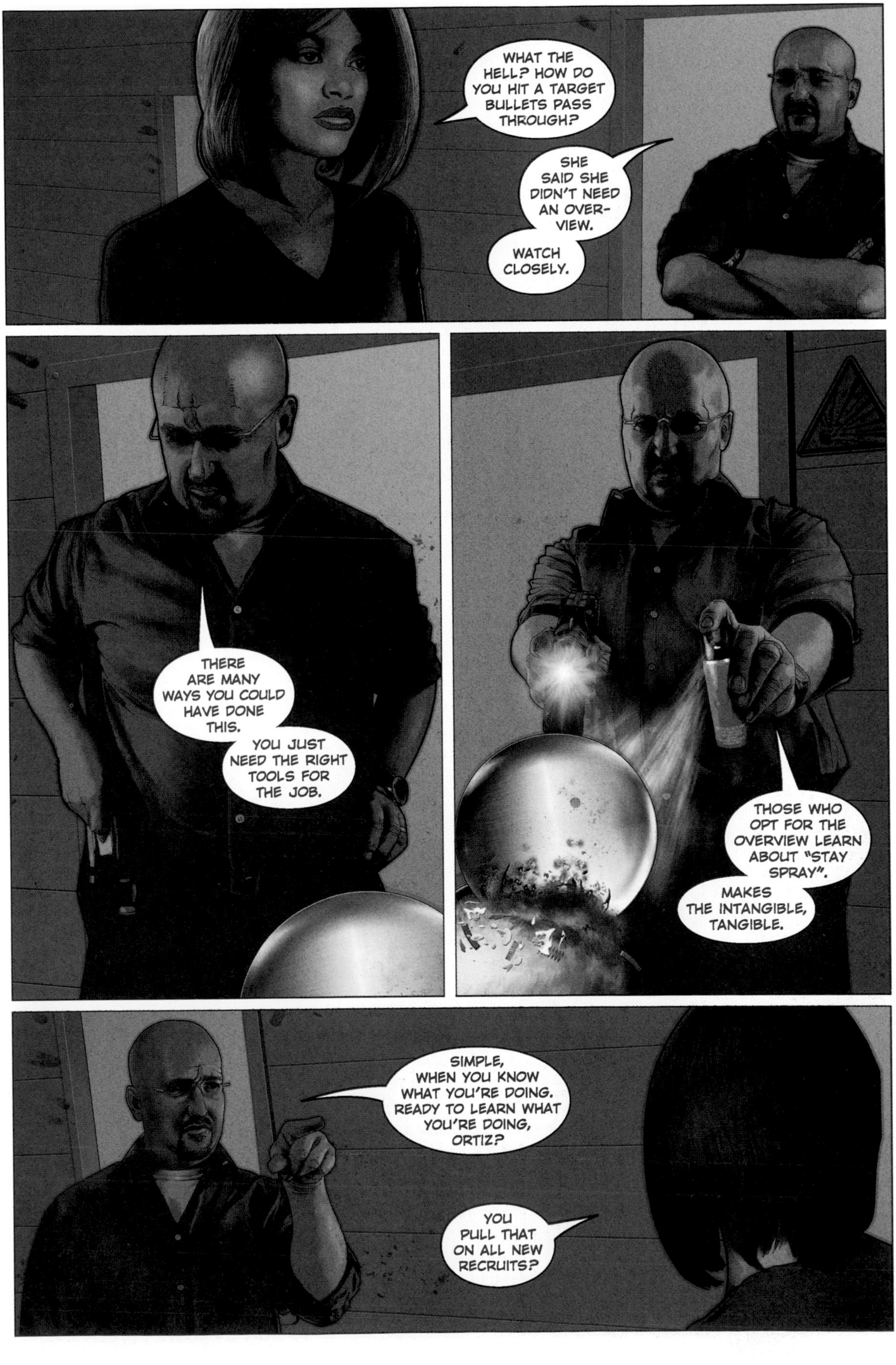
WHAT THE HELL? HOW DO YOU HIT A TARGET BULLETS PASS THROUGH?
SHE SAID SHE DIDN'T NEED AN OVER-VIEW.
WATCH CLOSELY.
THERE ARE MANY WAYS YOU COULD HAVE DONE THIS.
YOU JUST NEED THE RIGHT TOOLS FOR THE JOB.
THOSE WHO OPT FOR THE OVERVIEW LEARN ABOUT "STAY SPRAY".
MAKES THE INTANGIBLE, TANGIBLE.
SIMPLE, WHEN YOU KNOW WHAT YOU'RE DOING. READY TO LEARN WHAT YOU'RE DOING, ORTIZ?
YOU PULL THAT ON ALL NEW RECRUITS?

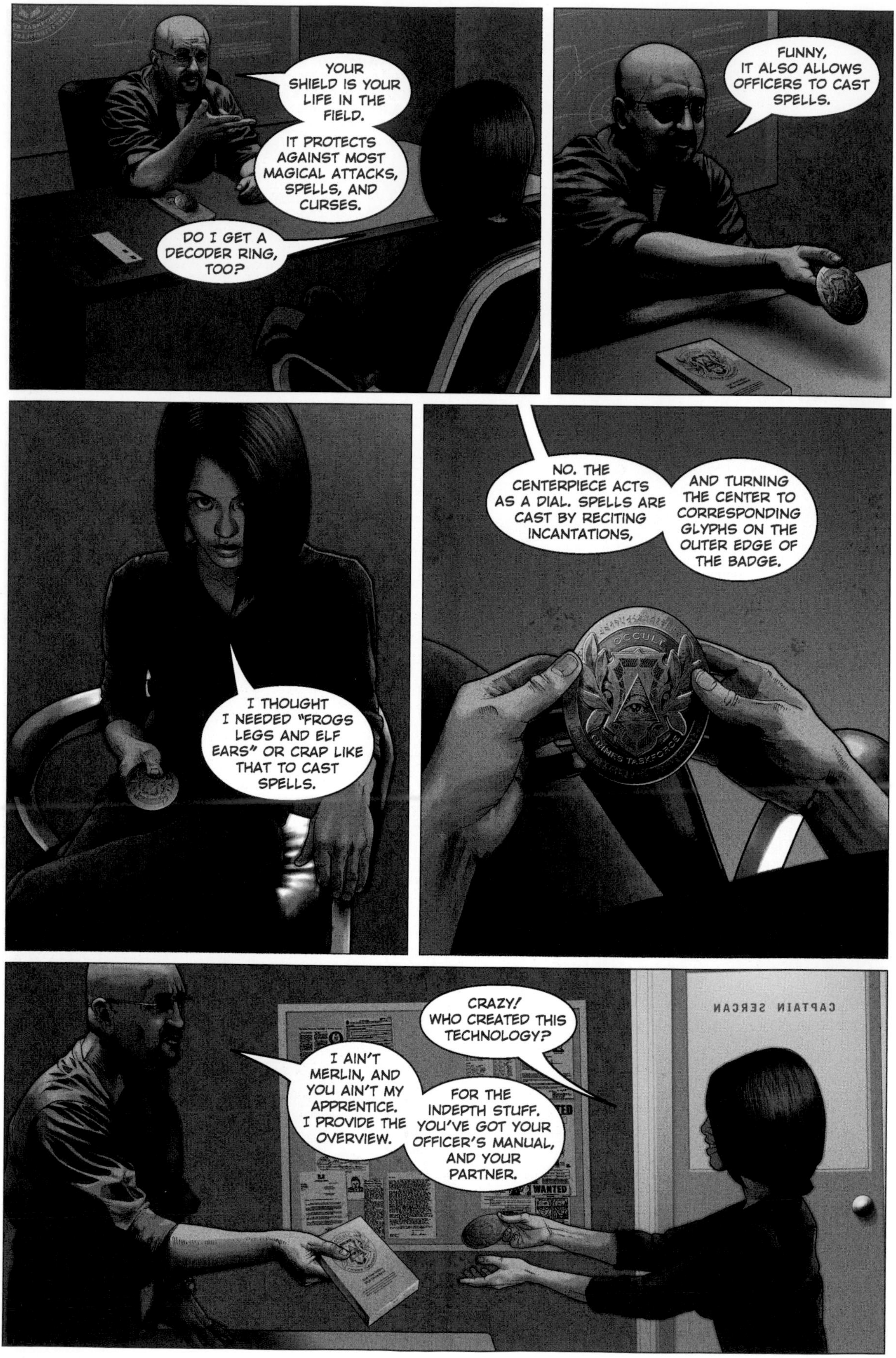
YOUR SHIELD IS YOUR LIFE IN THE FIELD.
IT PROTECTS AGAINST MOST MAGICAL ATTACKS, SPELLS, AND CURSES.
DO I GET A DECODER RING, TOO?
FUNNY, IT ALSO ALLOWS OFFICERS TO CAST SPELLS.
I THOUGHT I NEEDED "FROGS LEGS AND ELF EARS" OR CRAP LIKE THAT TO CAST SPELLS.
NO. THE CENTERPIECE ACTS AS A DIAL. SPELLS ARE CAST BY RECITING INCANTATIONS,
AND TURNING THE CENTER TO CORRESPONDING GLYPHS ON THE OUTER EDGE OF THE BADGE.
OCCULT
CRIMES TASKFORCE
CRAZY! WHO CREATED THIS TECHNOLOGY?
I AIN'T MERLIN, AND YOU AIN'T MY APPRENTICE. I PROVIDE THE OVERVIEW.
FOR THE INDEPTH STUFF. YOU'VE GOT YOUR OFFICER'S MANUAL, AND YOUR PARTNER.
CAPTAIN SERCAN
WANTED

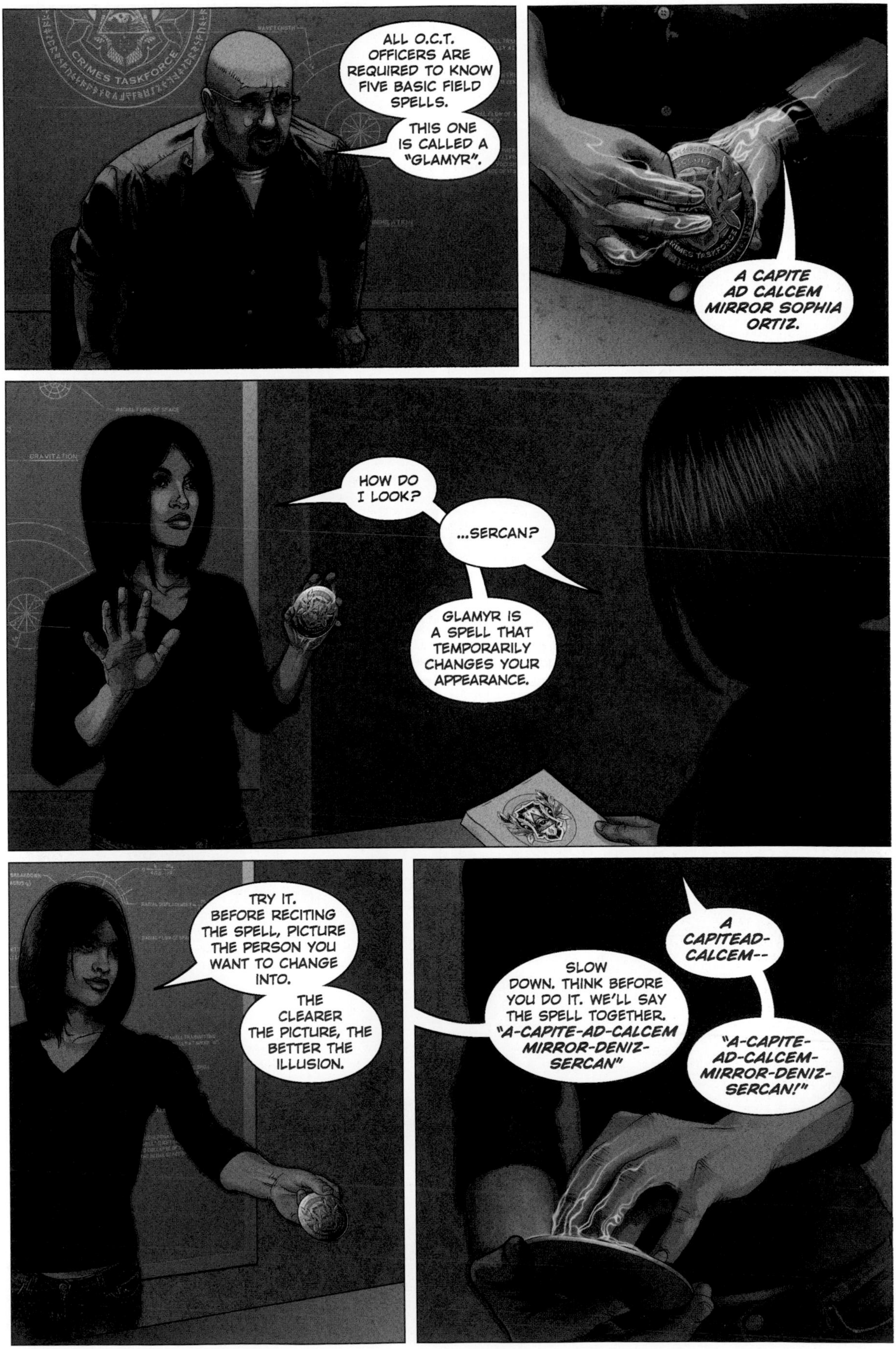

ALL O.C.T. OFFICERS ARE REQUIRED TO KNOW FIVE BASIC FIELD SPELLS.
THIS ONE IS CALLED A "GLAMYR".
CRIMES TASKFORCE
A CAPITE AD CALCEM MIRROR SOPHIA ORTIZ.
HOW DO I LOOK?
...SERCAN?
GLAMYR IS A SPELL THAT TEMPORARILY CHANGES YOUR APPEARANCE.
TRY IT. BEFORE RECITING THE SPELL, PICTURE THE PERSON YOU WANT TO CHANGE INTO.
THE CLEARER THE PICTURE, THE BETTER THE ILLUSION.
A CAPITEAD-CALCEM--
SLOW DOWN. THINK BEFORE YOU DO IT. WE'LL SAY THE SPELL TOGETHER. "A-CAPITE-AD-CALCEM MIRROR-DENIZ-SERCAN"
"A-CAPITE-AD-CALCEM-MIRROR-DENIZ-SERCAN!"

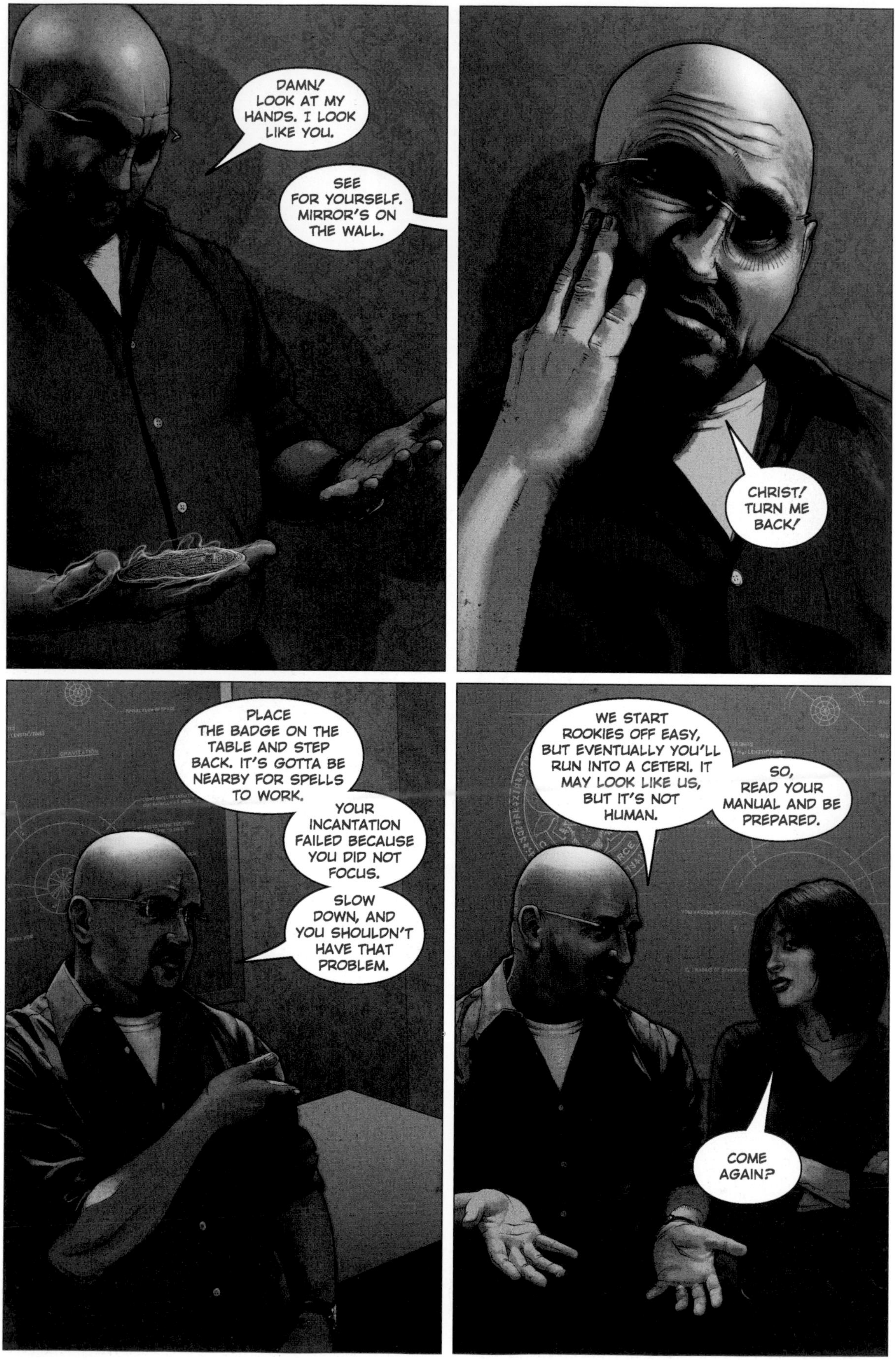
DAMN! LOOK AT MY HANDS. I LOOK LIKE YOU.
SEE FOR YOURSELF. MIRROR'S ON THE WALL.
CHRIST! TURN ME BACK!
PLACE THE BADGE ON THE TABLE AND STEP BACK. IT'S GOTTA BE NEARBY FOR SPELLS TO WORK.
YOUR INCANTATION FAILED BECAUSE YOU DID NOT FOCUS.
SLOW DOWN, AND YOU SHOULDN'T HAVE THAT PROBLEM.
WE START ROOKIES OFF EASY, BUT EVENTUALLY YOU'LL RUN INTO A CETERI. IT MAY LOOK LIKE US, BUT IT'S NOT HUMAN.
SO, READ YOUR MANUAL AND BE PREPARED.
COME AGAIN?

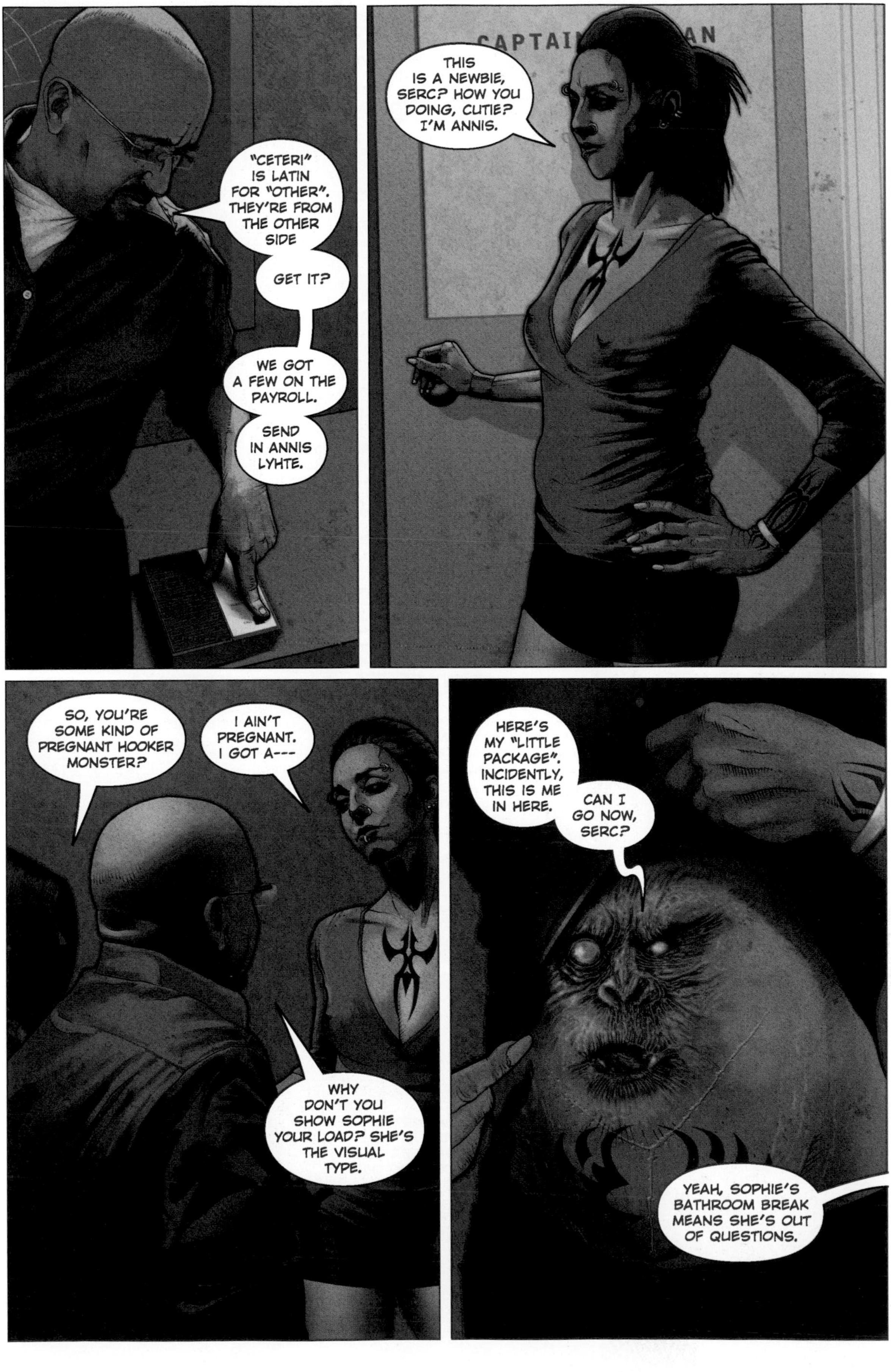
CAPTAIN AN
"CETERI" IS LATIN FOR "OTHER". THEY'RE FROM THE OTHER SIDE
GET IT?
WE GOT A FEW ON THE PAYROLL.
SEND IN ANNIS LYHTE.
THIS IS A NEWBIE, SERC? HOW YOU DOING, CUTIE? I'M ANNIS.
SO, YOU'RE SOME KIND OF PREGNANT HOOKER MONSTER?
I AIN'T PREGNANT. I GOT A---
WHY DON'T YOU SHOW SOPHIE YOUR LOAD? SHE'S THE VISUAL TYPE.
HERE'S MY "LITTLE PACKAGE". INCIDENTLY, THIS IS ME IN HERE.
CAN I GO NOW, SERC?
YEAH, SOPHIE'S BATHROOM BREAK MEANS SHE'S OUT OF QUESTIONS.

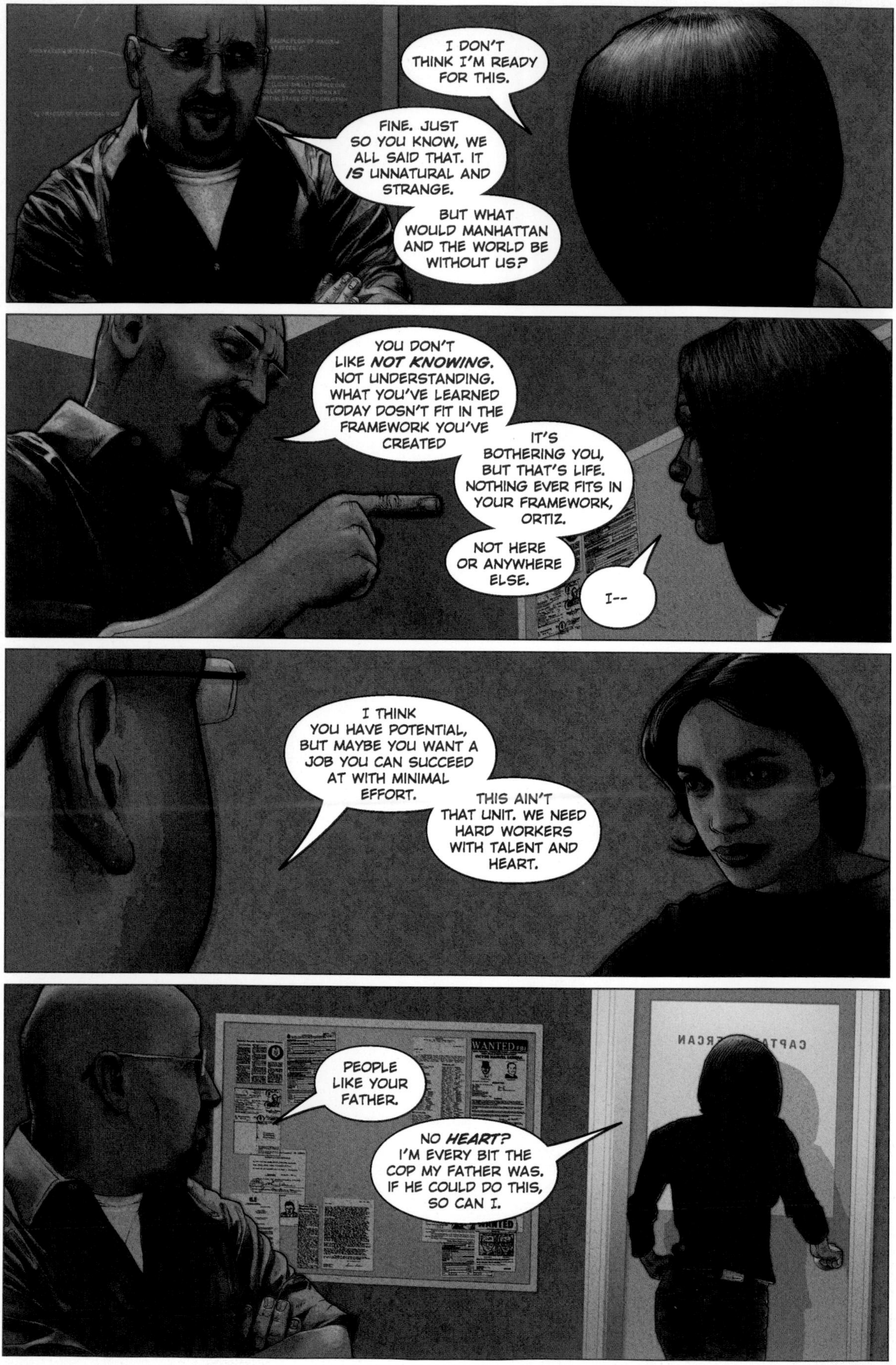
I DON'T THINK I'M READY FOR THIS.
FINE. JUST SO YOU KNOW, WE ALL SAID THAT. IT *IS* UNNATURAL AND STRANGE.
BUT WHAT WOULD MANHATTAN AND THE WORLD BE WITHOUT US?
YOU DON'T LIKE ***NOT KNOWING.*** NOT UNDERSTANDING. WHAT YOU'VE LEARNED TODAY DOSN'T FIT IN THE FRAMEWORK YOU'VE CREATED
IT'S BOTHERING YOU, BUT THAT'S LIFE. NOTHING EVER FITS IN YOUR FRAMEWORK, ORTIZ.
NOT HERE OR ANYWHERE ELSE.
I--
I THINK YOU HAVE POTENTIAL, BUT MAYBE YOU WANT A JOB YOU CAN SUCCEED AT WITH MINIMAL EFFORT.
THIS AIN'T THAT UNIT. WE NEED HARD WORKERS WITH TALENT AND HEART.
WANTED
PEOPLE LIKE YOUR FATHER.
NO ***HEART?*** I'M EVERY BIT THE COP MY FATHER WAS. IF HE COULD DO THIS, SO CAN I.

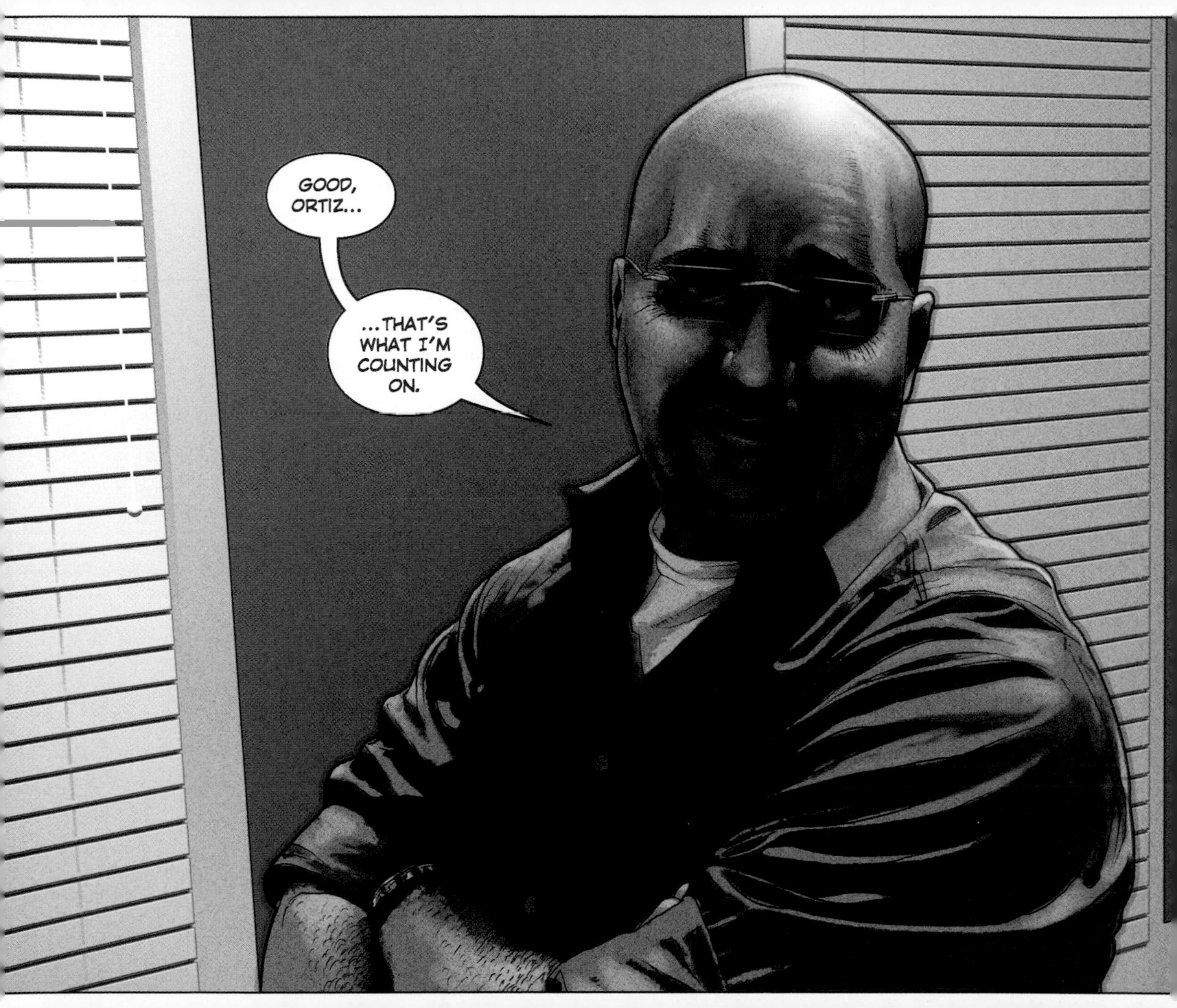
GOOD, ORTIZ...
...THAT'S WHAT I'M COUNTING ON.

Chapter Two

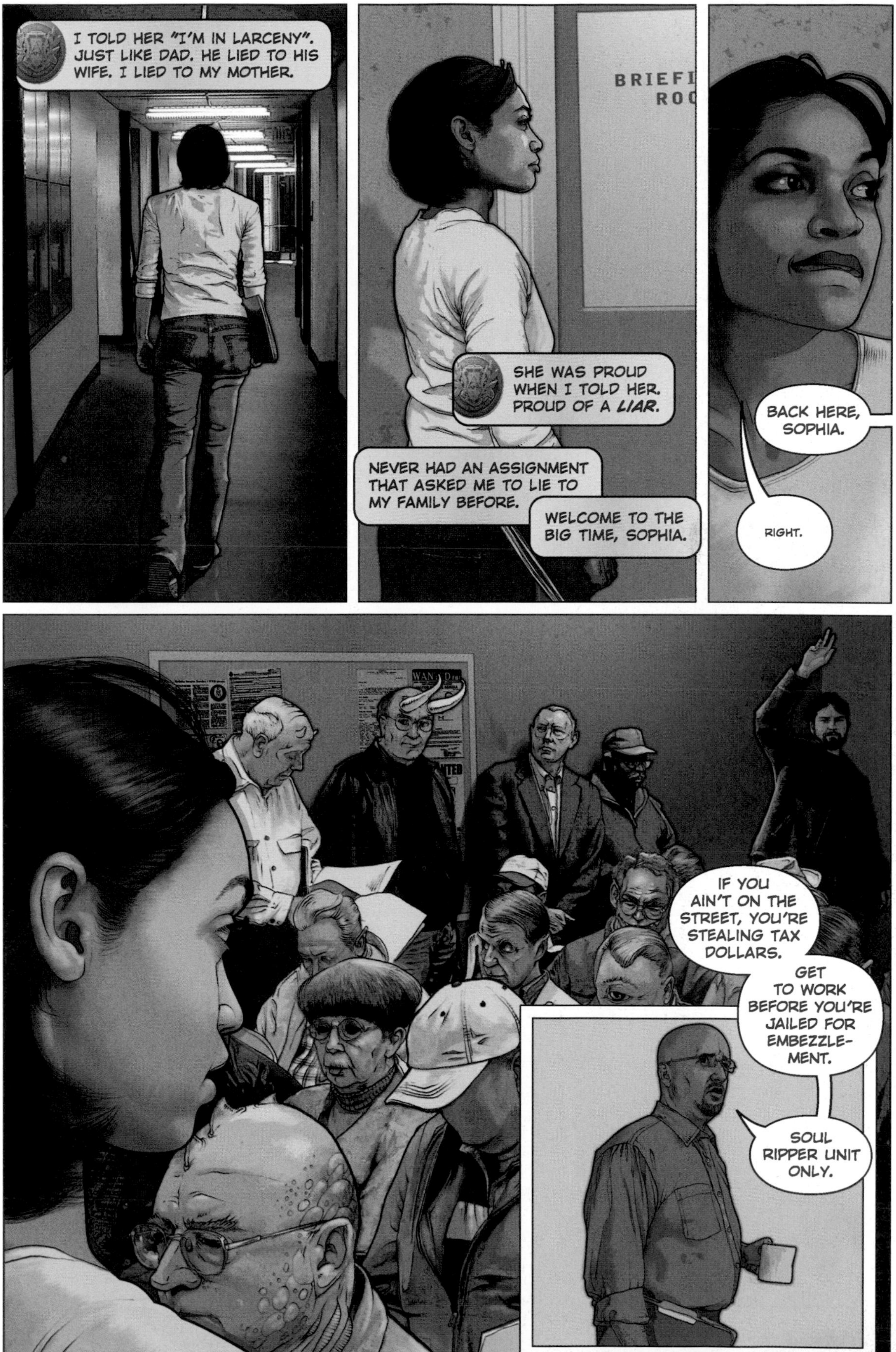
I TOLD HER "I'M IN LARCENY". JUST LIKE DAD. HE LIED TO HIS WIFE. I LIED TO MY MOTHER.
BRIEFI
ROO
SHE WAS PROUD WHEN I TOLD HER. PROUD OF A *LIAR*.
NEVER HAD AN ASSIGNMENT THAT ASKED ME TO LIE TO MY FAMILY BEFORE.
WELCOME TO THE BIG TIME, SOPHIA.
BACK HERE, SOPHIA.
RIGHT.
IF YOU AIN'T ON THE STREET, YOU'RE STEALING TAX DOLLARS.
GET TO WORK BEFORE YOU'RE JAILED FOR EMBEZZLE-MENT.
SOUL RIPPER UNIT ONLY.

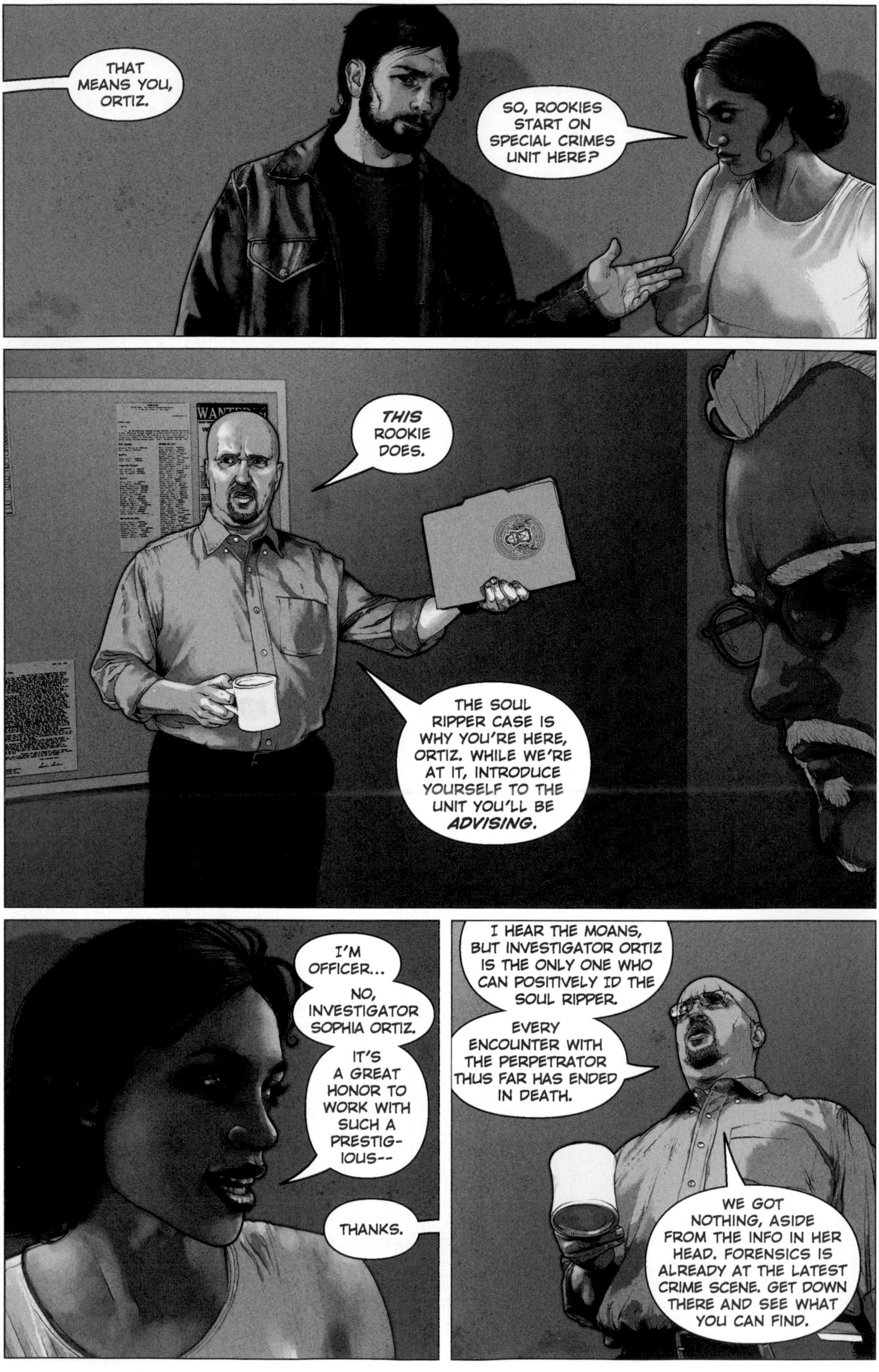
THAT MEANS YOU, ORTIZ.
SO, ROOKIES START ON SPECIAL CRIMES UNIT HERE?
THIS ROOKIE DOES.
THE SOUL RIPPER CASE IS WHY YOU'RE HERE, ORTIZ. WHILE WE'RE AT IT, INTRODUCE YOURSELF TO THE UNIT YOU'LL BE ADVISING.
I'M OFFICER...
NO, INVESTIGATOR SOPHIA ORTIZ.
IT'S A GREAT HONOR TO WORK WITH SUCH A PRESTIG-IOUS--
THANKS.
I HEAR THE MOANS, BUT INVESTIGATOR ORTIZ IS THE ONLY ONE WHO CAN POSITIVELY ID THE SOUL RIPPER.
EVERY ENCOUNTER WITH THE PERPETRATOR THUS FAR HAS ENDED IN DEATH.
WE GOT NOTHING, ASIDE FROM THE INFO IN HER HEAD. FORENSICS IS ALREADY AT THE LATEST CRIME SCENE. GET DOWN THERE AND SEE WHAT YOU CAN FIND.

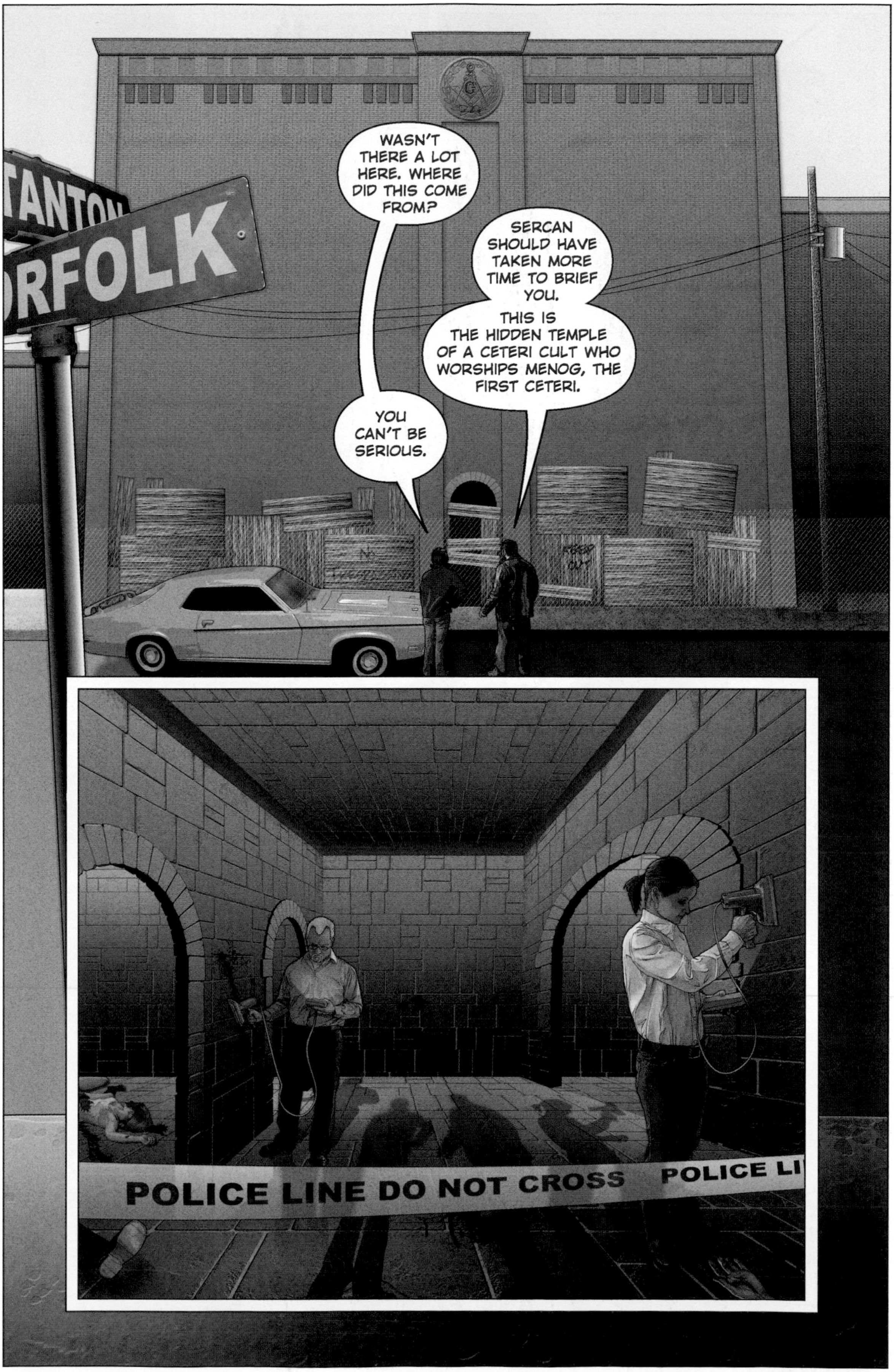
TANTON
ORFOLK
WASN'T THERE A LOT HERE. WHERE DID THIS COME FROM?
SERCAN SHOULD HAVE TAKEN MORE TIME TO BRIEF YOU.
THIS IS THE HIDDEN TEMPLE OF A CETERI CULT WHO WORSHIPS MENOG, THE FIRST CETERI.
YOU CAN'T BE SERIOUS.
POLICE LINE DO NOT CROSS
POLICE LI

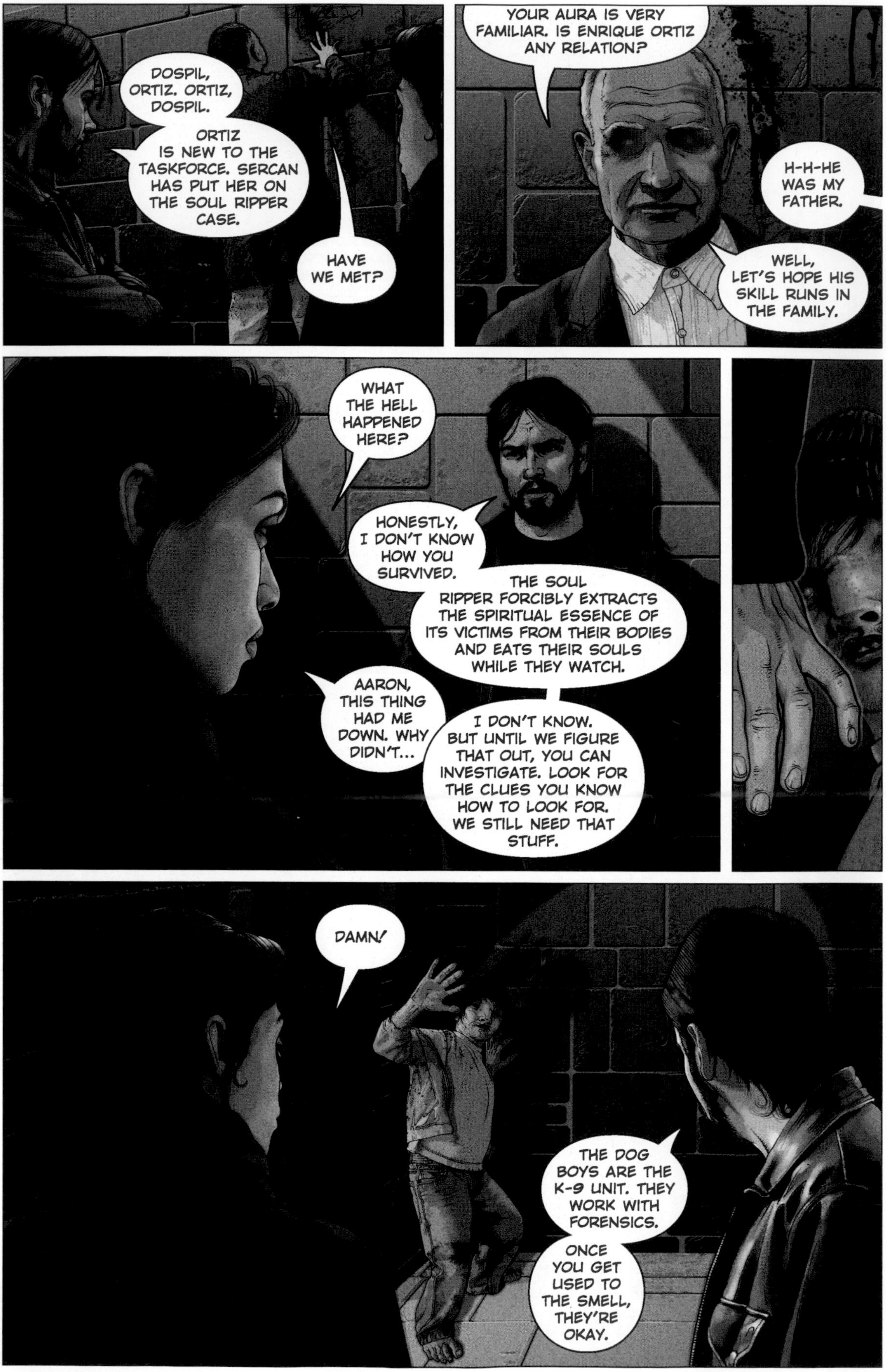
DOSPIL, ORTIZ. ORTIZ, DOSPIL.
ORTIZ IS NEW TO THE TASKFORCE. SERCAN HAS PUT HER ON THE SOUL RIPPER CASE.
HAVE WE MET?
YOUR AURA IS VERY FAMILIAR. IS ENRIQUE ORTIZ ANY RELATION?
H-H-HE WAS MY FATHER.
WELL, LET'S HOPE HIS SKILL RUNS IN THE FAMILY.
WHAT THE HELL HAPPENED HERE?
HONESTLY, I DON'T KNOW HOW YOU SURVIVED.
THE SOUL RIPPER FORCIBLY EXTRACTS THE SPIRITUAL ESSENCE OF ITS VICTIMS FROM THEIR BODIES AND EATS THEIR SOULS WHILE THEY WATCH.
AARON, THIS THING HAD ME DOWN. WHY DIDN'T...
I DON'T KNOW. BUT UNTIL WE FIGURE THAT OUT, YOU CAN INVESTIGATE. LOOK FOR THE CLUES YOU KNOW HOW TO LOOK FOR. WE STILL NEED THAT STUFF.
DAMN!
THE DOG BOYS ARE THE K-9 UNIT. THEY WORK WITH FORENSICS.
ONCE YOU GET USED TO THE SMELL, THEY'RE OKAY.

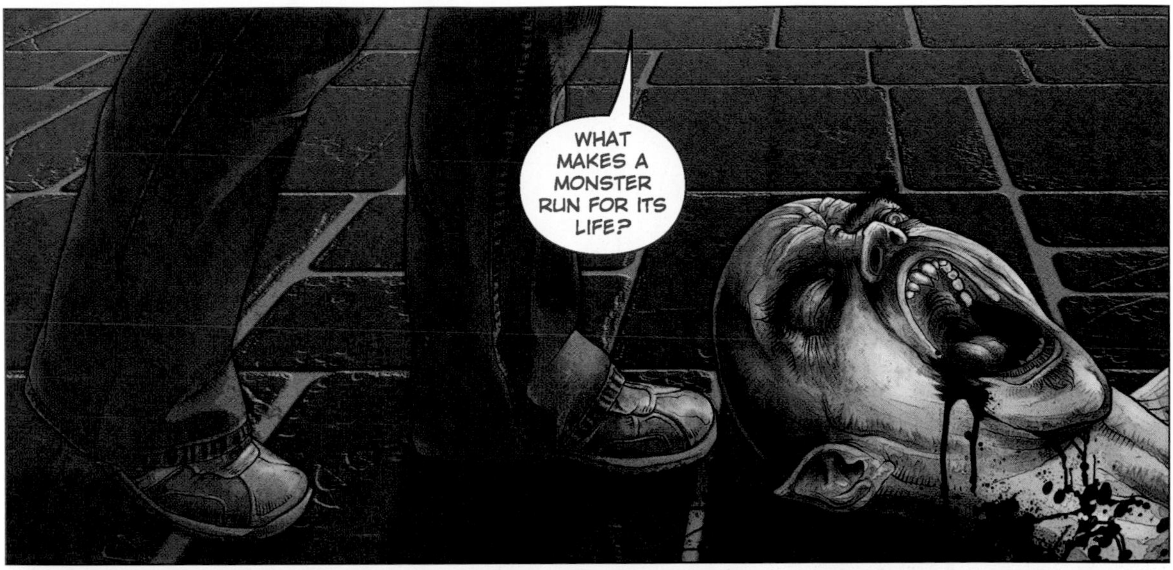
WHAT MAKES A MONSTER RUN FOR ITS LIFE?
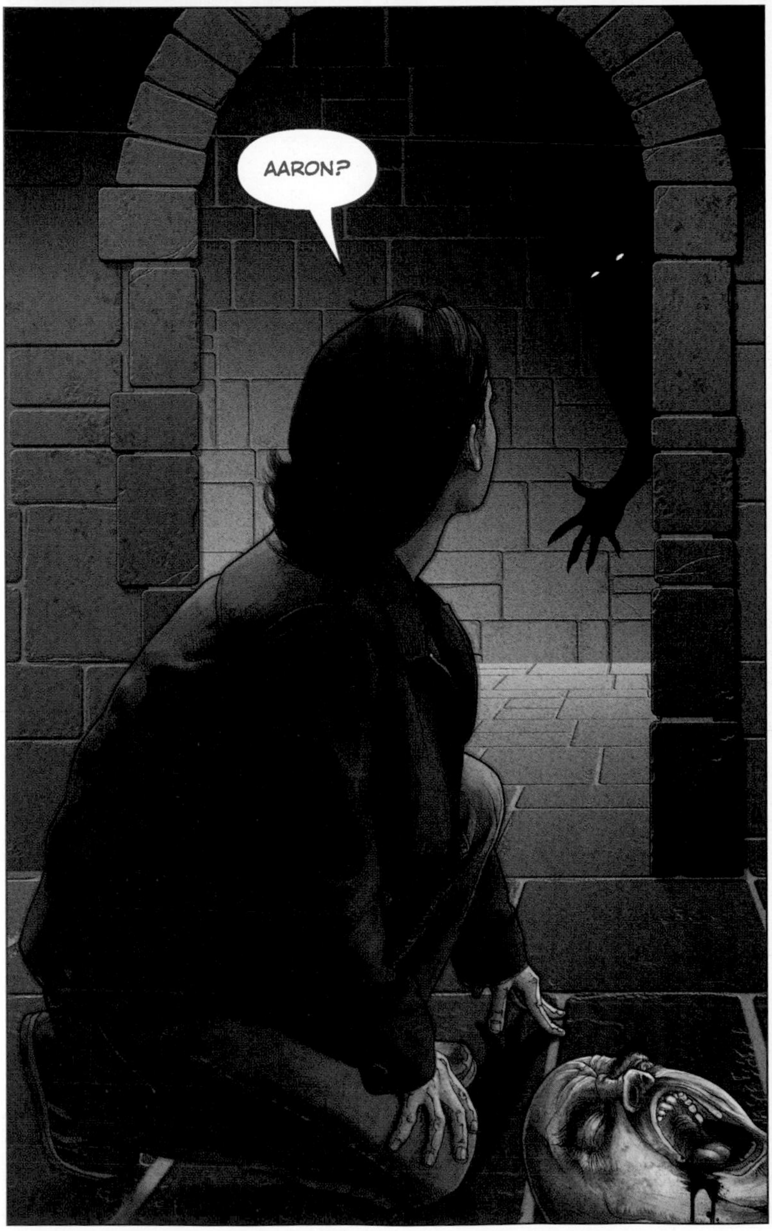
AARON?
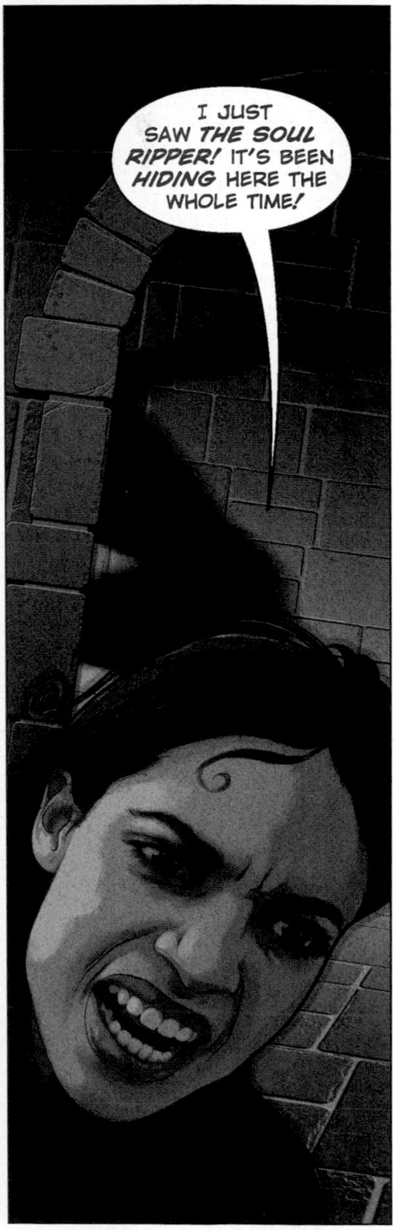
I JUST SAW *THE SOUL RIPPER!* IT'S BEEN *HIDING* HERE THE WHOLE TIME*!*

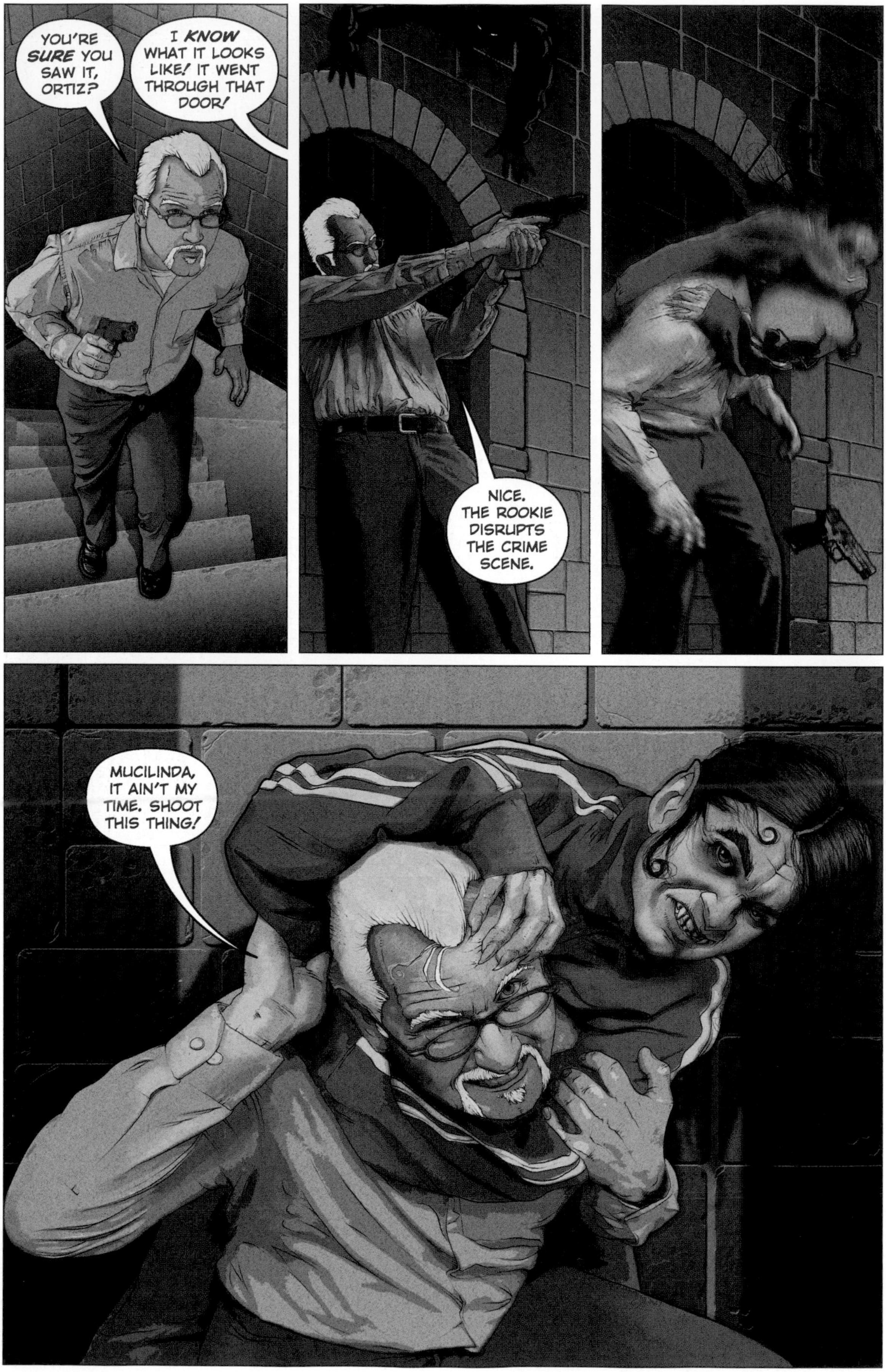

YOU'RE SURE YOU SAW IT, ORTIZ?
I KNOW WHAT IT LOOKS LIKE! IT WENT THROUGH THAT DOOR!
NICE. THE ROOKIE DISRUPTS THE CRIME SCENE.
MUCILINDA, IT AIN'T MY TIME. SHOOT THIS THING!

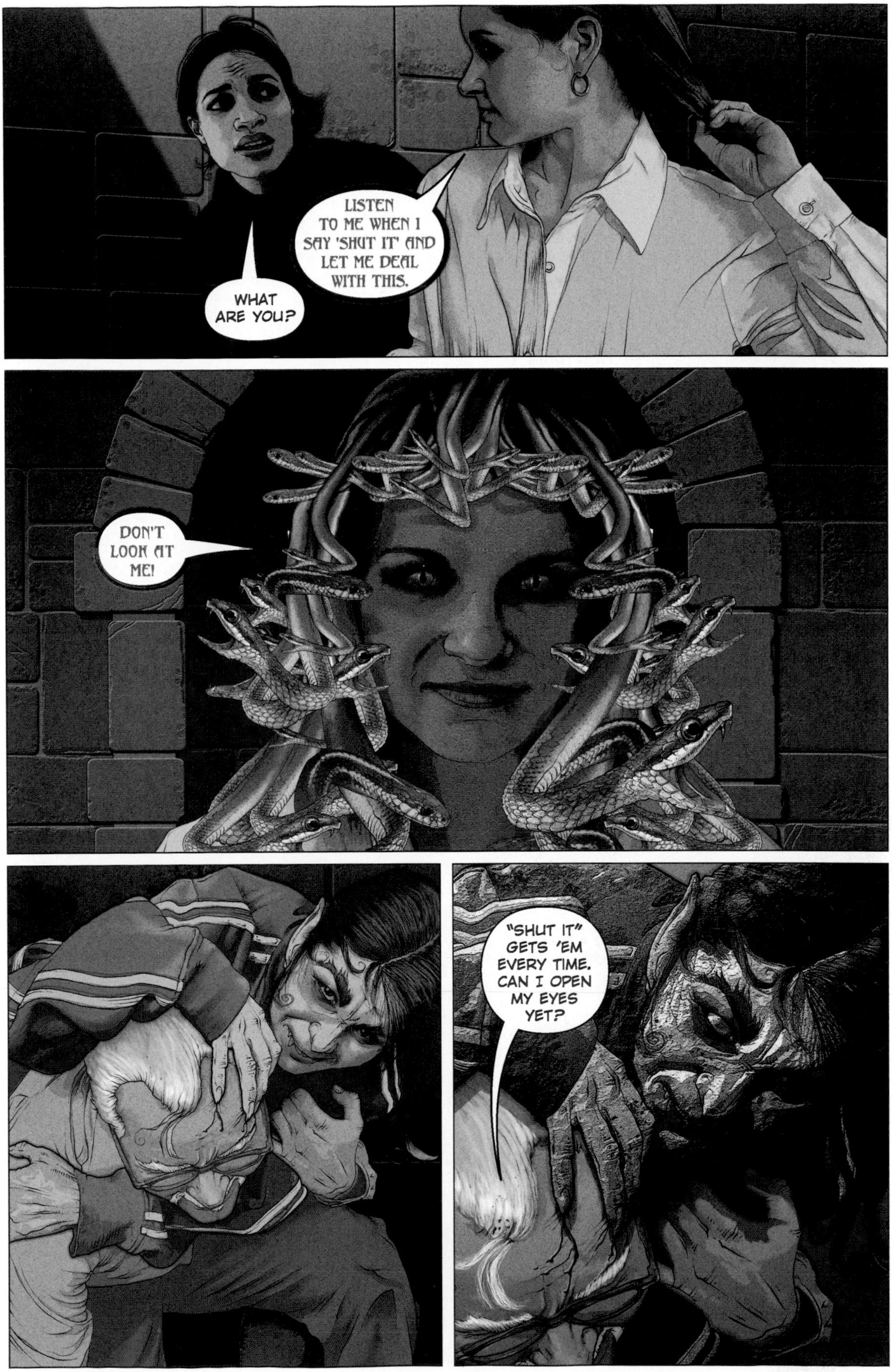
WHAT ARE YOU?
LISTEN TO ME WHEN I SAY 'SHUT IT' AND LET ME DEAL WITH THIS.
DON'T LOOK AT ME!
"SHUT IT" GETS 'EM EVERY TIME. CAN I OPEN MY EYES YET?

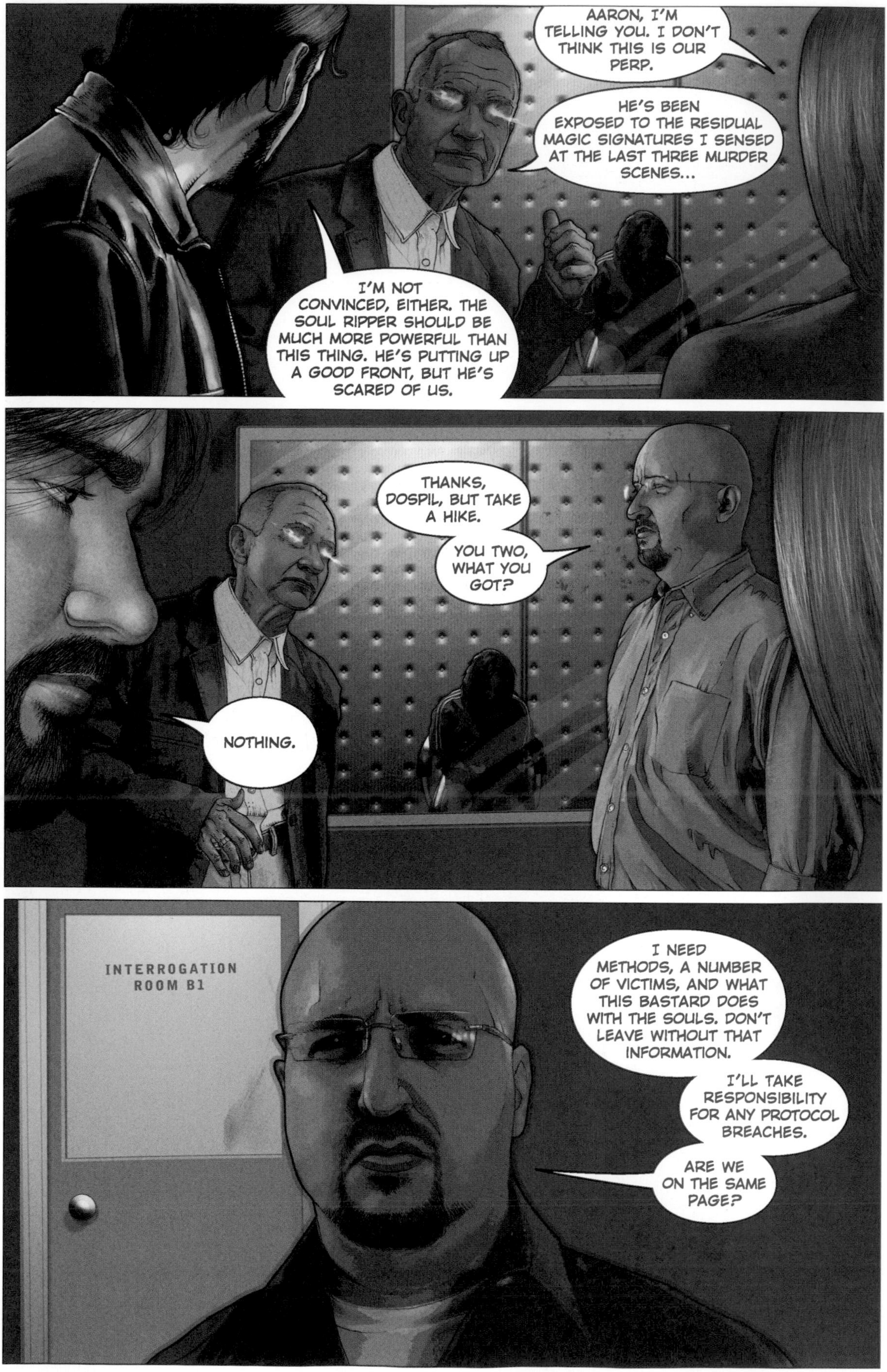
AARON, I'M TELLING YOU. I DON'T THINK THIS IS OUR PERP.
HE'S BEEN EXPOSED TO THE RESIDUAL MAGIC SIGNATURES I SENSED AT THE LAST THREE MURDER SCENES...
I'M NOT CONVINCED, EITHER. THE SOUL RIPPER SHOULD BE MUCH MORE POWERFUL THAN THIS THING. HE'S PUTTING UP A GOOD FRONT, BUT HE'S SCARED OF US.
THANKS, DOSPIL, BUT TAKE A HIKE.
YOU TWO, WHAT YOU GOT?
NOTHING.
INTERROGATION ROOM B1
I NEED METHODS, A NUMBER OF VICTIMS, AND WHAT THIS BASTARD DOES WITH THE SOULS. DON'T LEAVE WITHOUT THAT INFORMATION.
I'LL TAKE RESPONSIBILITY FOR ANY PROTOCOL BREACHES.
ARE WE ON THE SAME PAGE?

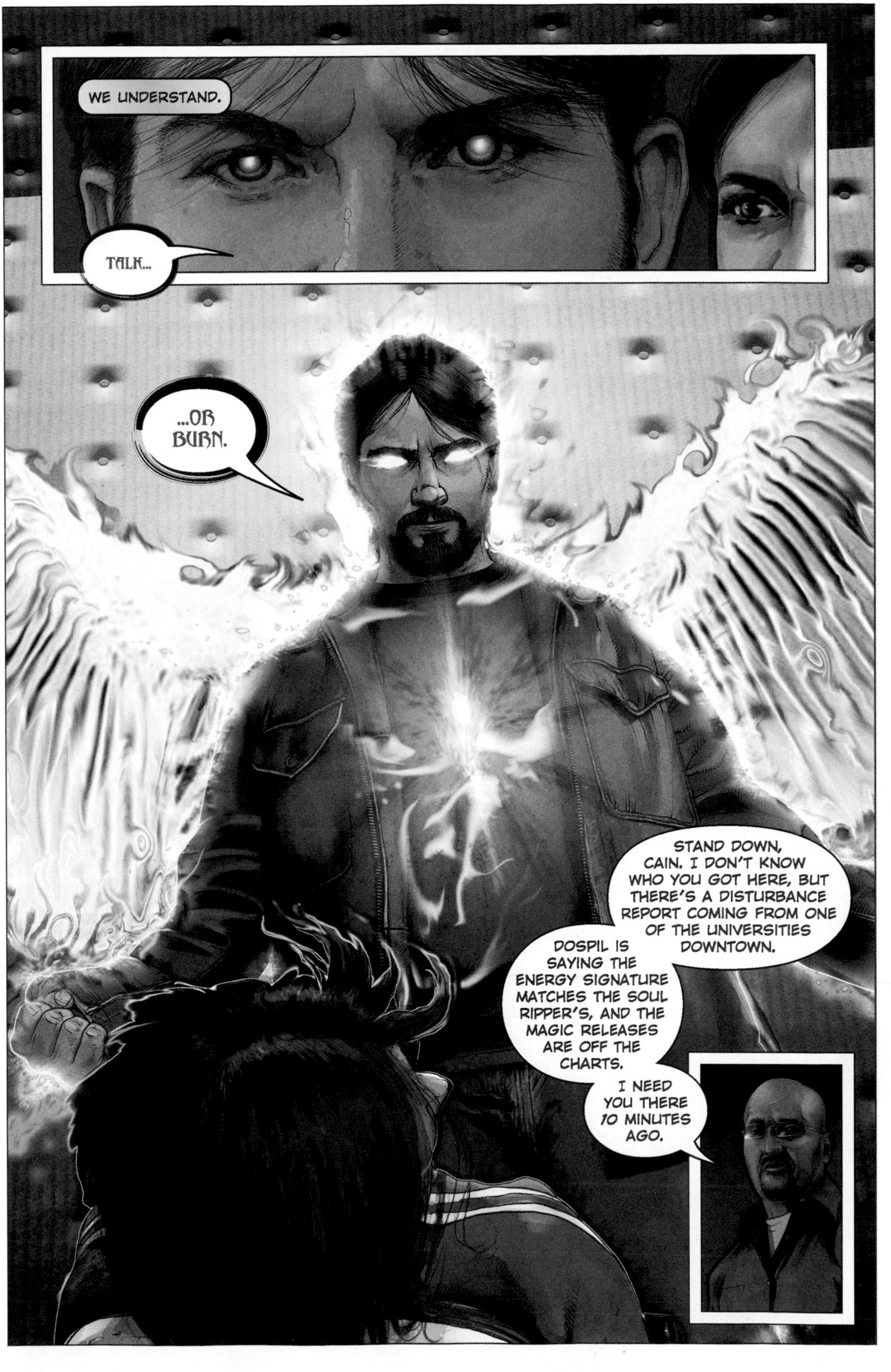
WE UNDERSTAND.
TALK...
...OR BURN.
STAND DOWN, CAIN. I DON'T KNOW WHO YOU GOT HERE, BUT THERE'S A DISTURBANCE REPORT COMING FROM ONE OF THE UNIVERSITIES DOWNTOWN.
DOSPIL IS SAYING THE ENERGY SIGNATURE MATCHES THE SOUL RIPPER'S, AND THE MAGIC RELEASES ARE OFF THE CHARTS.
I NEED YOU THERE 10 MINUTES AGO.

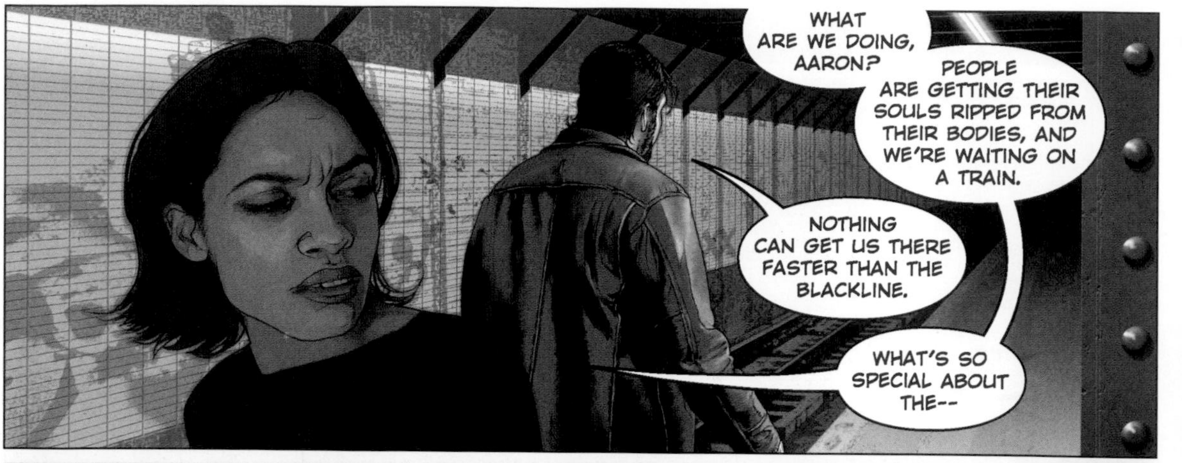
WHAT ARE WE DOING, AARON?
PEOPLE ARE GETTING THEIR SOULS RIPPED FROM THEIR BODIES, AND WE'RE WAITING ON A TRAIN.
NOTHING CAN GET US THERE FASTER THAN THE BLACKLINE.
WHAT'S SO SPECIAL ABOUT THE--

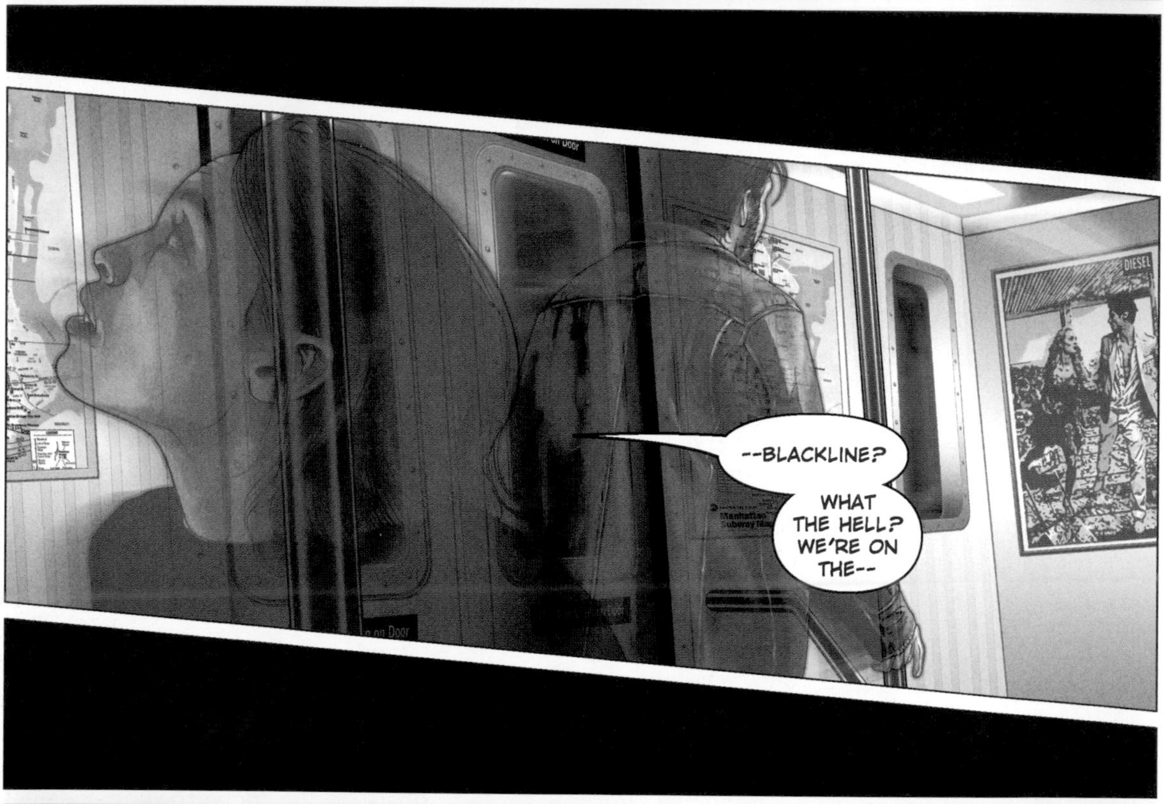
--BLACKLINE?
WHAT THE HELL? WE'RE ON THE--

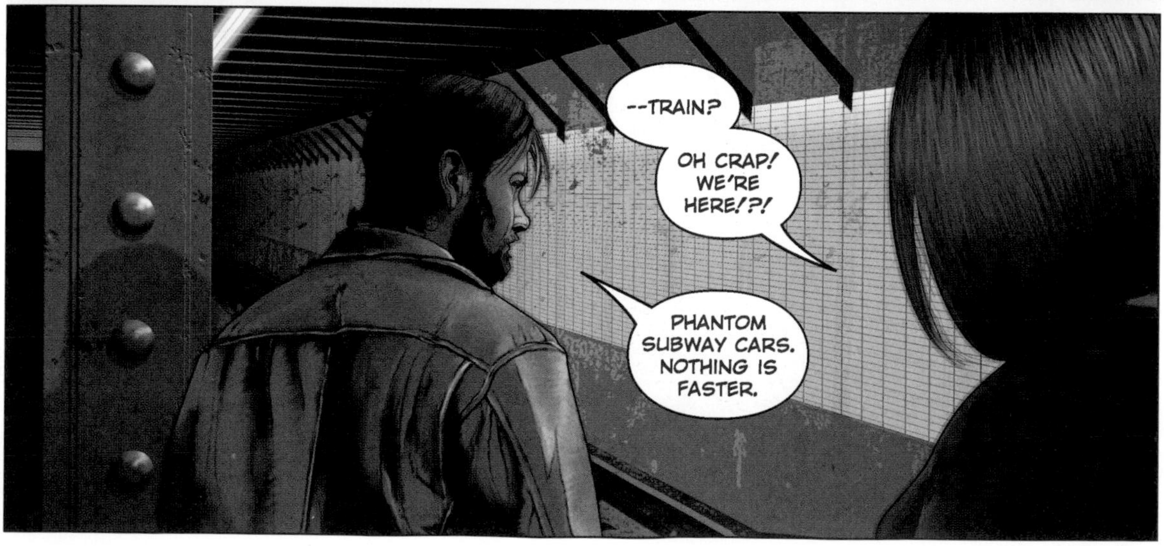
--TRAIN?
OH CRAP! WE'RE HERE!?!
PHANTOM SUBWAY CARS. NOTHING IS FASTER.

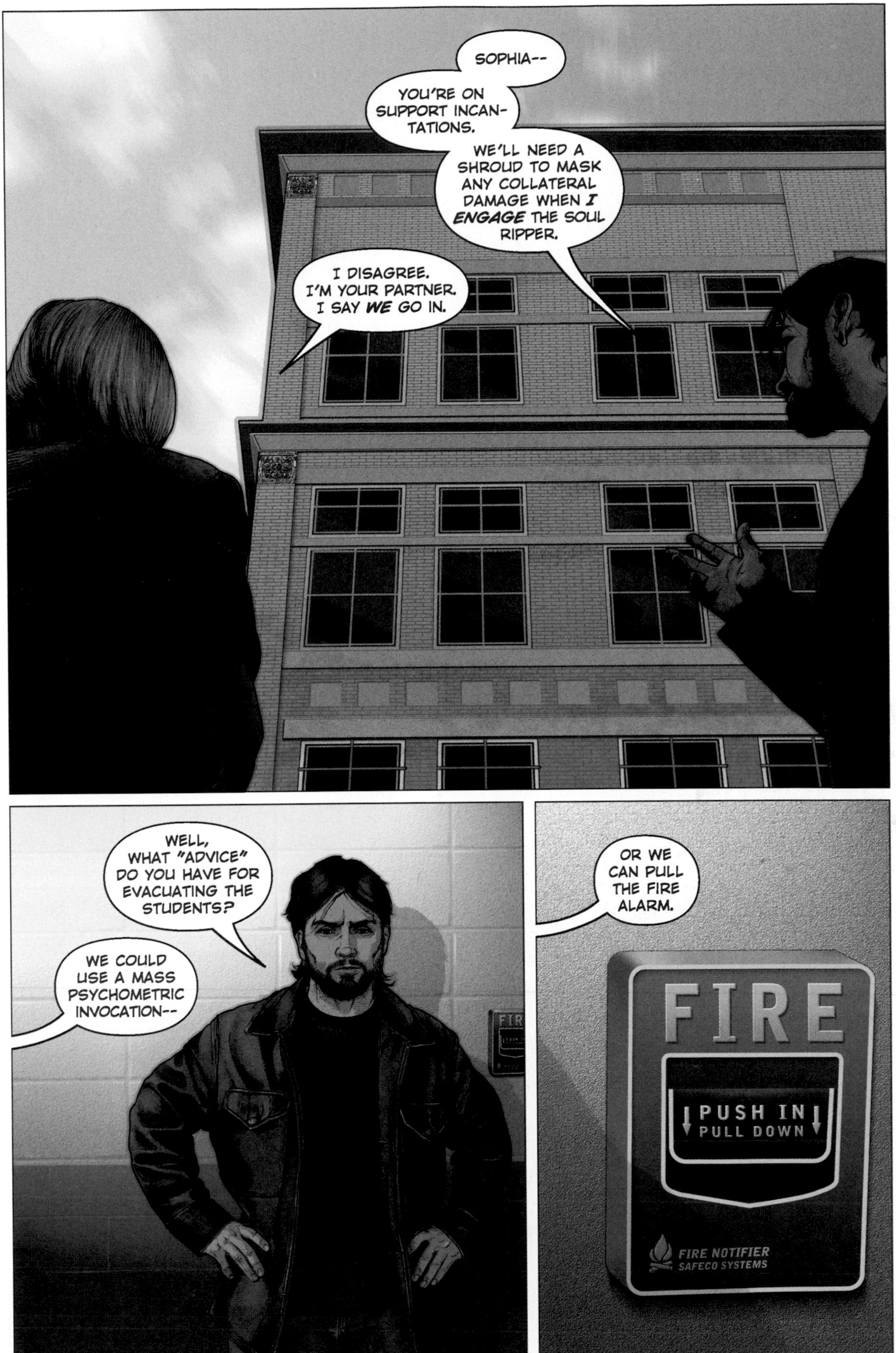
SOPHIA--
YOU'RE ON SUPPORT INCAN-TATIONS.
WE'LL NEED A SHROUD TO MASK ANY COLLATERAL DAMAGE WHEN *I* *ENGAGE* THE SOUL RIPPER.
I DISAGREE. I'M YOUR PARTNER. I SAY *WE* GO IN.
WELL, WHAT "ADVICE" DO YOU HAVE FOR EVACUATING THE STUDENTS?
WE COULD USE A MASS PSYCHOMETRIC INVOCATION--
OR WE CAN PULL THE FIRE ALARM.
FIRE
PUSH IN
PULL DOWN
FIRE NOTIFIER
SAFECO SYSTEMS

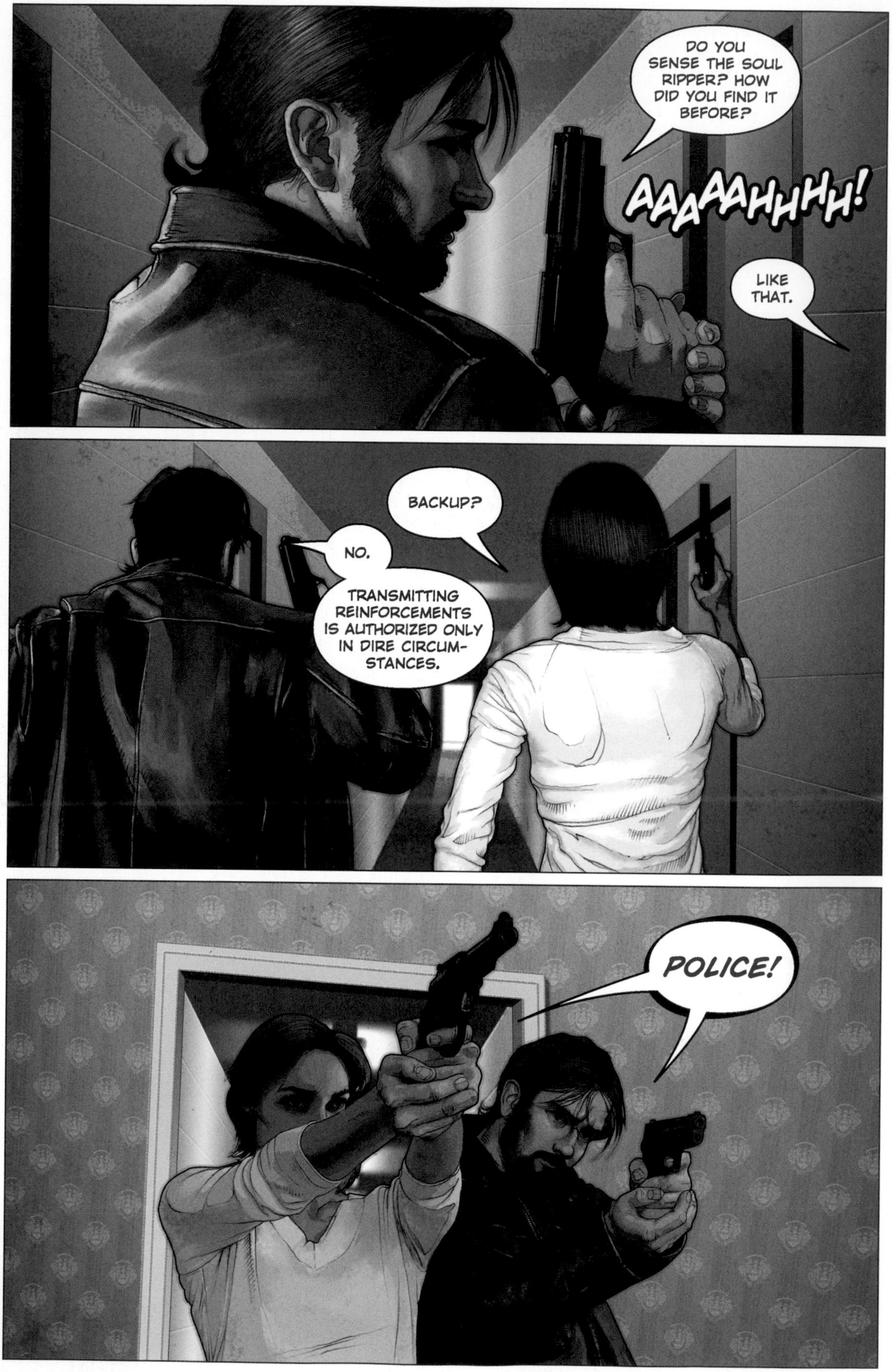
DO YOU SENSE THE SOUL RIPPER? HOW DID YOU FIND IT BEFORE?
AAAAAHHHHH!
LIKE THAT.
BACKUP?
NO.
TRANSMITTING REINFORCEMENTS IS AUTHORIZED ONLY IN DIRE CIRCUM-STANCES.
POLICE!

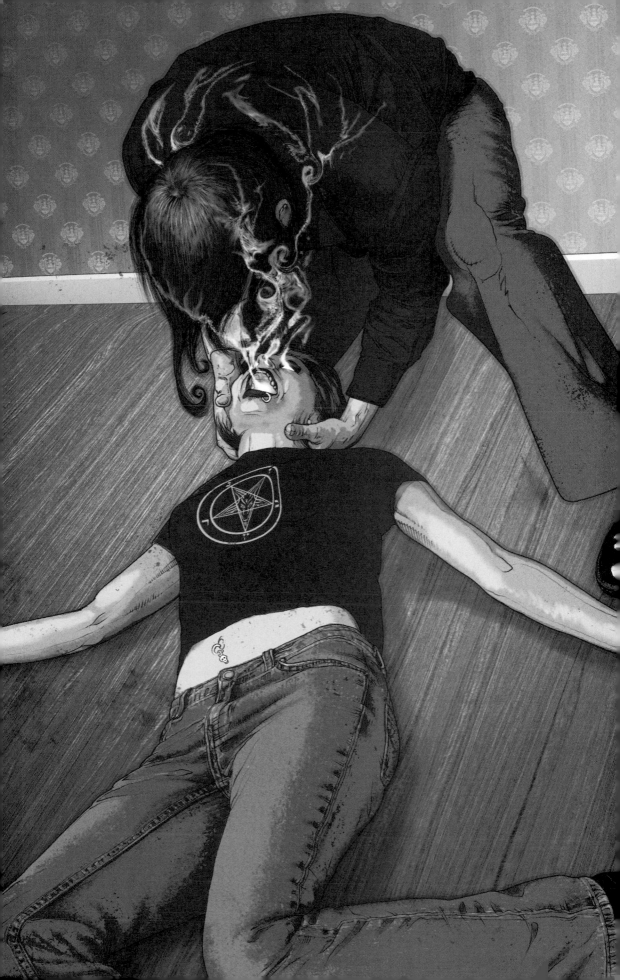

A POSSE AD ESSE AD HOC AD REM.

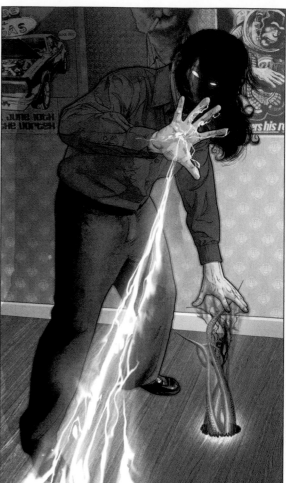

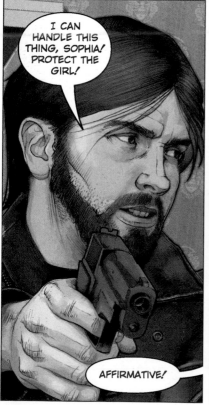

I CAN HANDLE THIS THING, SOPHIA! PROTECT THE GIRL!

AFFIRMATIVE!

AD PROTESTOR!

KILL ME! MENOG HAS FORSAKEN ME! THE THING ATE A PART OF MY SOUL!

ARE YOU BLEEDING?!?

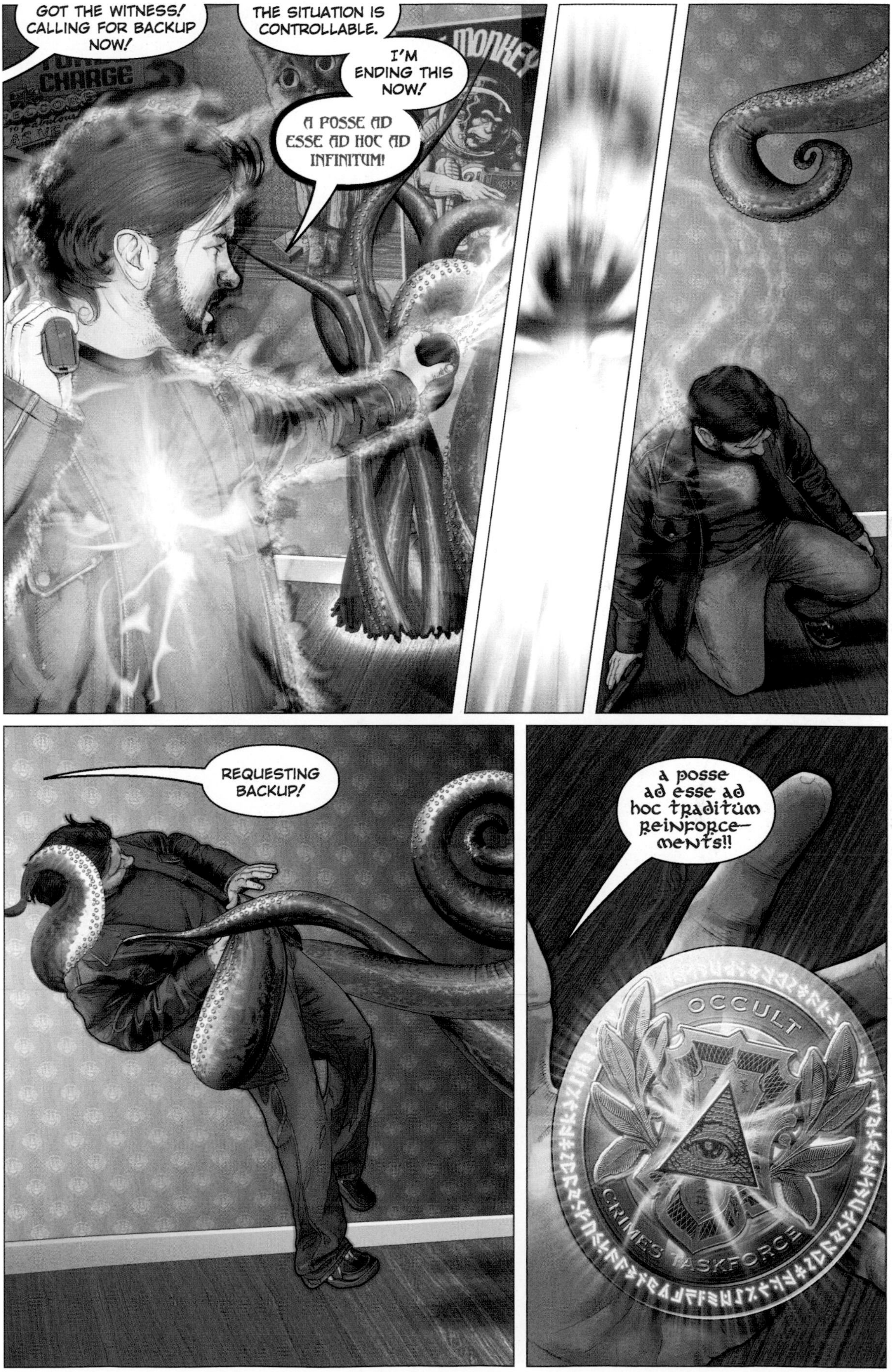

GOT THE WITNESS! CALLING FOR BACKUP NOW!
THE SITUATION IS CONTROLLABLE.
I'M ENDING THIS NOW!
A POSSE AD ESSE AD HOC AD INFINITUM!
REQUESTING BACKUP!
a posse ad esse ad hoc traditum reinforce-ments!!
OCCULT CRIMES TASKFORCE

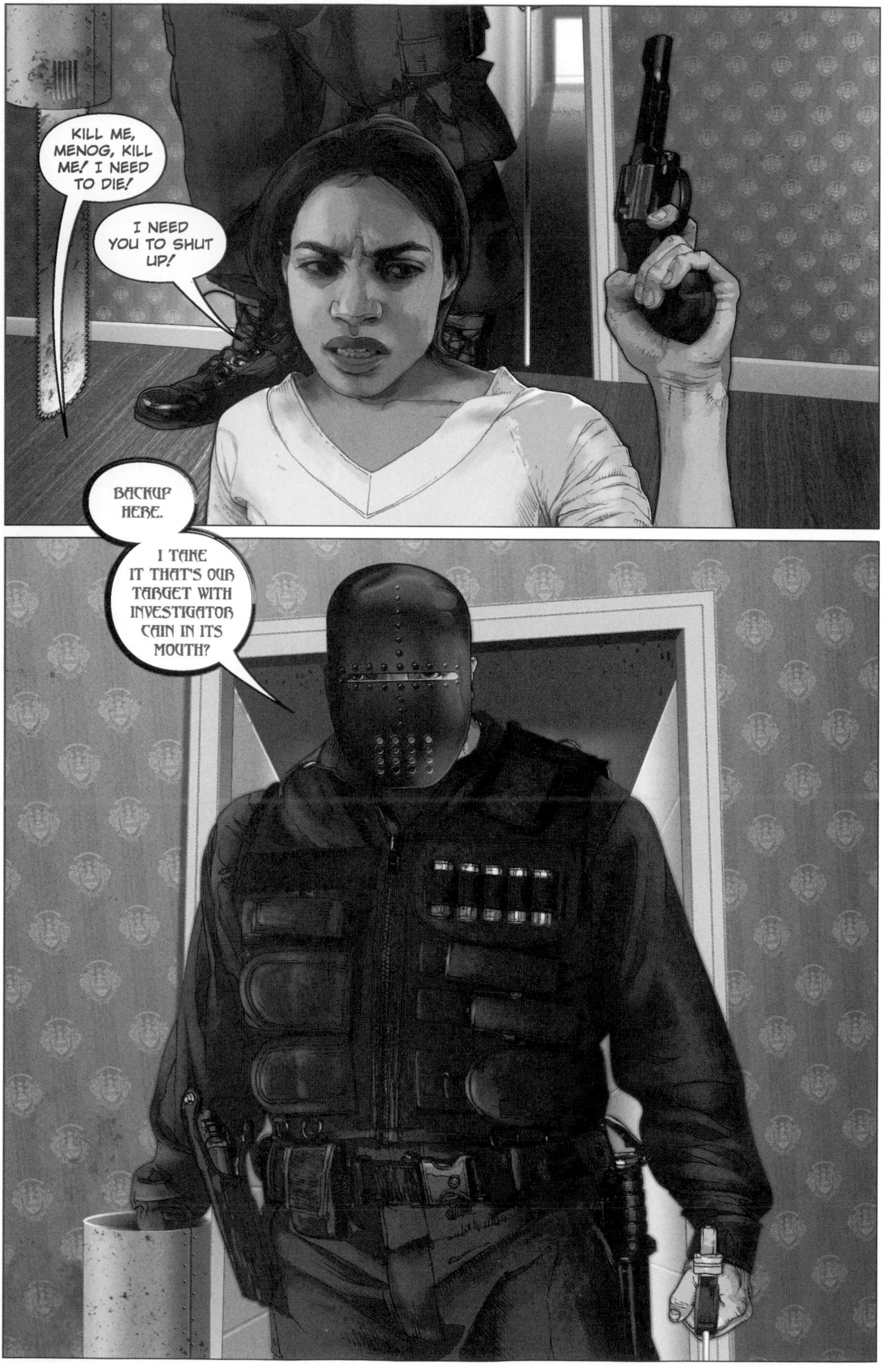
KILL ME, MENOG, KILL ME! I NEED TO DIE!
I NEED YOU TO SHUT UP!
BACKUP HERE.
I TAKE IT THAT'S OUR TARGET WITH INVESTIGATOR CAIN IN ITS MOUTH?

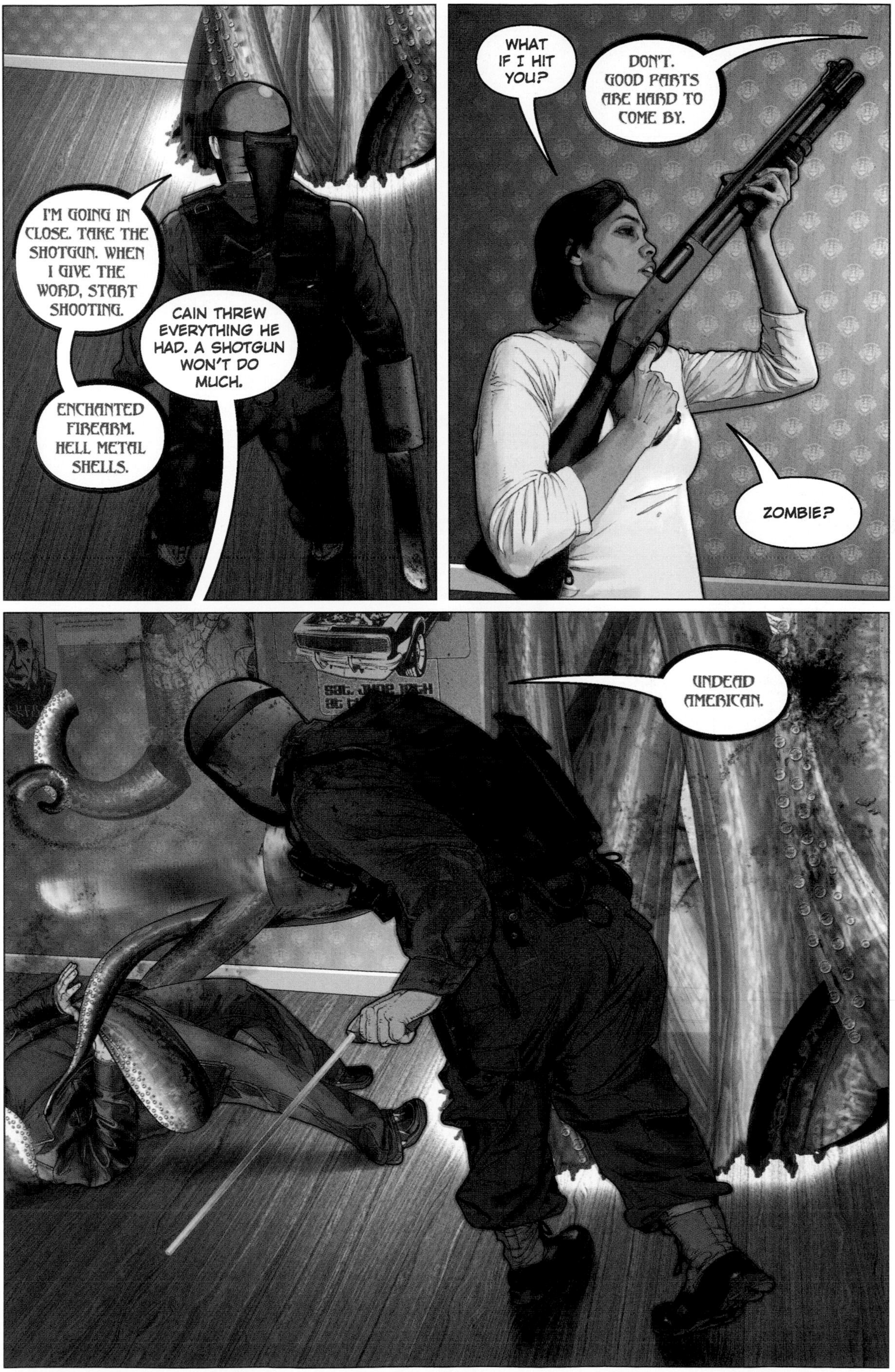
I'M GOING IN CLOSE. TAKE THE SHOTGUN. WHEN I GIVE THE WORD, START SHOOTING.
CAIN THREW EVERYTHING HE HAD. A SHOTGUN WON'T DO MUCH.
ENCHANTED FIREARM. HELL METAL SHELLS.
WHAT IF I HIT YOU?
DON'T. GOOD PARTS ARE HARD TO COME BY.
ZOMBIE?
UNDEAD AMERICAN.

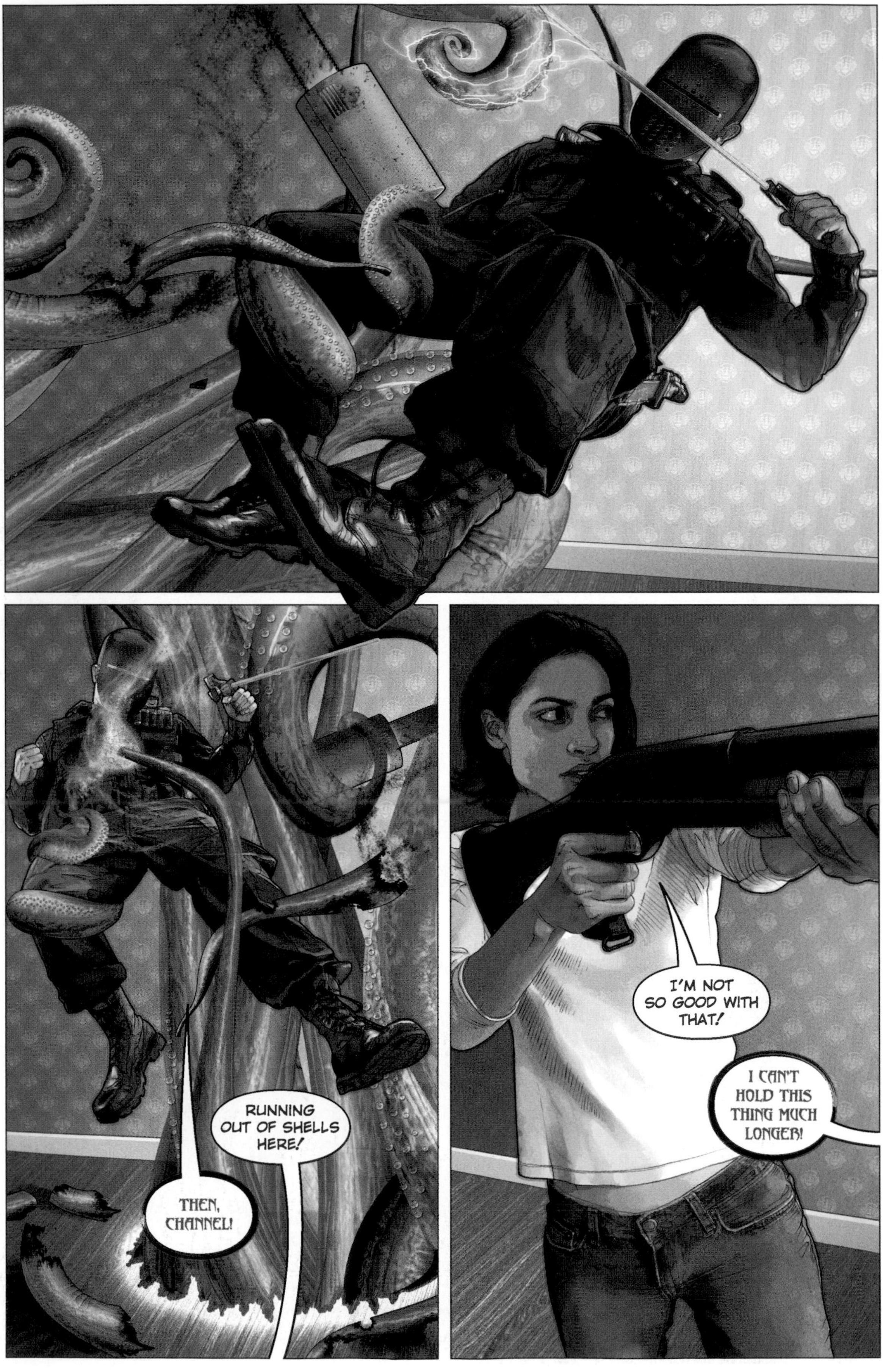
RUNNING OUT OF SHELLS HERE!
THEN, CHANNEL!
I'M NOT SO GOOD WITH THAT!
I CAN'T HOLD THIS THING MUCH LONGER!

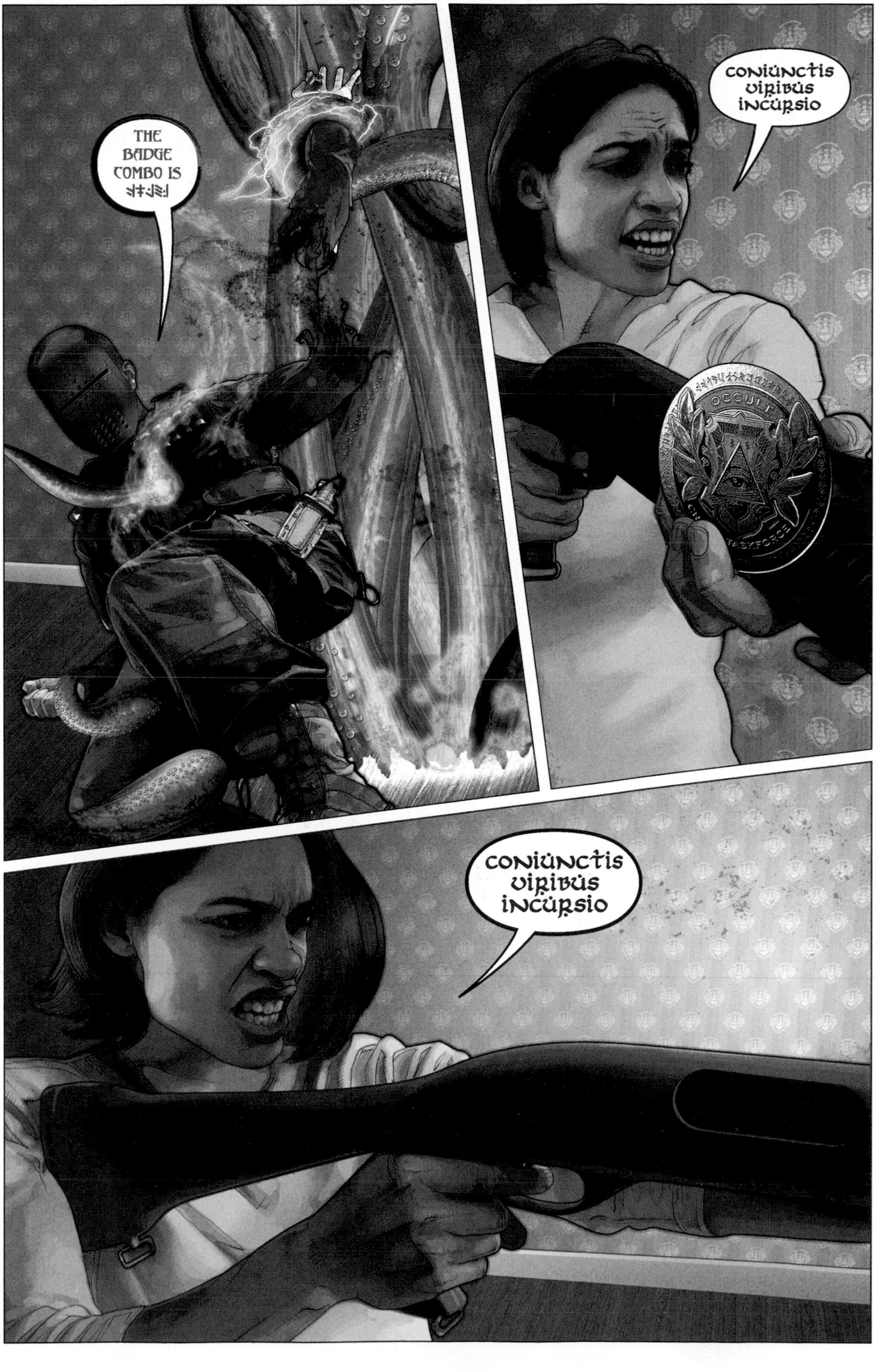
THE BADGE COMBO IS
OCCULT
TASKFORCE
CONIUNCTIS VIRIBUS INCURSIO
CONIUNCTIS VIRIBUS INCURSIO

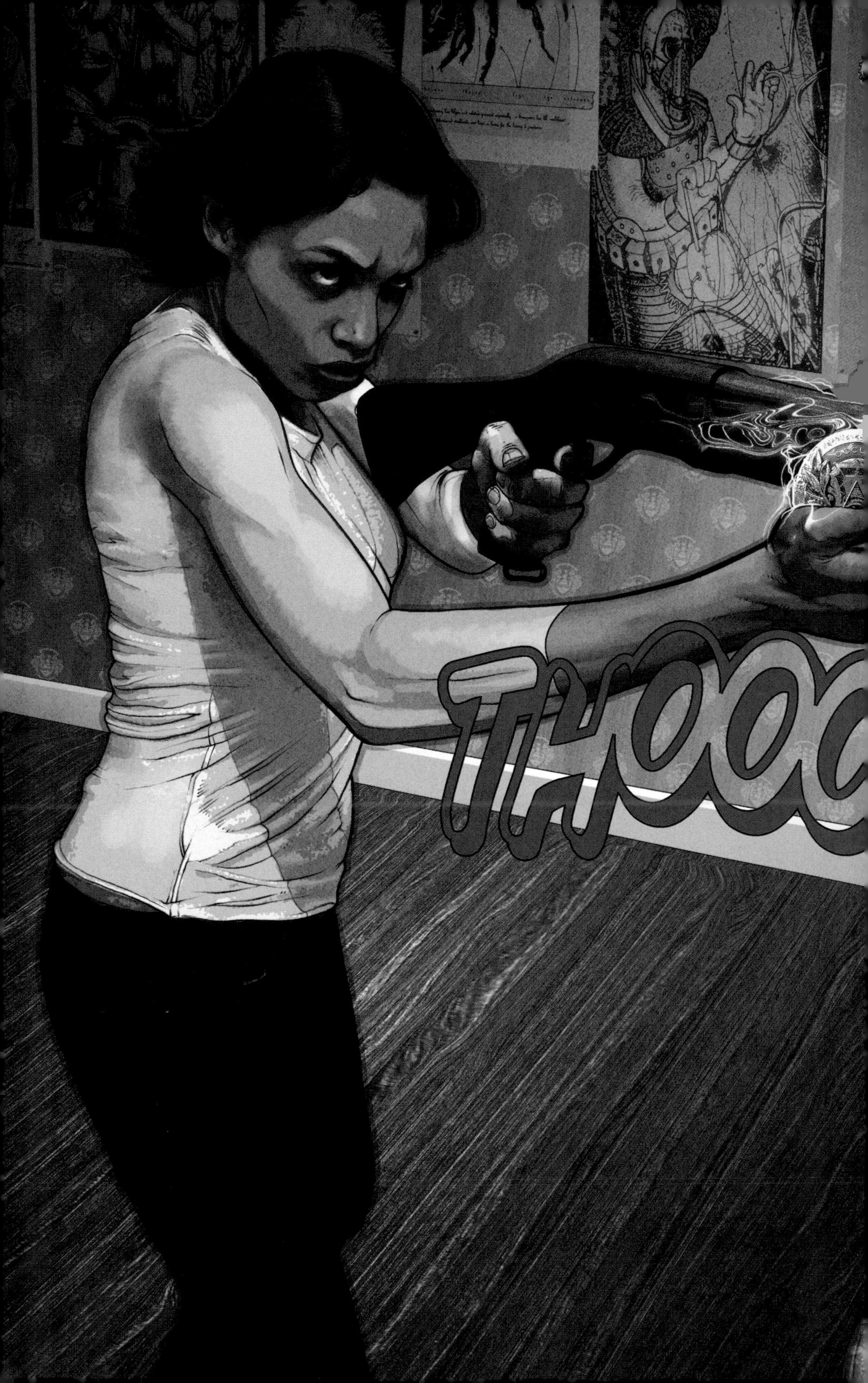
THOO

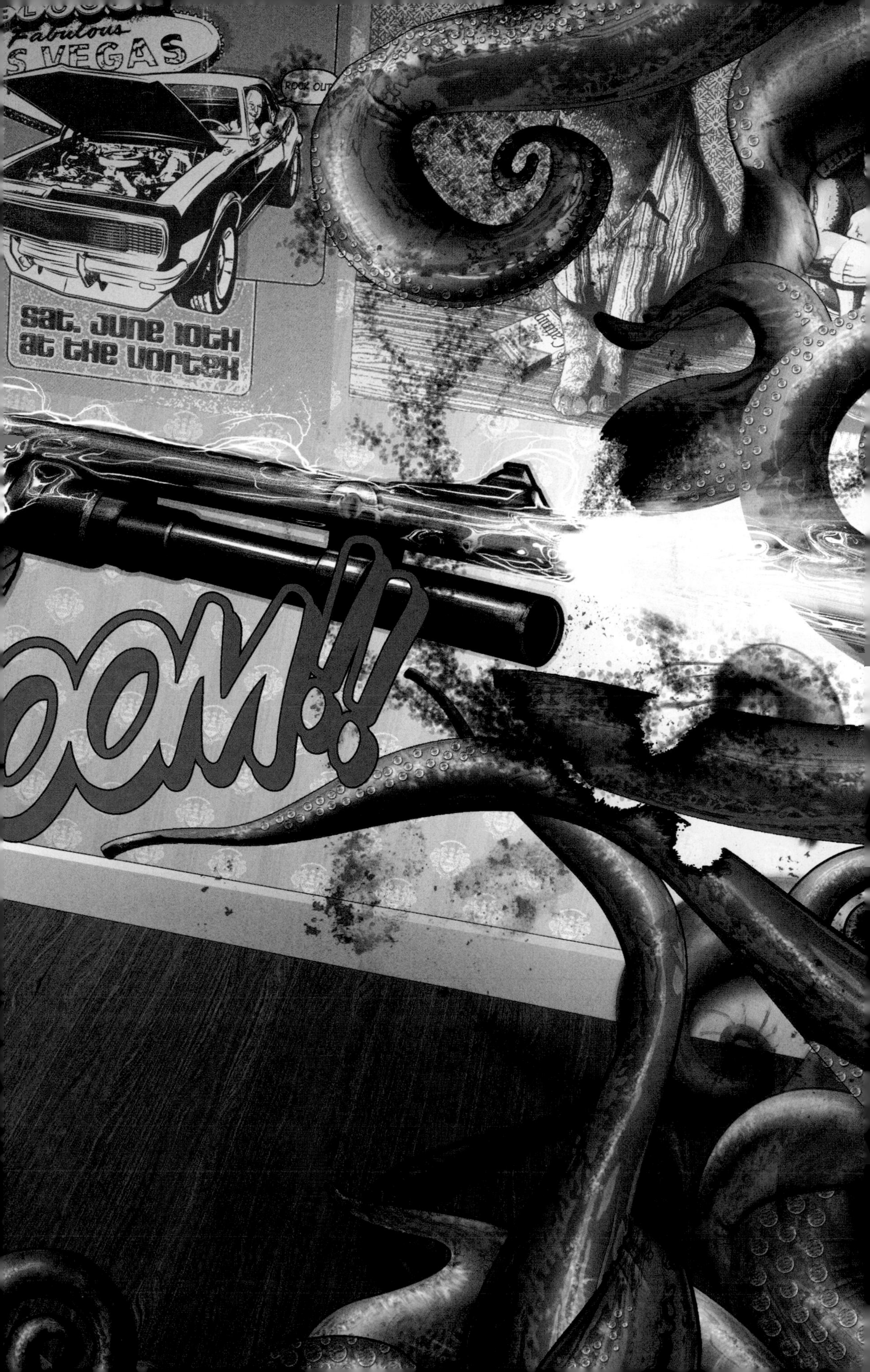
Fabulous
S VEGAS
ROCK OUT
SAT. JUNE 10TH
AT THE VORTEX

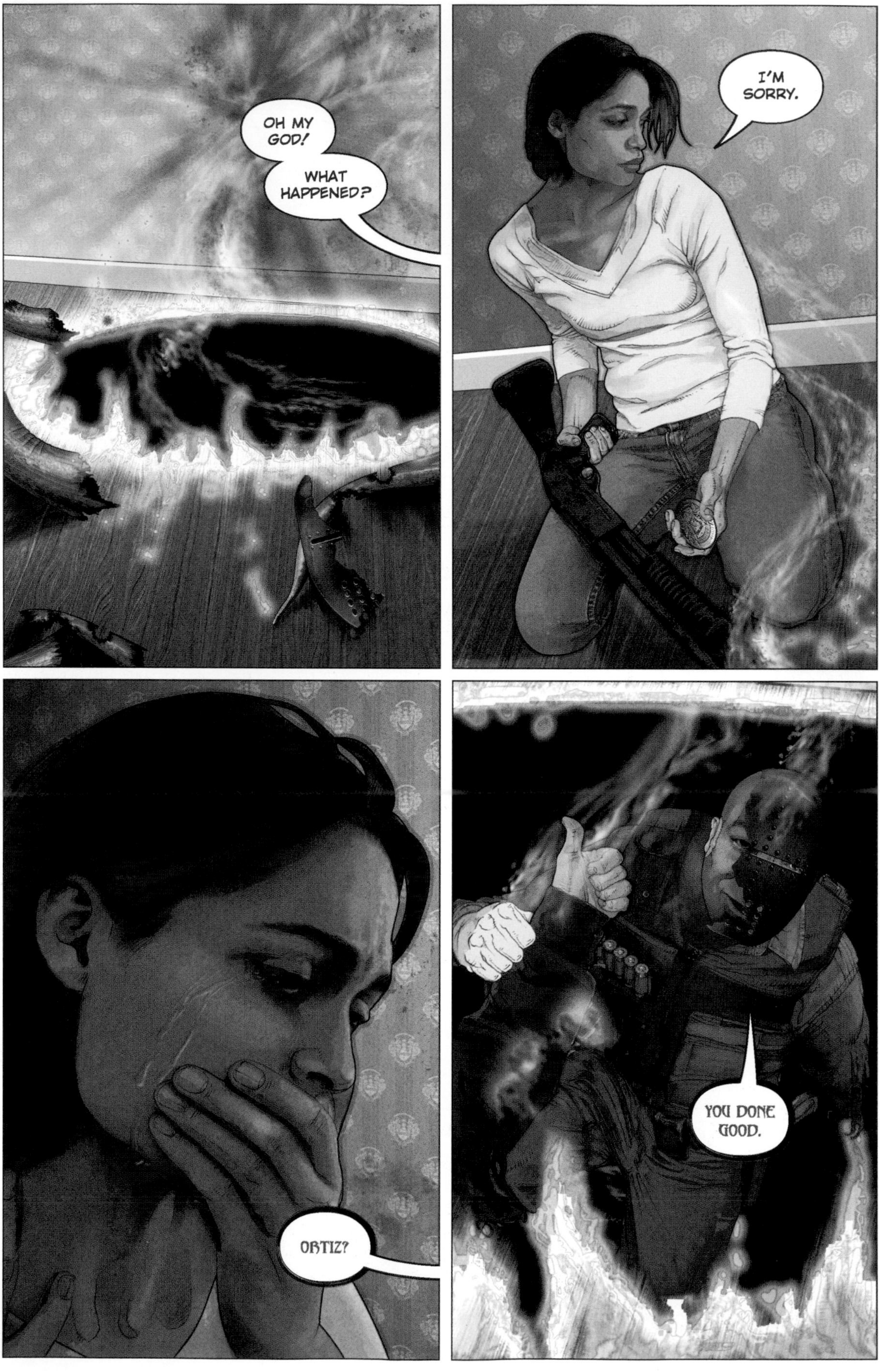
OH MY GOD!
WHAT HAPPENED?
I'M SORRY.
ORTIZ?
YOU DONE GOOD.

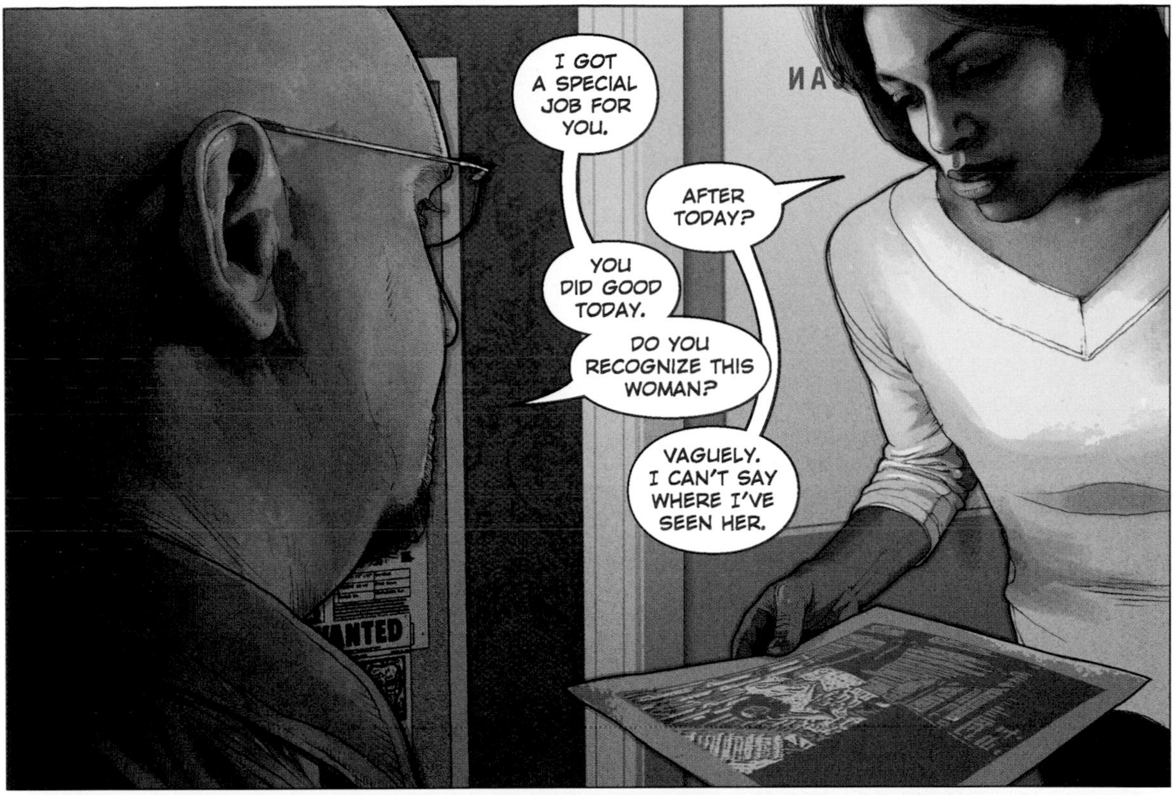
I GOT A SPECIAL JOB FOR YOU.
AFTER TODAY?
YOU DID GOOD TODAY.
DO YOU RECOGNIZE THIS WOMAN?
VAGUELY. I CAN'T SAY WHERE I'VE SEEN HER.
WANTED

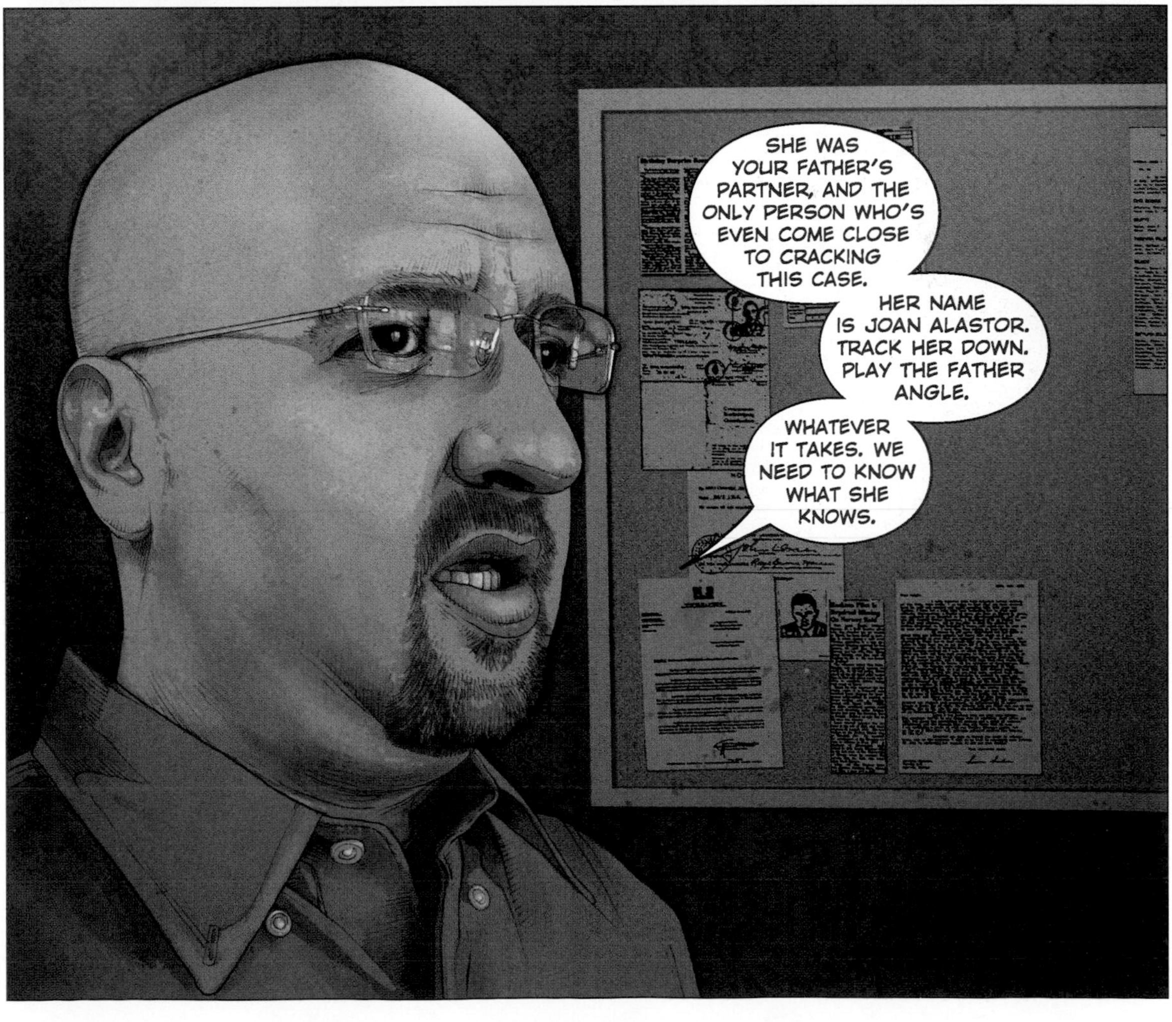
SHE WAS YOUR FATHER'S PARTNER, AND THE ONLY PERSON WHO'S EVEN COME CLOSE TO CRACKING THIS CASE.
HER NAME IS JOAN ALASTOR. TRACK HER DOWN. PLAY THE FATHER ANGLE.
WHATEVER IT TAKES. WE NEED TO KNOW WHAT SHE KNOWS.

Chapter Three

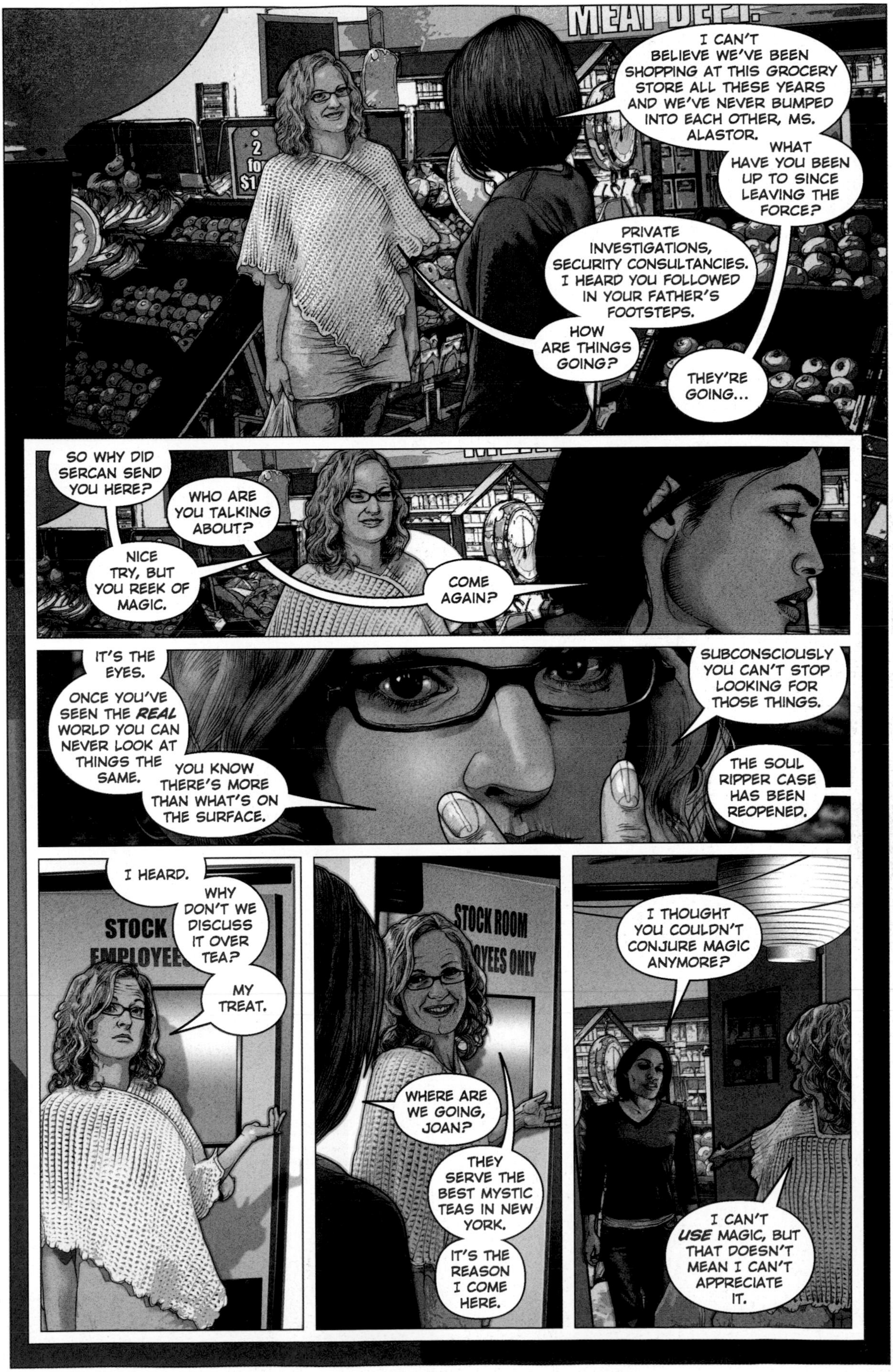
MEAT DEPT.
2 for $1
I CAN'T BELIEVE WE'VE BEEN SHOPPING AT THIS GROCERY STORE ALL THESE YEARS AND WE'VE NEVER BUMPED INTO EACH OTHER, MS. ALASTOR.
WHAT HAVE YOU BEEN UP TO SINCE LEAVING THE FORCE?
PRIVATE INVESTIGATIONS, SECURITY CONSULTANCIES. I HEARD YOU FOLLOWED IN YOUR FATHER'S FOOTSTEPS.
HOW ARE THINGS GOING?
THEY'RE GOING...
SO WHY DID SERCAN SEND YOU HERE?
WHO ARE YOU TALKING ABOUT?
NICE TRY, BUT YOU REEK OF MAGIC.
COME AGAIN?
IT'S THE EYES.
ONCE YOU'VE SEEN THE *REAL* WORLD YOU CAN NEVER LOOK AT THINGS THE SAME.
YOU KNOW THERE'S MORE THAN WHAT'S ON THE SURFACE.
SUBCONSCIOUSLY YOU CAN'T STOP LOOKING FOR THOSE THINGS.
THE SOUL RIPPER CASE HAS BEEN REOPENED.
I HEARD.
WHY DON'T WE DISCUSS IT OVER TEA?
MY TREAT.
STOCK ROOM
EMPLOYEES ONLY
WHERE ARE WE GOING, JOAN?
THEY SERVE THE BEST MYSTIC TEAS IN NEW YORK.
IT'S THE REASON I COME HERE.
I THOUGHT YOU COULDN'T CONJURE MAGIC ANYMORE?
I CAN'T *USE* MAGIC, BUT THAT DOESN'T MEAN I CAN'T APPRECIATE IT.

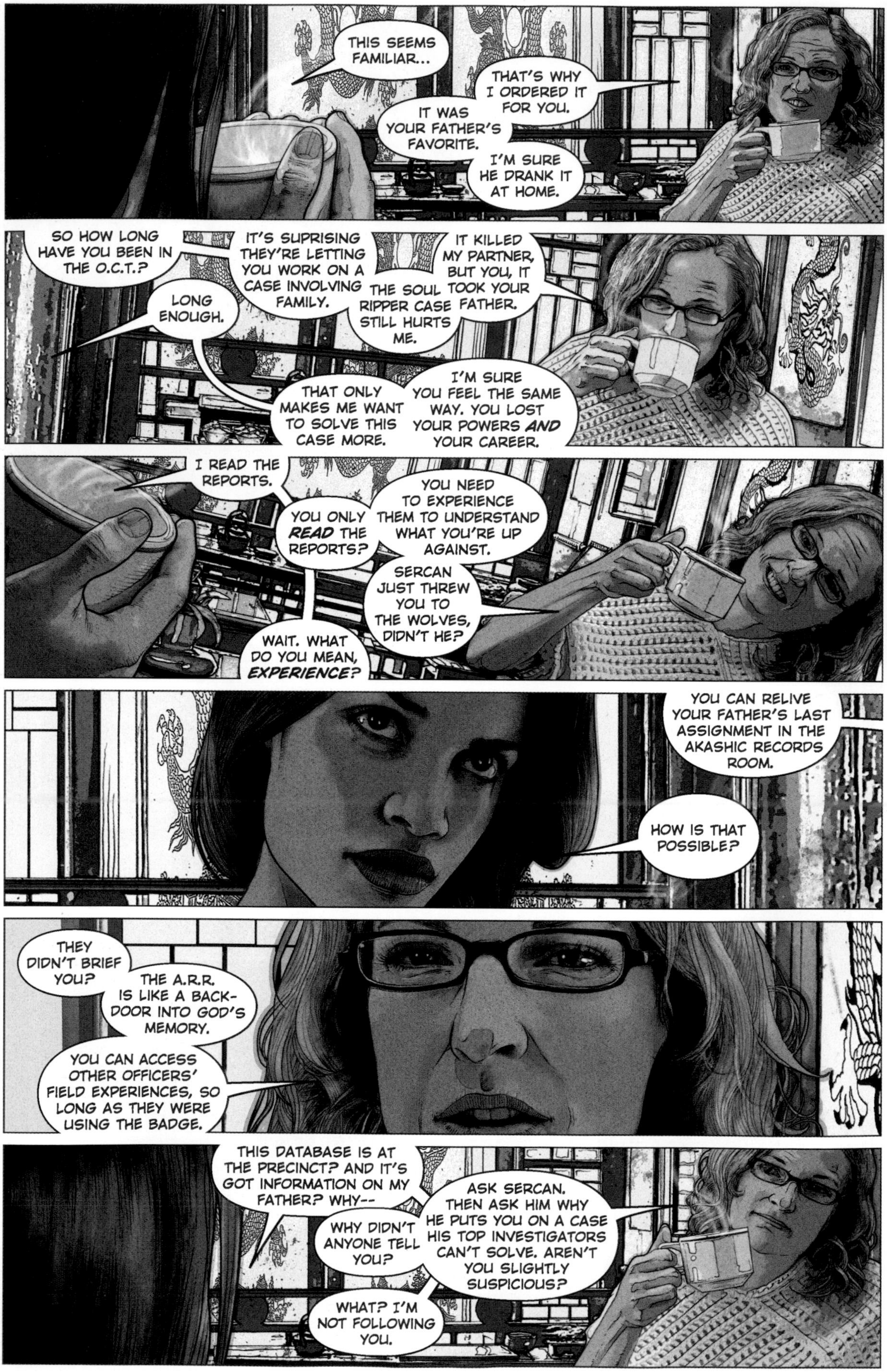
THIS SEEMS FAMILIAR...
THAT'S WHY I ORDERED IT FOR YOU.
IT WAS YOUR FATHER'S FAVORITE.
I'M SURE HE DRANK IT AT HOME.
SO HOW LONG HAVE YOU BEEN IN THE O.C.T.?
LONG ENOUGH.
IT'S SUPRISING THEY'RE LETTING YOU WORK ON A CASE INVOLVING FAMILY.
THE SOUL RIPPER CASE STILL HURTS ME.
IT KILLED MY PARTNER, BUT YOU, IT TOOK YOUR FATHER.
THAT ONLY MAKES ME WANT TO SOLVE THIS CASE MORE.
I'M SURE YOU FEEL THE SAME WAY. YOU LOST YOUR POWERS AND YOUR CAREER.
I READ THE REPORTS.
YOU ONLY READ THE REPORTS?
YOU NEED TO EXPERIENCE THEM TO UNDERSTAND WHAT YOU'RE UP AGAINST.
SERCAN JUST THREW YOU TO THE WOLVES, DIDN'T HE?
WAIT. WHAT DO YOU MEAN, EXPERIENCE?
YOU CAN RELIVE YOUR FATHER'S LAST ASSIGNMENT IN THE AKASHIC RECORDS ROOM.
HOW IS THAT POSSIBLE?
THEY DIDN'T BRIEF YOU?
THE A.R.R. IS LIKE A BACK-DOOR INTO GOD'S MEMORY.
YOU CAN ACCESS OTHER OFFICERS' FIELD EXPERIENCES, SO LONG AS THEY WERE USING THE BADGE.
THIS DATABASE IS AT THE PRECINCT? AND IT'S GOT INFORMATION ON MY FATHER? WHY--
WHY DIDN'T ANYONE TELL YOU?
ASK SERCAN. THEN ASK HIM WHY HE PUTS YOU ON A CASE HIS TOP INVESTIGATORS CAN'T SOLVE. AREN'T YOU SLIGHTLY SUSPICIOUS?
WHAT? I'M NOT FOLLOWING YOU.

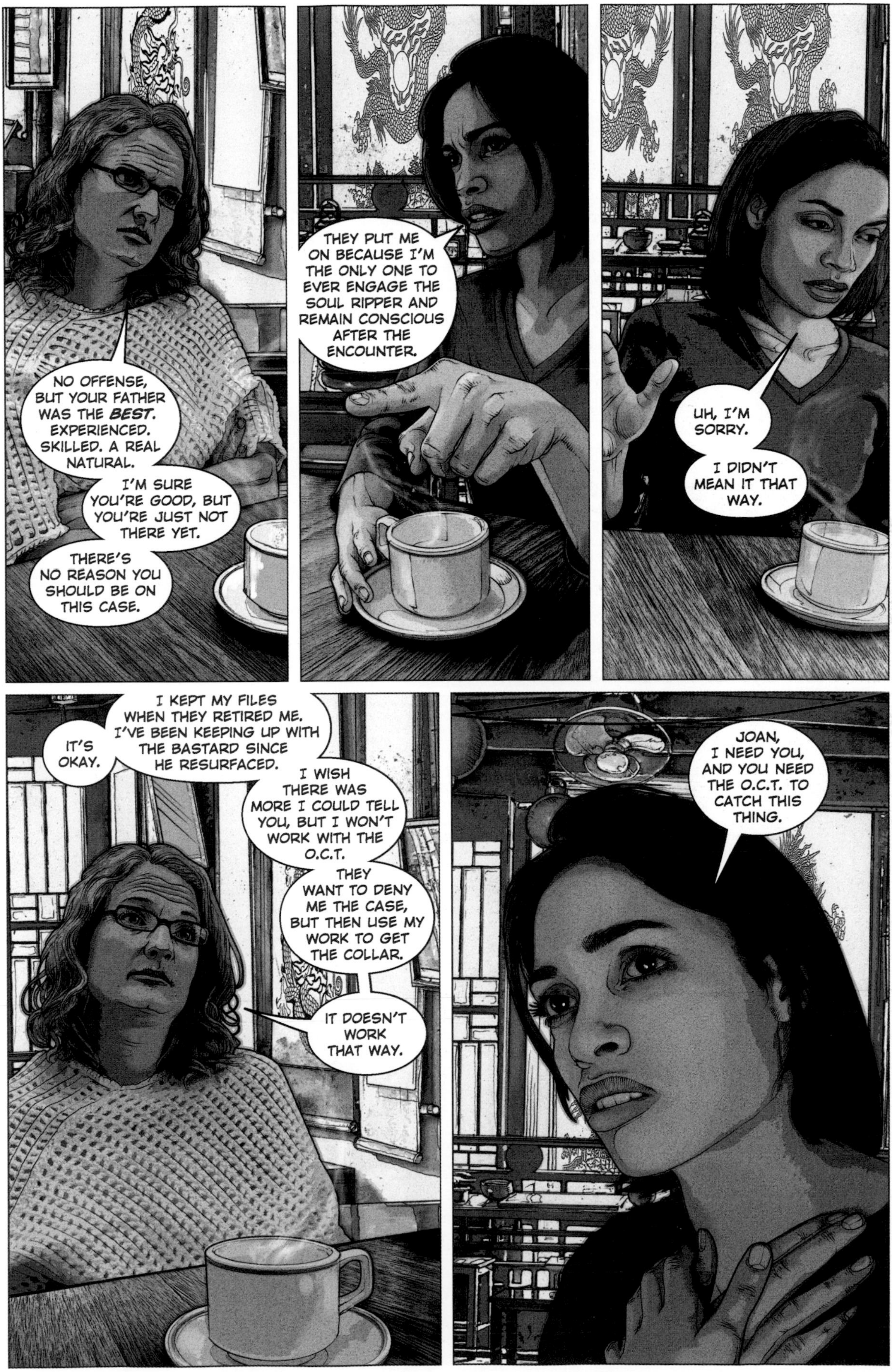
NO OFFENSE, BUT YOUR FATHER WAS THE *BEST*. EXPERIENCED. SKILLED. A REAL NATURAL.
I'M SURE YOU'RE GOOD, BUT YOU'RE JUST NOT THERE YET.
THERE'S NO REASON YOU SHOULD BE ON THIS CASE.
THEY PUT ME ON BECAUSE I'M THE ONLY ONE TO EVER ENGAGE THE SOUL RIPPER AND REMAIN CONSCIOUS AFTER THE ENCOUNTER.
UH, I'M SORRY.
I DIDN'T MEAN IT THAT WAY.
IT'S OKAY.
I KEPT MY FILES WHEN THEY RETIRED ME. I'VE BEEN KEEPING UP WITH THE BASTARD SINCE HE RESURFACED.
I WISH THERE WAS MORE I COULD TELL YOU, BUT I WON'T WORK WITH THE O.C.T.
THEY WANT TO DENY ME THE CASE, BUT THEN USE MY WORK TO GET THE COLLAR.
IT DOESN'T WORK THAT WAY.
JOAN, I NEED YOU, AND YOU NEED THE O.C.T. TO CATCH THIS THING.

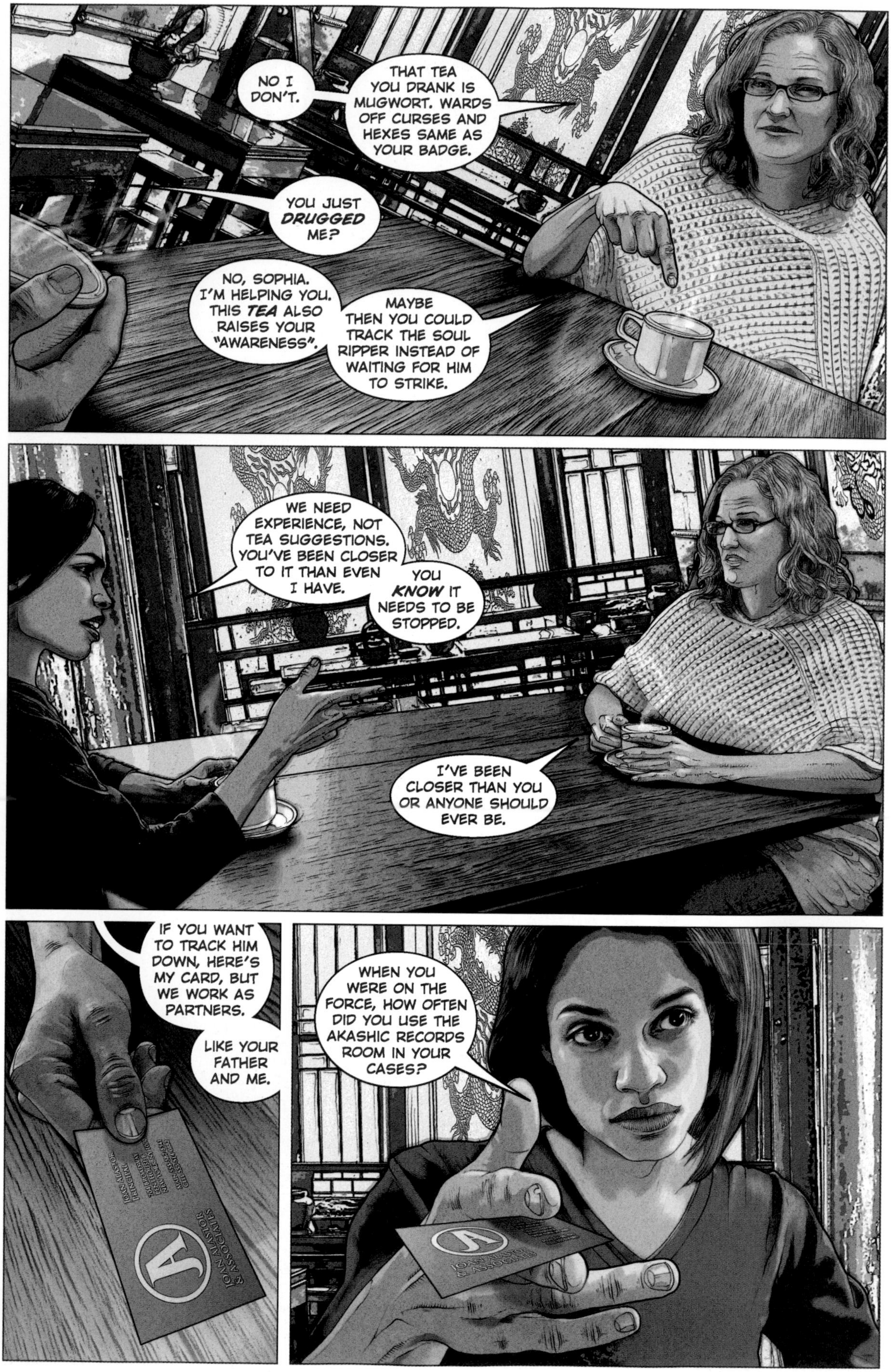

THAT TEA YOU DRANK IS MUGWORT. WARDS OFF CURSES AND HEXES SAME AS YOUR BADGE.
NO I DON'T.
YOU JUST *DRUGGED* ME?
NO, SOPHIA. I'M HELPING YOU. THIS *TEA* ALSO RAISES YOUR "AWARENESS".
MAYBE THEN YOU COULD TRACK THE SOUL RIPPER INSTEAD OF WAITING FOR HIM TO STRIKE.
WE NEED EXPERIENCE, NOT TEA SUGGESTIONS. YOU'VE BEEN CLOSER TO IT THAN EVEN I HAVE.
YOU *KNOW* IT NEEDS TO BE STOPPED.
I'VE BEEN CLOSER THAN YOU OR ANYONE SHOULD EVER BE.
IF YOU WANT TO TRACK HIM DOWN, HERE'S MY CARD, BUT WE WORK AS PARTNERS.
LIKE YOUR FATHER AND ME.
JOAN ALASTOR & ASSOCIATES
WHEN YOU WERE ON THE FORCE, HOW OFTEN DID YOU USE THE AKASHIC RECORDS ROOM IN YOUR CASES?

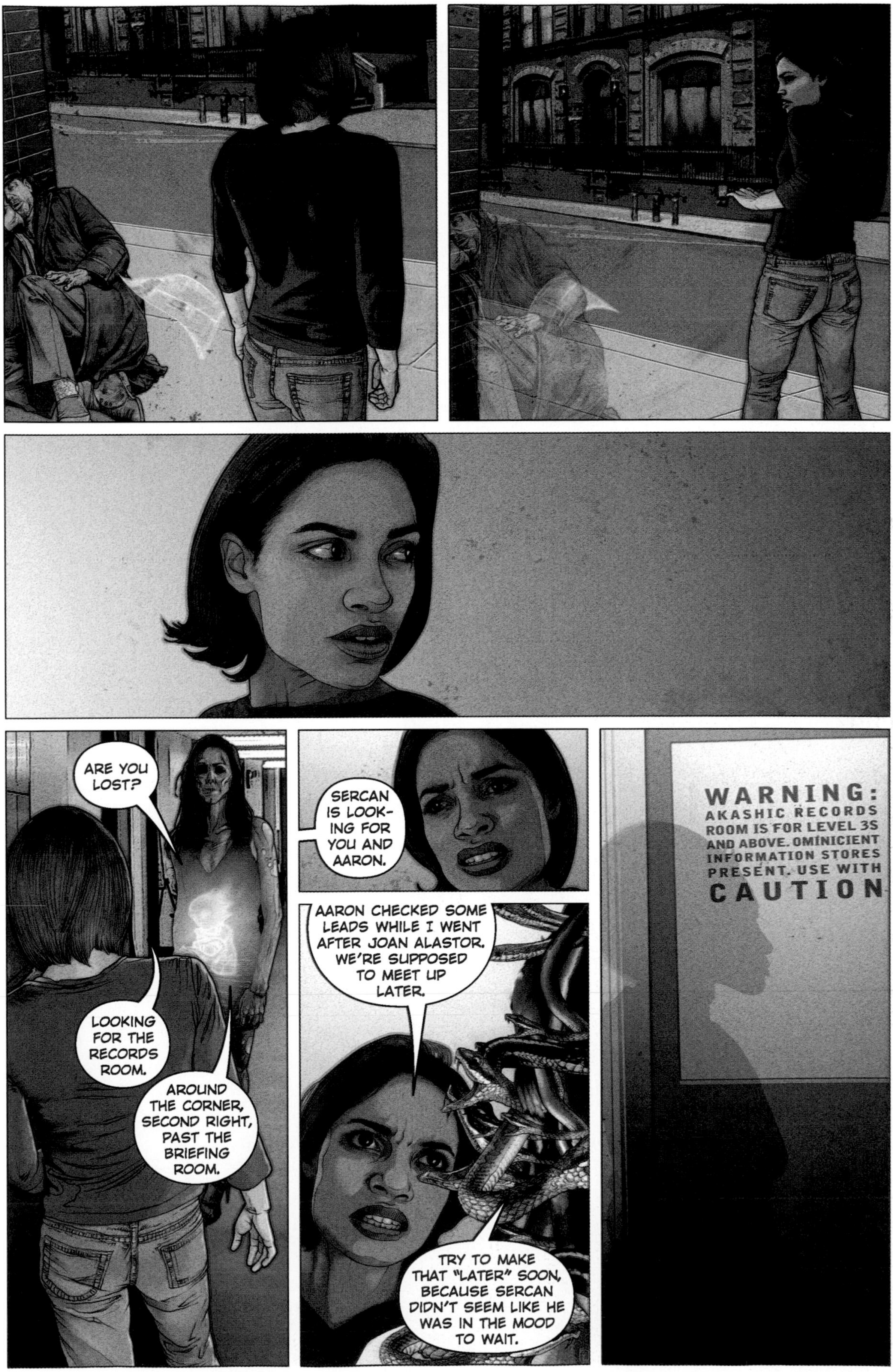
ARE YOU LOST?
LOOKING FOR THE RECORDS ROOM.
AROUND THE CORNER, SECOND RIGHT, PAST THE BRIEFING ROOM.
SERCAN IS LOOKING FOR YOU AND AARON.
AARON CHECKED SOME LEADS WHILE I WENT AFTER JOAN ALASTOR. WE'RE SUPPOSED TO MEET UP LATER.
TRY TO MAKE THAT "LATER" SOON, BECAUSE SERCAN DIDN'T SEEM LIKE HE WAS IN THE MOOD TO WAIT.
WARNING: AKASHIC RECORDS ROOM IS FOR LEVEL 3S AND ABOVE. OMINICIENT INFORMATION STORES PRESENT. USE WITH CAUTION

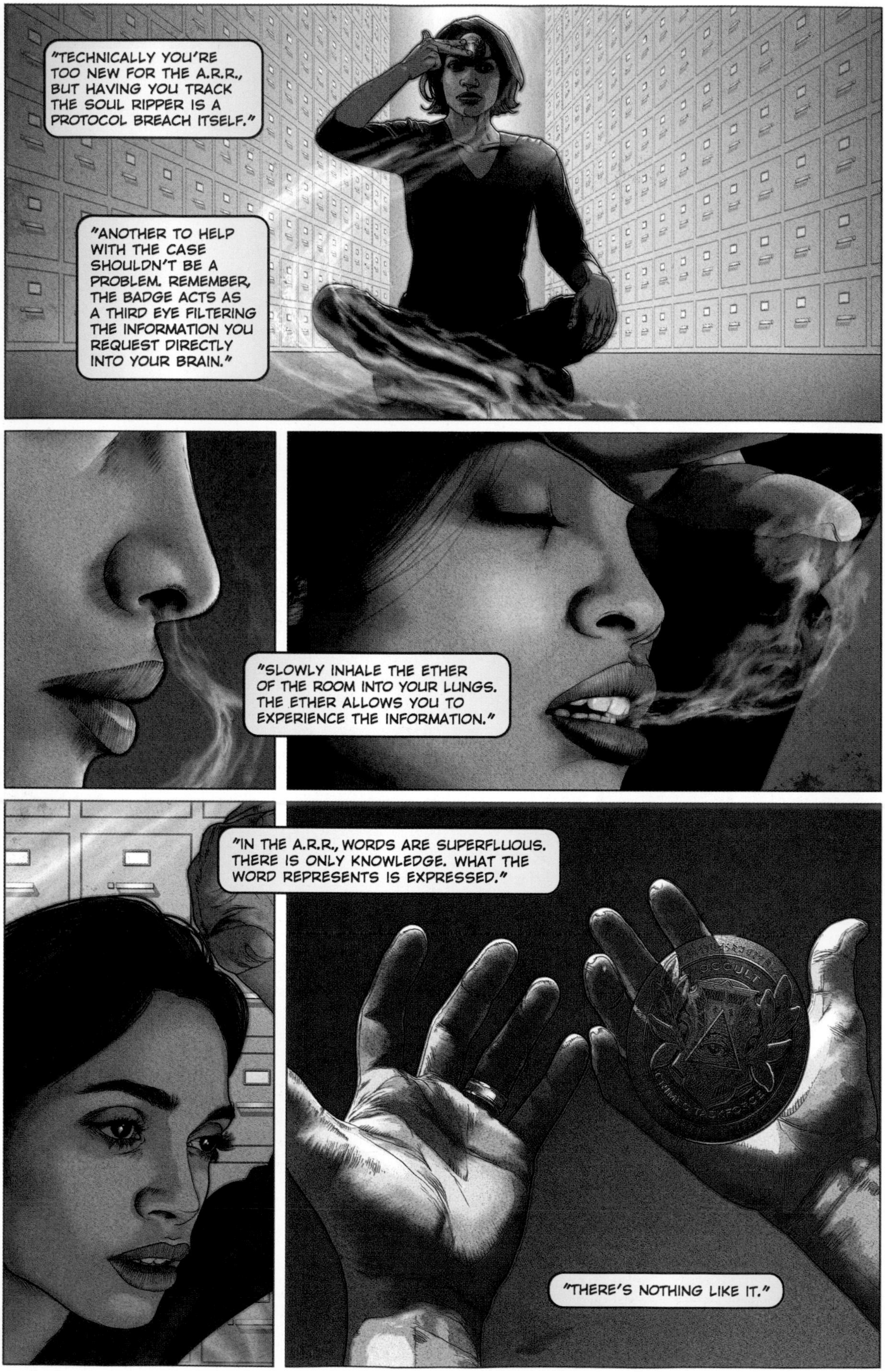
"TECHNICALLY YOU'RE TOO NEW FOR THE A.R.R., BUT HAVING YOU TRACK THE SOUL RIPPER IS A PROTOCOL BREACH ITSELF."
"ANOTHER TO HELP WITH THE CASE SHOULDN'T BE A PROBLEM. REMEMBER, THE BADGE ACTS AS A THIRD EYE FILTERING THE INFORMATION YOU REQUEST DIRECTLY INTO YOUR BRAIN."
"SLOWLY INHALE THE ETHER OF THE ROOM INTO YOUR LUNGS. THE ETHER ALLOWS YOU TO EXPERIENCE THE INFORMATION."
"IN THE A.R.R., WORDS ARE SUPERFLUOUS. THERE IS ONLY KNOWLEDGE. WHAT THE WORD REPRESENTS IS EXPRESSED."
"THERE'S NOTHING LIKE IT."

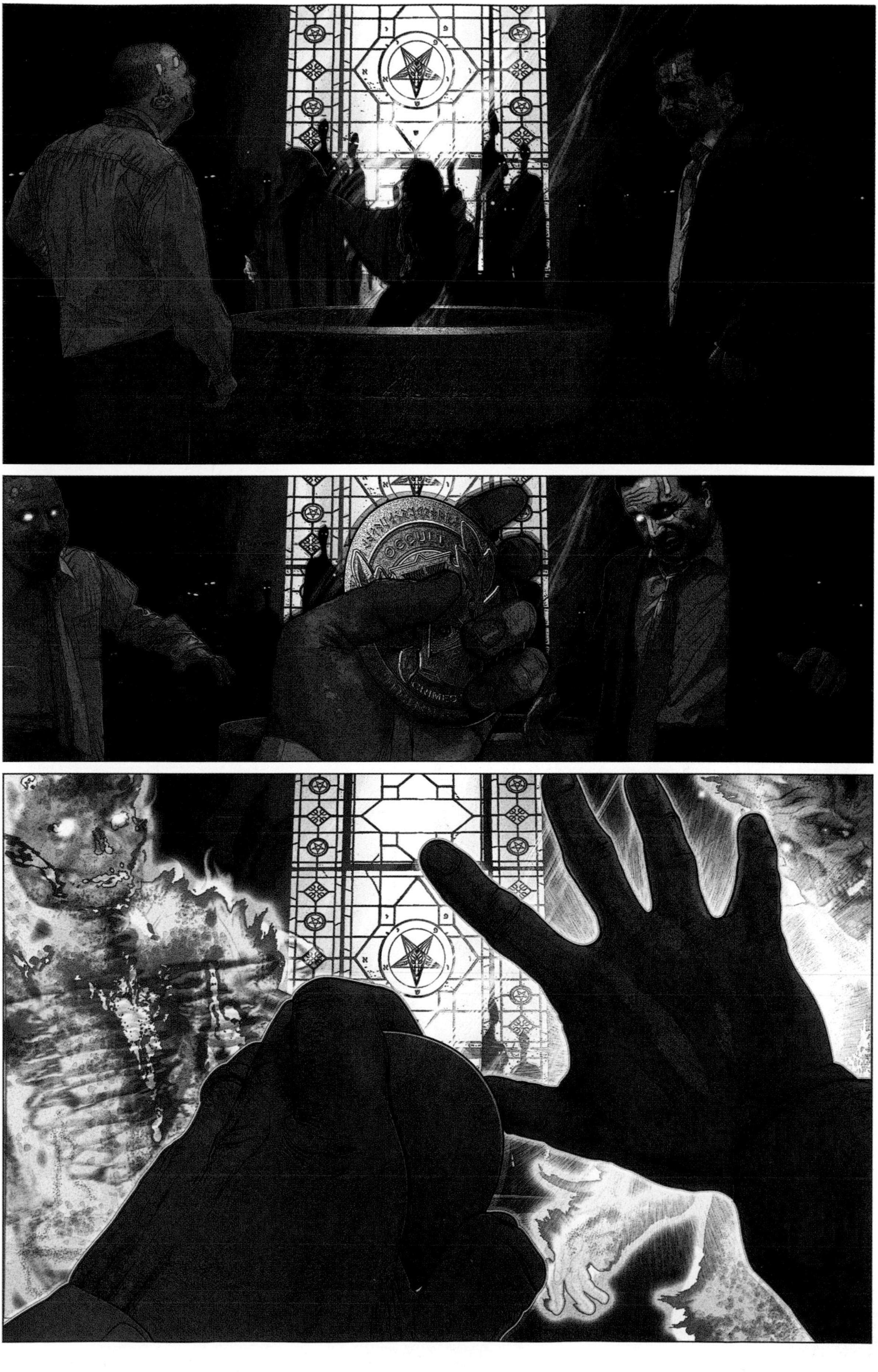
OCCULT
CRIMES

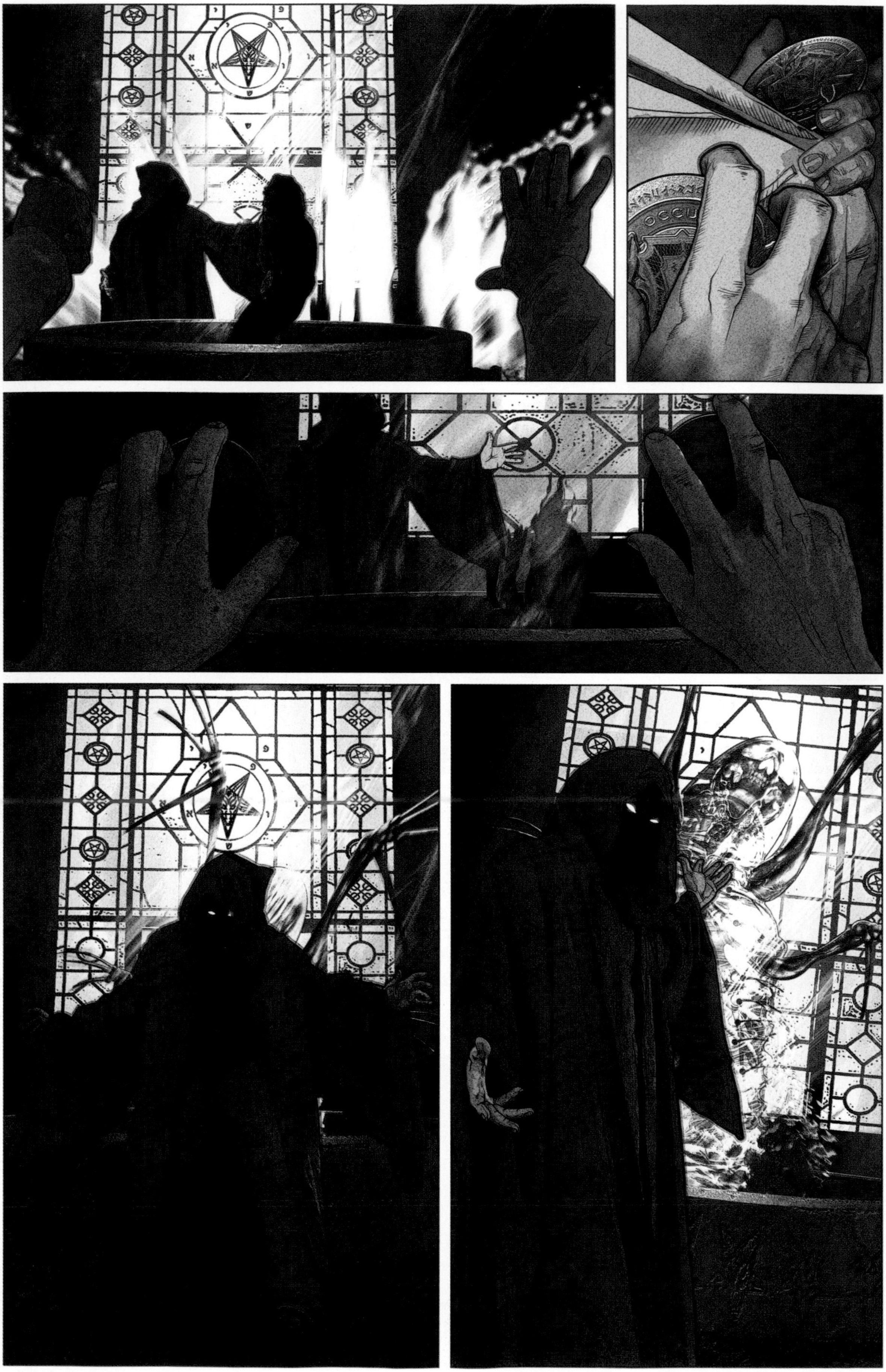

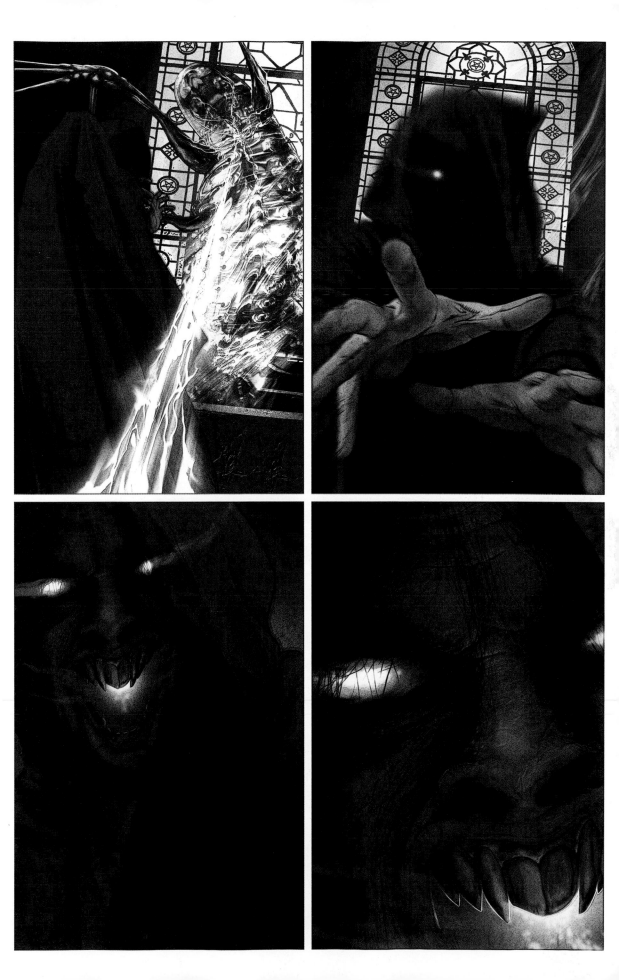

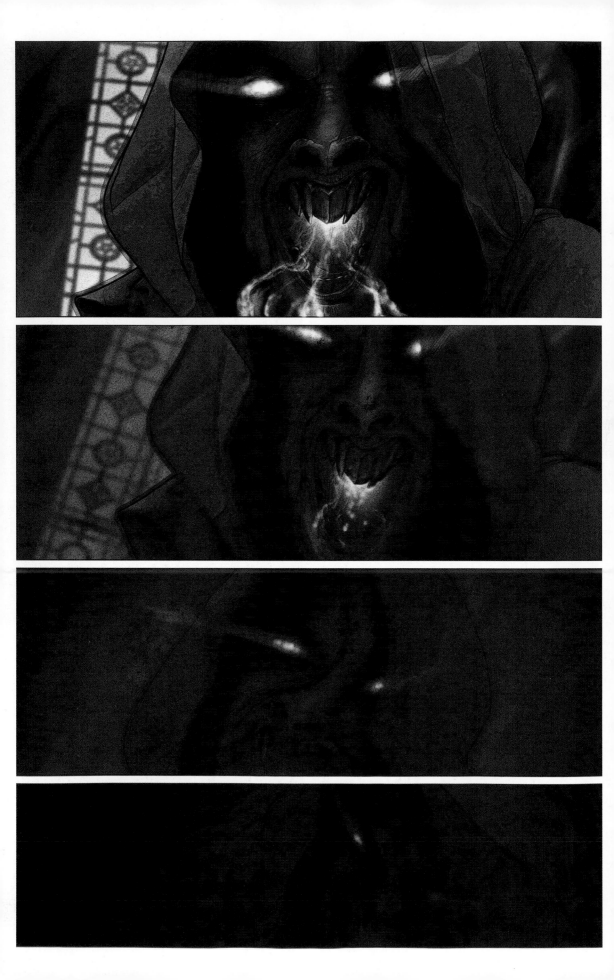

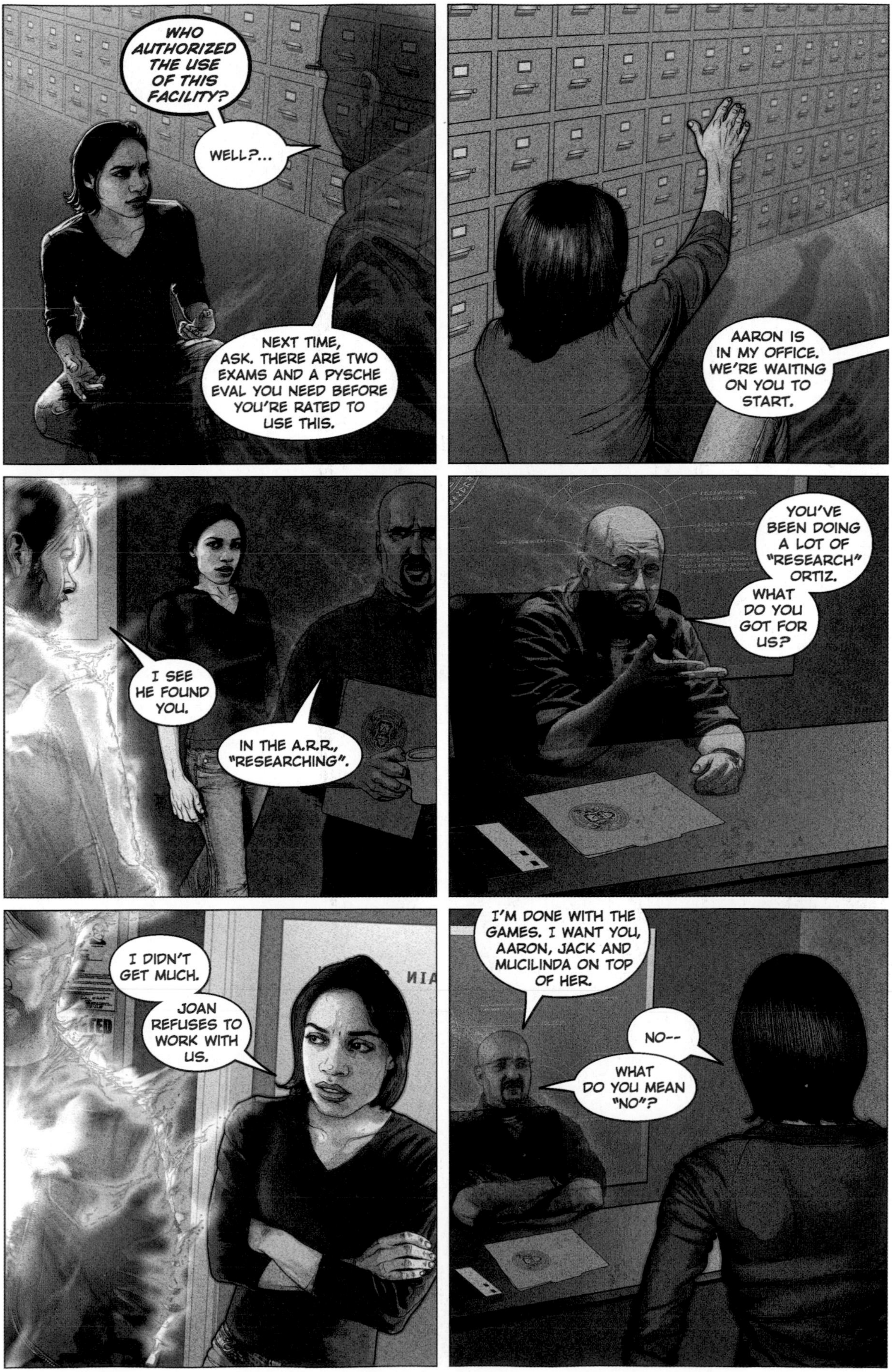
WHO AUTHORIZED THE USE OF THIS FACILITY?
WELL?...
NEXT TIME, ASK. THERE ARE TWO EXAMS AND A PYSCHE EVAL YOU NEED BEFORE YOU'RE RATED TO USE THIS.
AARON IS IN MY OFFICE. WE'RE WAITING ON YOU TO START.
I SEE HE FOUND YOU.
IN THE A.R.R., "RESEARCHING".
YOU'VE BEEN DOING A LOT OF "RESEARCH" ORTIZ.
WHAT DO YOU GOT FOR US?
I DIDN'T GET MUCH.
JOAN REFUSES TO WORK WITH US.
I'M DONE WITH THE GAMES. I WANT YOU, AARON, JACK AND MUCILINDA ON TOP OF HER.
NO--
WHAT DO YOU MEAN "NO"?

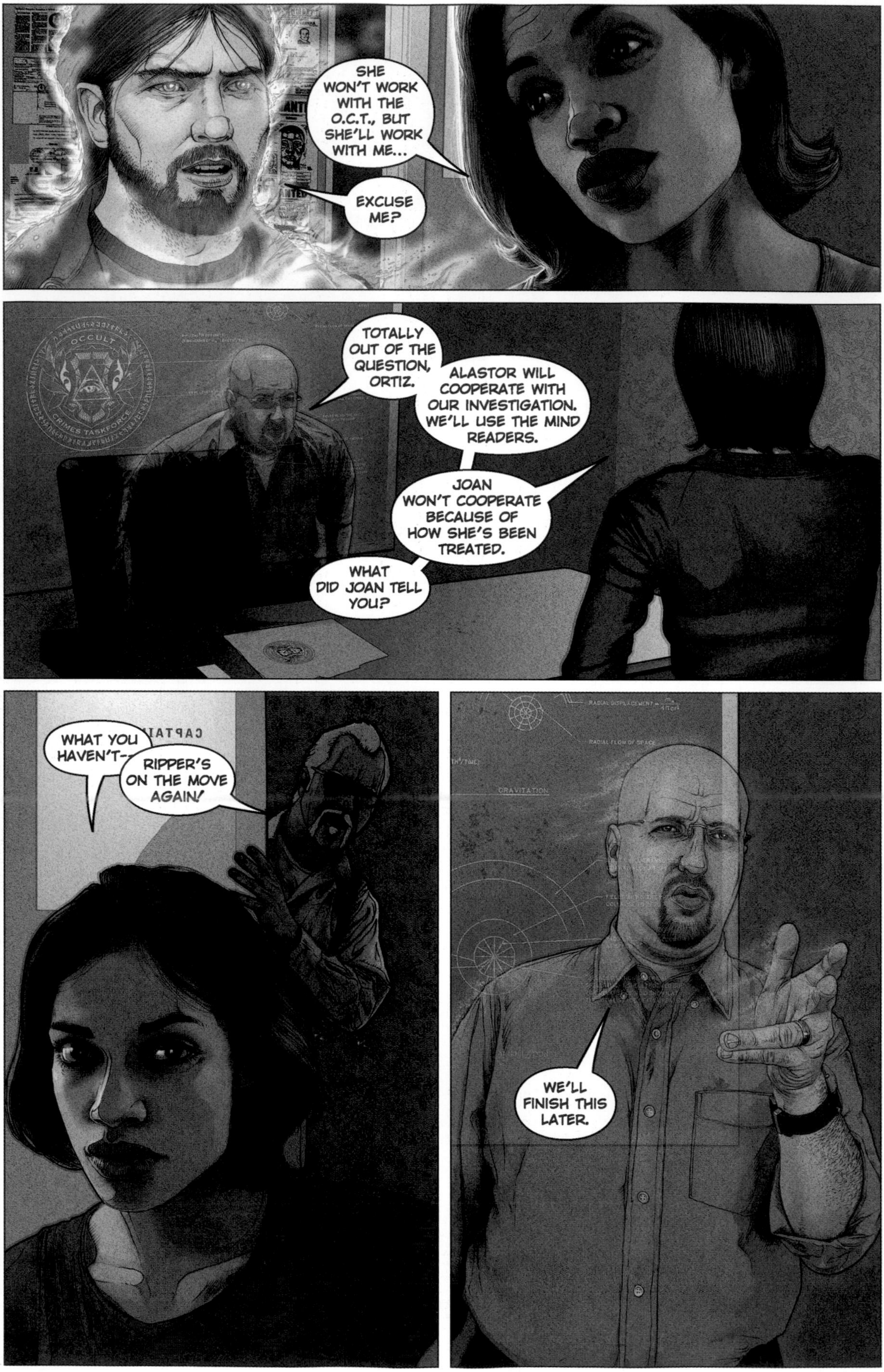
SHE WON'T WORK WITH THE O.C.T., BUT SHE'LL WORK WITH ME...
EXCUSE ME?
OCCULT CRIMES TASKFORCE
TOTALLY OUT OF THE QUESTION, ORTIZ.
ALASTOR WILL COOPERATE WITH OUR INVESTIGATION. WE'LL USE THE MIND READERS.
JOAN WON'T COOPERATE BECAUSE OF HOW SHE'S BEEN TREATED.
WHAT DID JOAN TELL YOU?
CAPTAI
WHAT YOU HAVEN'T--
RIPPER'S ON THE MOVE AGAIN!
RADIAL DISPLACEMENT
RADIAL FLOW OF SPACE
GRAVITATION
WE'LL FINISH THIS LATER.

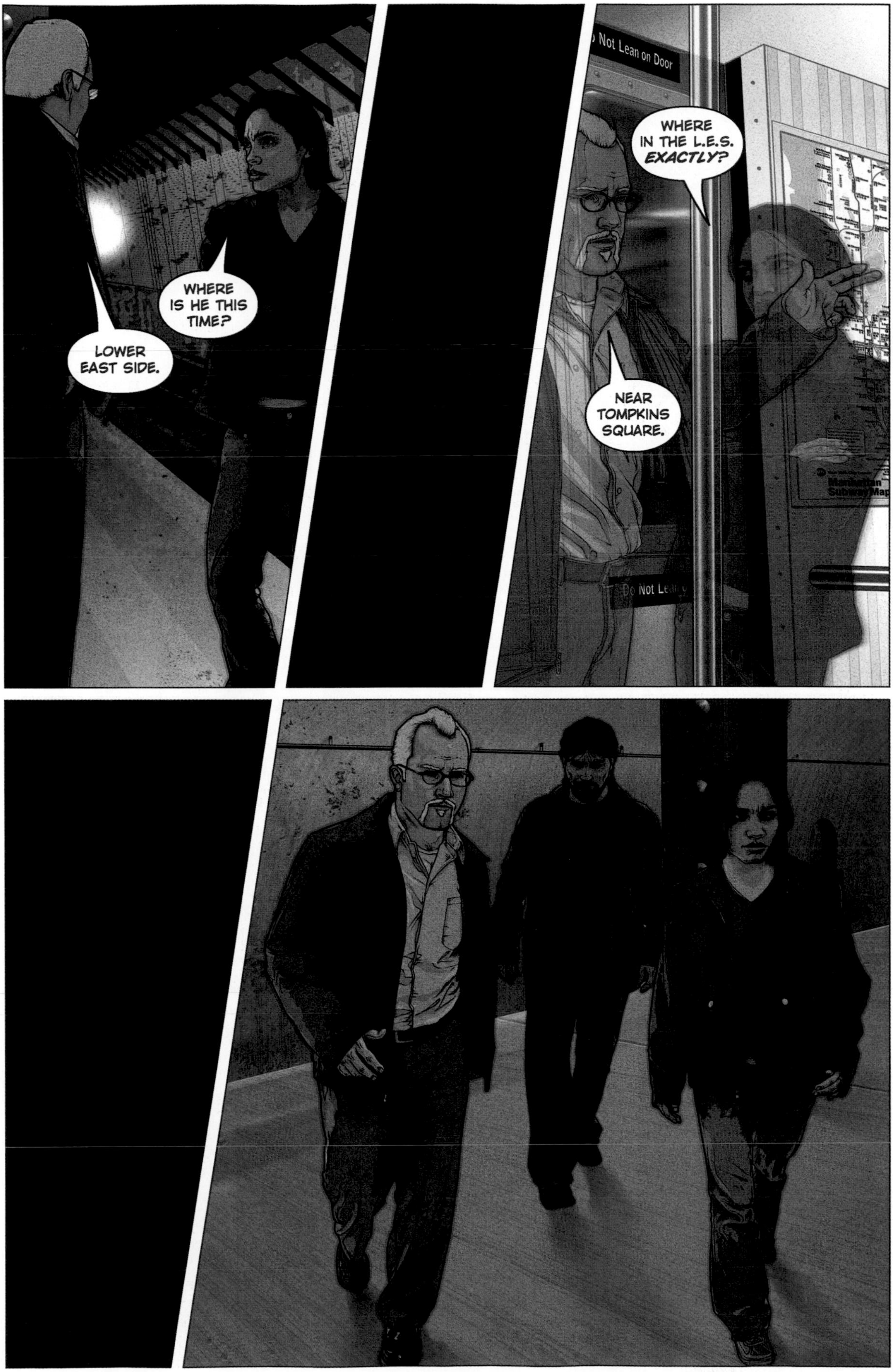

WHERE IS HE THIS TIME?
LOWER EAST SIDE.
Do Not Lean on Door
WHERE IN THE L.E.S. *EXACTLY?*
NEAR TOMPKINS SQUARE.
Manhattan Subway Map

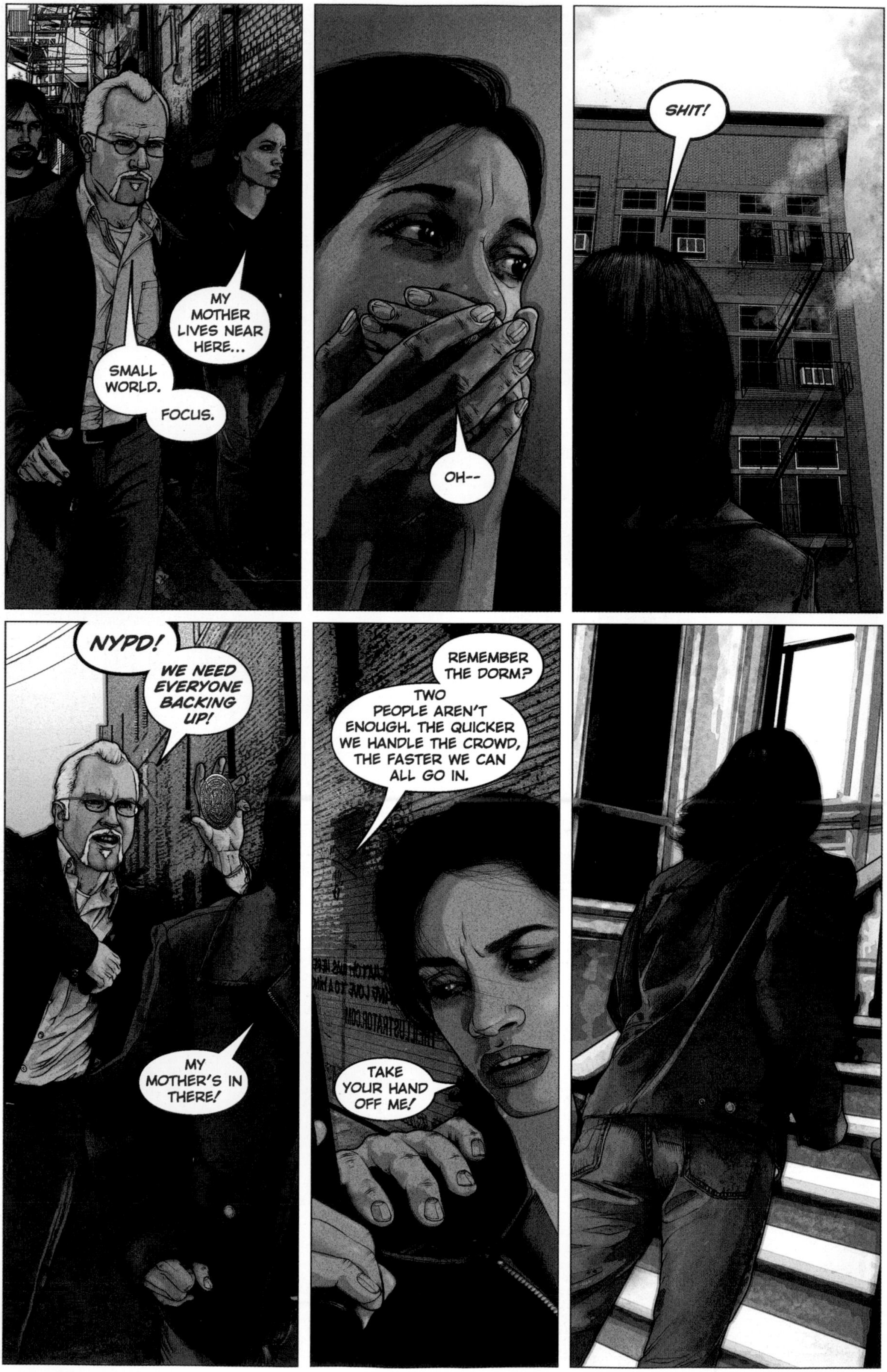
MY MOTHER LIVES NEAR HERE...
SMALL WORLD.
FOCUS.
OH--
SHIT!
NYPD!
WE NEED EVERYONE BACKING UP!
MY MOTHER'S IN THERE!
REMEMBER THE DORM?
TWO PEOPLE AREN'T ENOUGH. THE QUICKER WE HANDLE THE CROWD, THE FASTER WE CAN ALL GO IN.
TAKE YOUR HAND OFF ME!

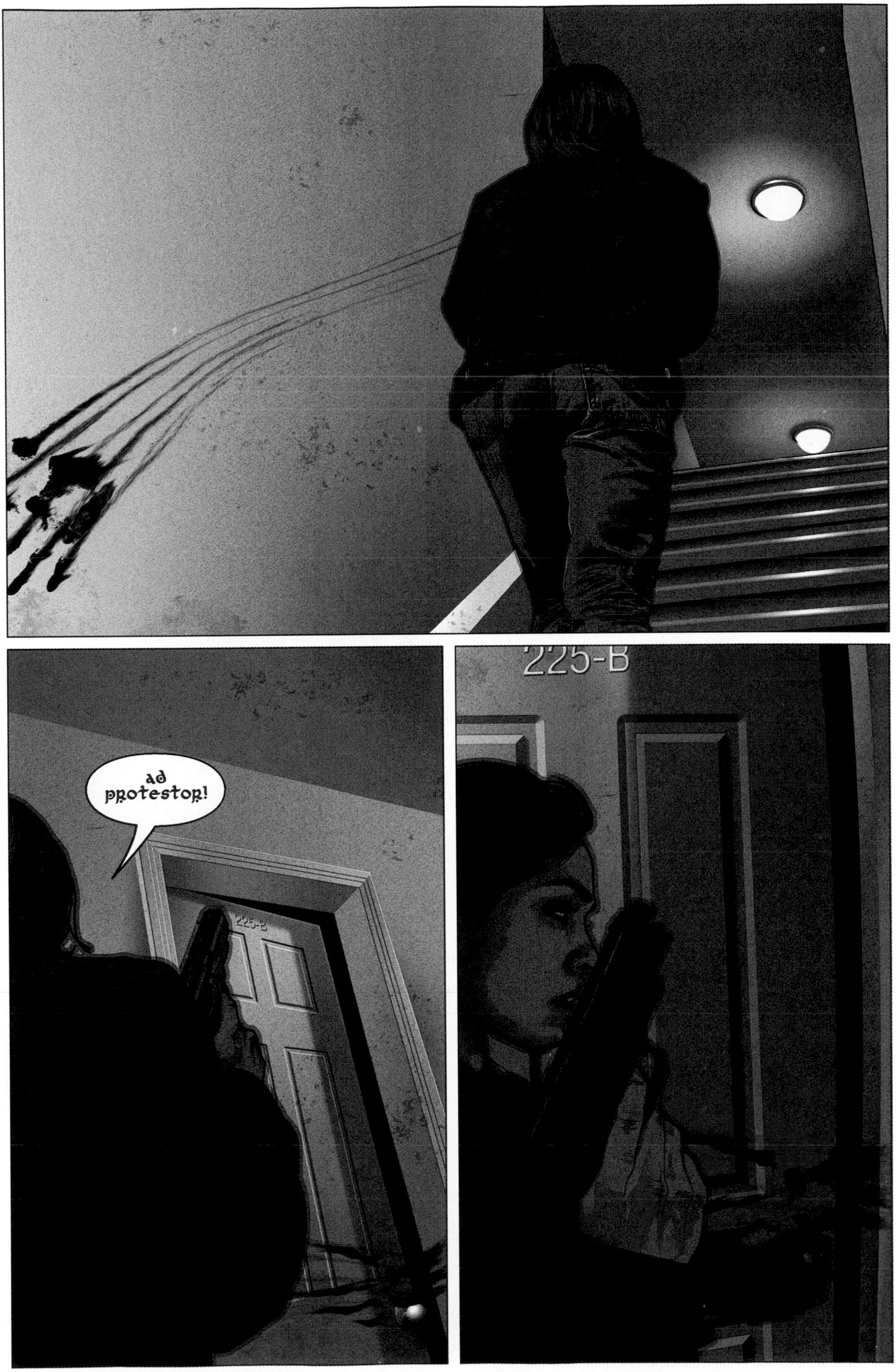
ad protestor!
225-B
225-B

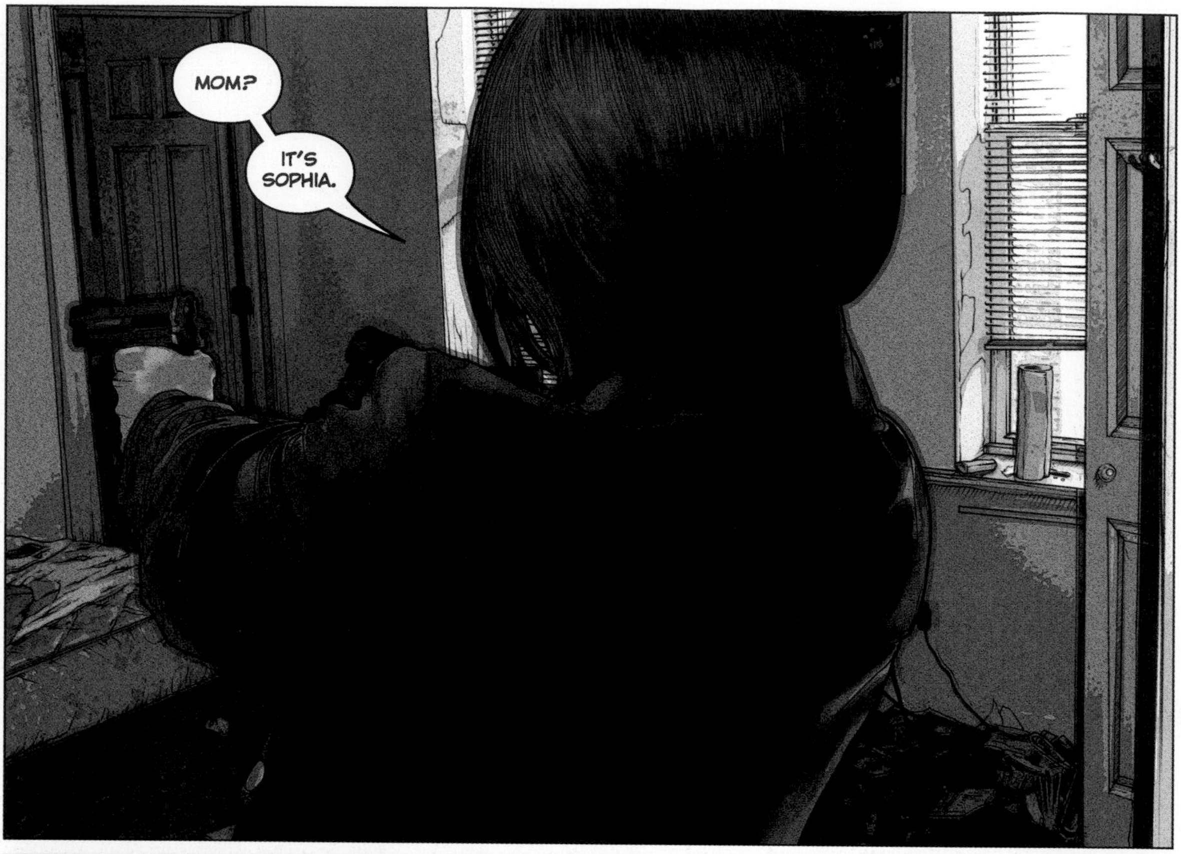
MOM?
IT'S SOPHIA.

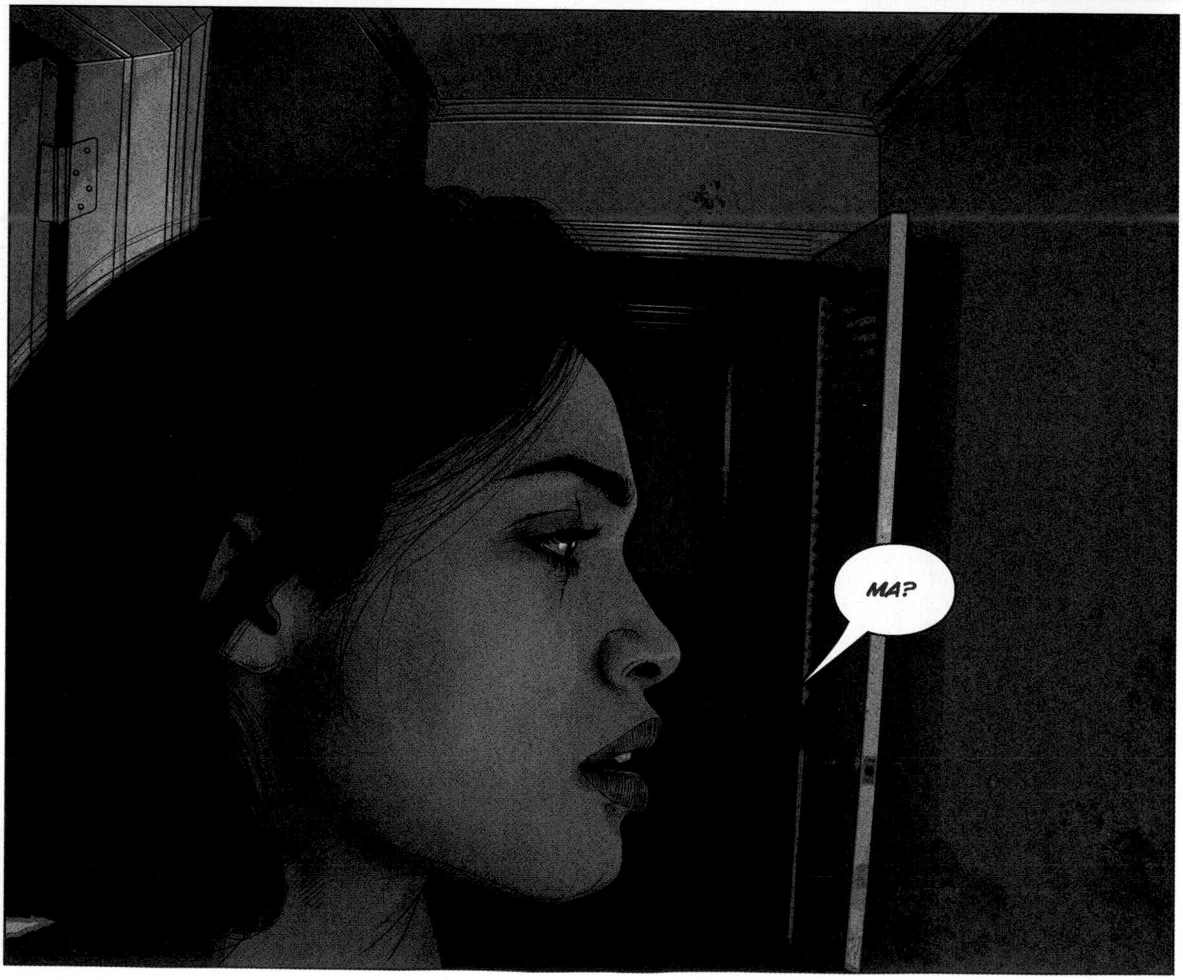
MA?

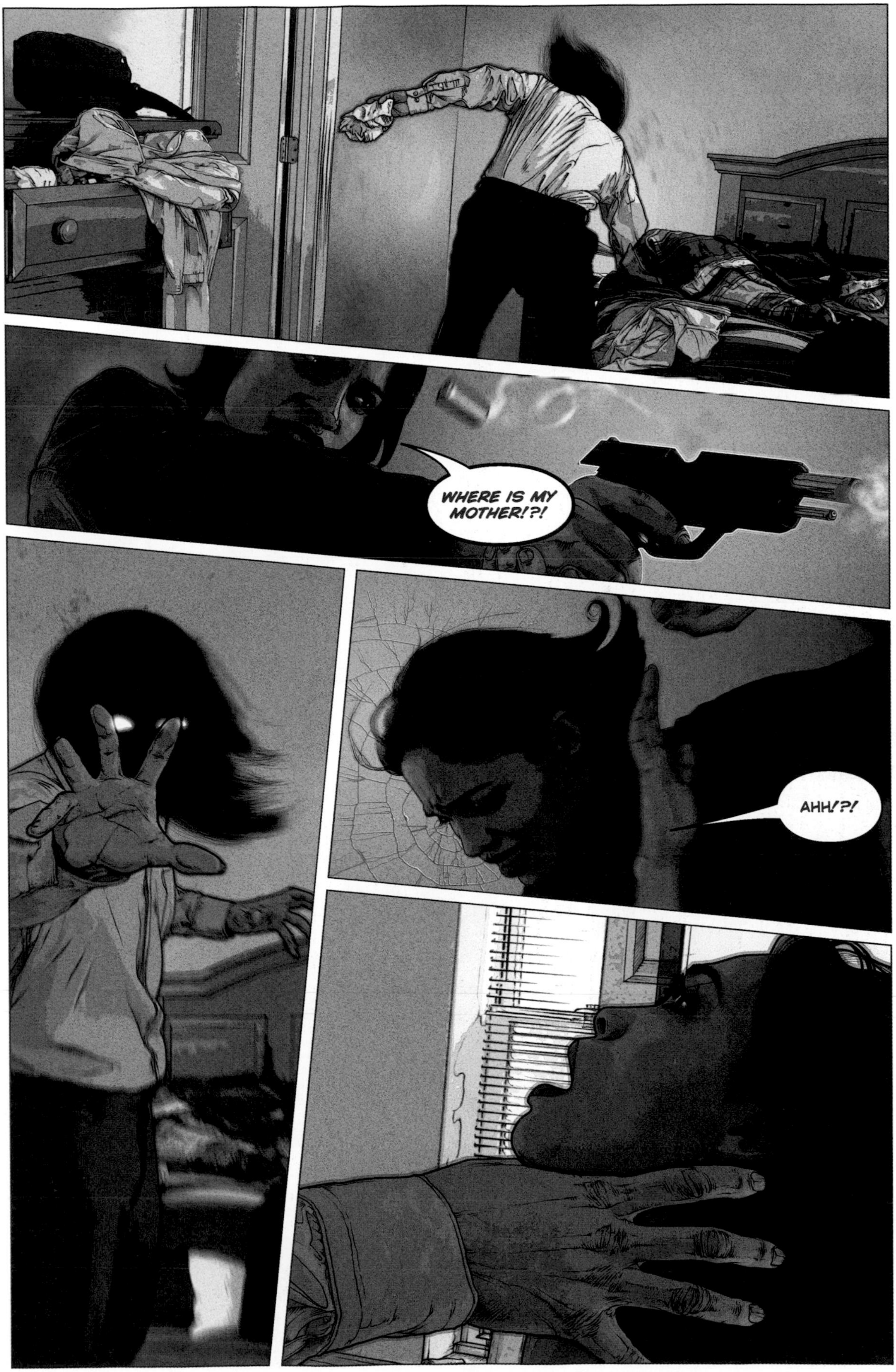
WHERE IS MY MOTHER!?!
AHH!?!

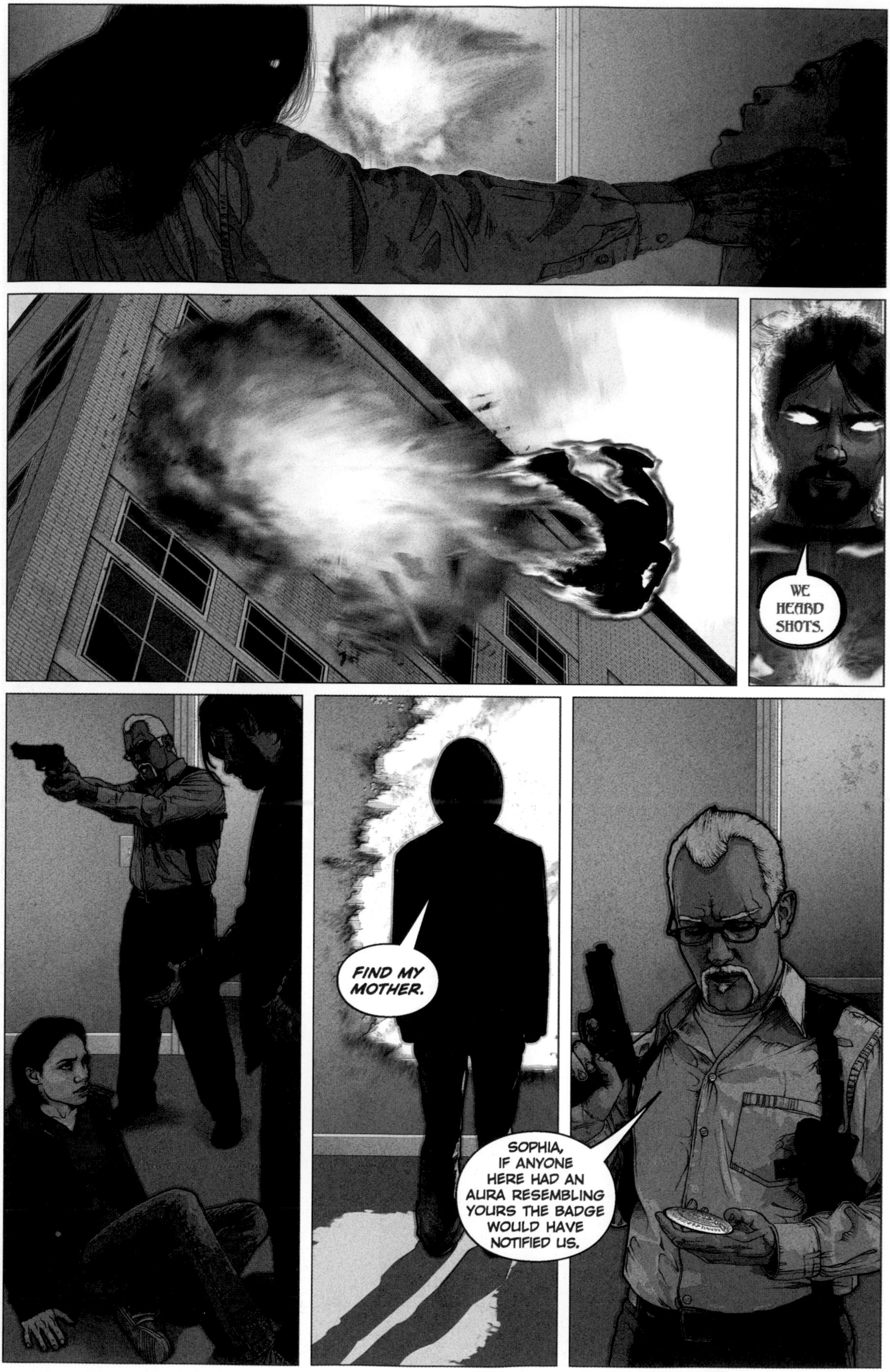
WE HEARD SHOTS.
FIND MY MOTHER.
SOPHIA, IF ANYONE HERE HAD AN AURA RESEMBLING YOURS THE BADGE WOULD HAVE NOTIFIED US.

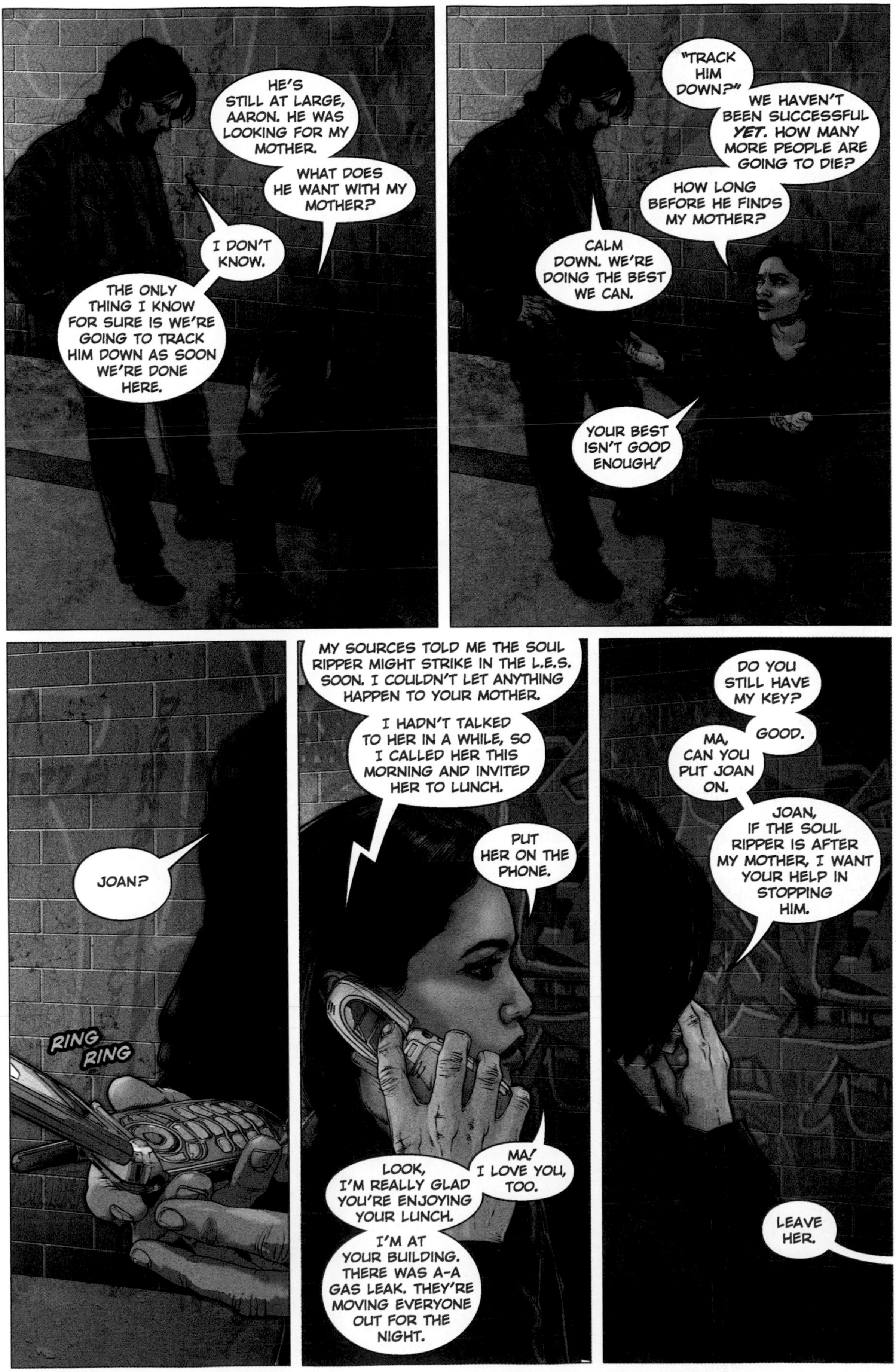
HE'S STILL AT LARGE, AARON. HE WAS LOOKING FOR MY MOTHER.
WHAT DOES HE WANT WITH MY MOTHER?
I DON'T KNOW.
THE ONLY THING I KNOW FOR SURE IS WE'RE GOING TO TRACK HIM DOWN AS SOON WE'RE DONE HERE.
"TRACK HIM DOWN?"
WE HAVEN'T BEEN SUCCESSFUL *YET*. HOW MANY MORE PEOPLE ARE GOING TO DIE?
HOW LONG BEFORE HE FINDS MY MOTHER?
CALM DOWN. WE'RE DOING THE BEST WE CAN.
YOUR BEST ISN'T GOOD ENOUGH!
JOAN?
RING RING
MY SOURCES TOLD ME THE SOUL RIPPER MIGHT STRIKE IN THE L.E.S. SOON. I COULDN'T LET ANYTHING HAPPEN TO YOUR MOTHER.
I HADN'T TALKED TO HER IN A WHILE, SO I CALLED HER THIS MORNING AND INVITED HER TO LUNCH.
PUT HER ON THE PHONE.
MA! I LOVE YOU, TOO.
LOOK, I'M REALLY GLAD YOU'RE ENJOYING YOUR LUNCH.
I'M AT YOUR BUILDING. THERE WAS A-A GAS LEAK. THEY'RE MOVING EVERYONE OUT FOR THE NIGHT.
DO YOU STILL HAVE MY KEY?
GOOD.
MA, CAN YOU PUT JOAN ON.
JOAN, IF THE SOUL RIPPER IS AFTER MY MOTHER, I WANT YOUR HELP IN STOPPING HIM.
LEAVE HER.

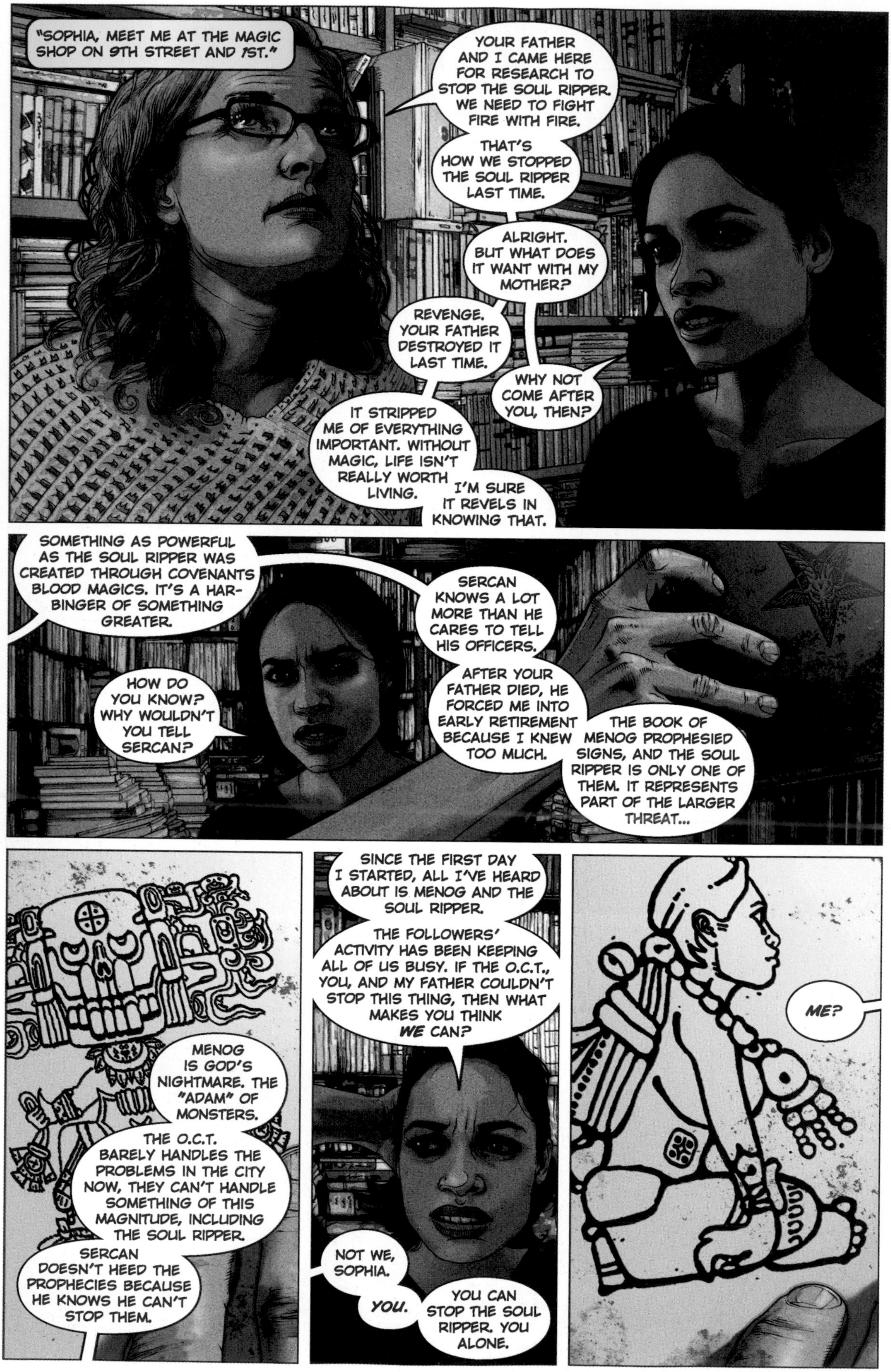
"SOPHIA, MEET ME AT THE MAGIC SHOP ON 9TH STREET AND 1ST."
YOUR FATHER AND I CAME HERE FOR RESEARCH TO STOP THE SOUL RIPPER. WE NEED TO FIGHT FIRE WITH FIRE.
THAT'S HOW WE STOPPED THE SOUL RIPPER LAST TIME.
ALRIGHT. BUT WHAT DOES IT WANT WITH MY MOTHER?
REVENGE. YOUR FATHER DESTROYED IT LAST TIME.
WHY NOT COME AFTER YOU, THEN?
IT STRIPPED ME OF EVERYTHING IMPORTANT. WITHOUT MAGIC, LIFE ISN'T REALLY WORTH LIVING.
I'M SURE IT REVELS IN KNOWING THAT.
SOMETHING AS POWERFUL AS THE SOUL RIPPER WAS CREATED THROUGH COVENANTS BLOOD MAGICS. IT'S A HARBINGER OF SOMETHING GREATER.
HOW DO YOU KNOW? WHY WOULDN'T YOU TELL SERCAN?
SERCAN KNOWS A LOT MORE THAN HE CARES TO TELL HIS OFFICERS.
AFTER YOUR FATHER DIED, HE FORCED ME INTO EARLY RETIREMENT BECAUSE I KNEW TOO MUCH.
THE BOOK OF MENOG PROPHESIED SIGNS, AND THE SOUL RIPPER IS ONLY ONE OF THEM. IT REPRESENTS PART OF THE LARGER THREAT...
MENOG IS GOD'S NIGHTMARE. THE "ADAM" OF MONSTERS.
THE O.C.T. BARELY HANDLES THE PROBLEMS IN THE CITY NOW, THEY CAN'T HANDLE SOMETHING OF THIS MAGNITUDE, INCLUDING THE SOUL RIPPER.
SERCAN DOESN'T HEED THE PROPHECIES BECAUSE HE KNOWS HE CAN'T STOP THEM.
SINCE THE FIRST DAY I STARTED, ALL I'VE HEARD ABOUT IS MENOG AND THE SOUL RIPPER.
THE FOLLOWERS' ACTIVITY HAS BEEN KEEPING ALL OF US BUSY. IF THE O.C.T., YOU, AND MY FATHER COULDN'T STOP THIS THING, THEN WHAT MAKES YOU THINK *WE* CAN?
NOT WE, SOPHIA.
YOU.
YOU CAN STOP THE SOUL RIPPER. YOU ALONE.
ME?

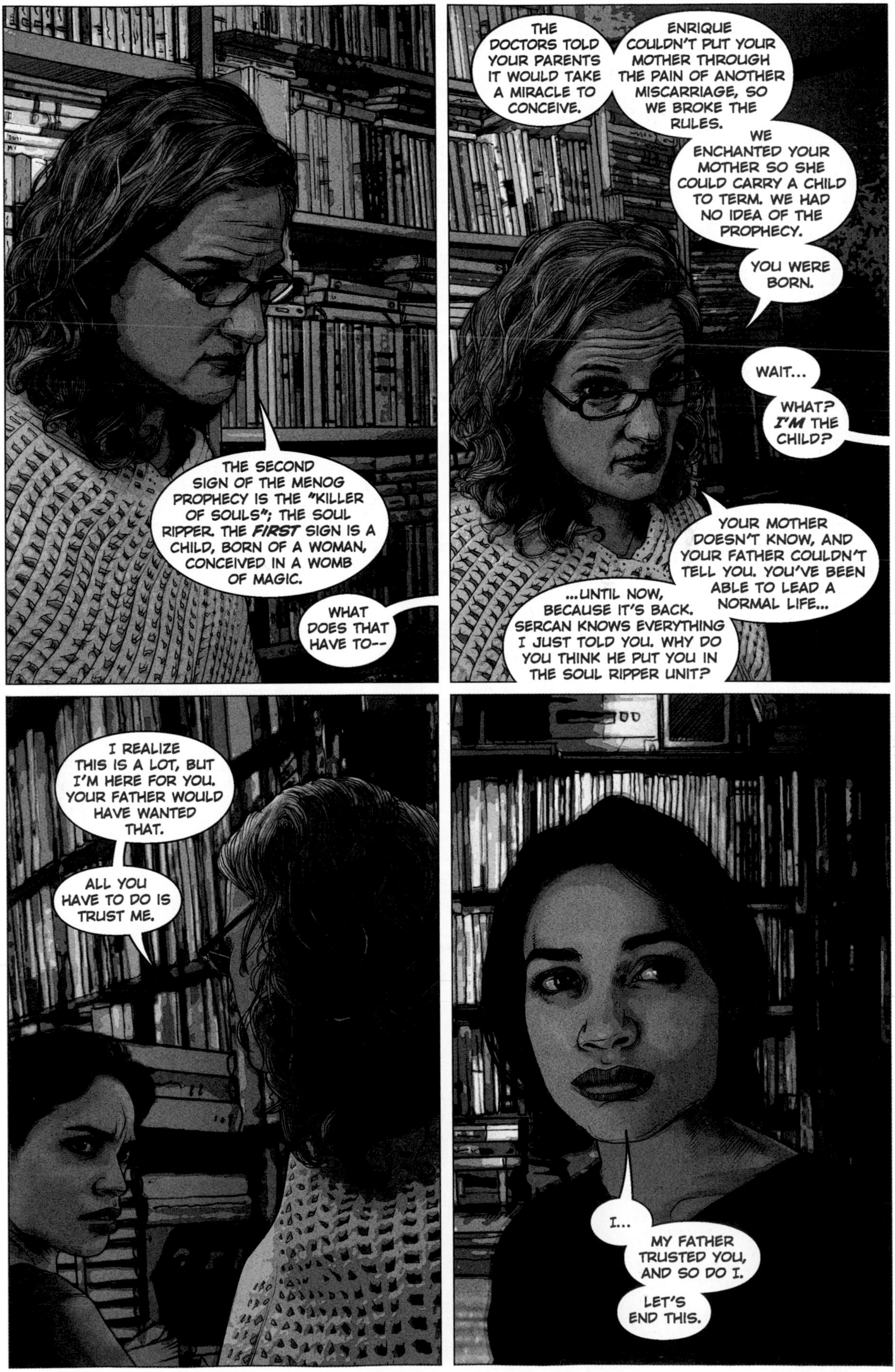
THE SECOND SIGN OF THE MENOG PROPHECY IS THE "KILLER OF SOULS"; THE SOUL RIPPER. THE *FIRST* SIGN IS A CHILD, BORN OF A WOMAN, CONCEIVED IN A WOMB OF MAGIC.
WHAT DOES THAT HAVE TO--
THE DOCTORS TOLD YOUR PARENTS IT WOULD TAKE A MIRACLE TO CONCEIVE.
ENRIQUE COULDN'T PUT YOUR MOTHER THROUGH THE PAIN OF ANOTHER MISCARRIAGE, SO WE BROKE THE RULES.
WE ENCHANTED YOUR MOTHER SO SHE COULD CARRY A CHILD TO TERM. WE HAD NO IDEA OF THE PROPHECY.
YOU WERE BORN.
WAIT...
WHAT? *I'M* THE CHILD?
YOUR MOTHER DOESN'T KNOW, AND YOUR FATHER COULDN'T TELL YOU. YOU'VE BEEN ABLE TO LEAD A NORMAL LIFE...
...UNTIL NOW, BECAUSE IT'S BACK. SERCAN KNOWS EVERYTHING I JUST TOLD YOU. WHY DO YOU THINK HE PUT YOU IN THE SOUL RIPPER UNIT?
I REALIZE THIS IS A LOT, BUT I'M HERE FOR YOU. YOUR FATHER WOULD HAVE WANTED THAT.
ALL YOU HAVE TO DO IS TRUST ME.
I...
MY FATHER TRUSTED YOU, AND SO DO I.
LET'S END THIS.

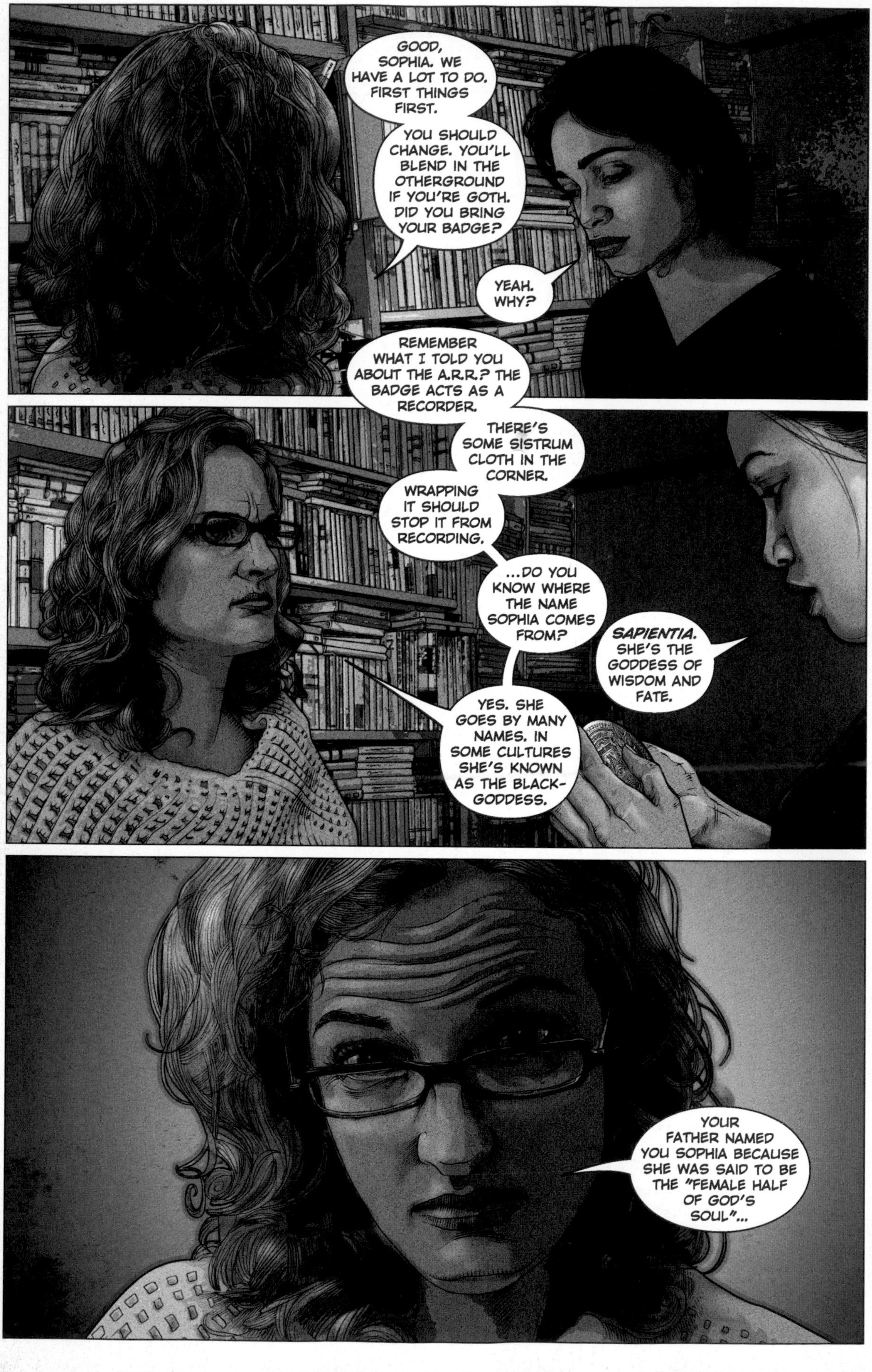
GOOD, SOPHIA. WE HAVE A LOT TO DO. FIRST THINGS FIRST.
YOU SHOULD CHANGE. YOU'LL BLEND IN THE OTHERGROUND IF YOU'RE GOTH. DID YOU BRING YOUR BADGE?
YEAH. WHY?
REMEMBER WHAT I TOLD YOU ABOUT THE A.R.R.? THE BADGE ACTS AS A RECORDER.
THERE'S SOME SISTRUM CLOTH IN THE CORNER.
WRAPPING IT SHOULD STOP IT FROM RECORDING.
...DO YOU KNOW WHERE THE NAME SOPHIA COMES FROM?
SAPIENTIA. SHE'S THE GODDESS OF WISDOM AND FATE.
YES. SHE GOES BY MANY NAMES. IN SOME CULTURES SHE'S KNOWN AS THE BLACK-GODDESS.
YOUR FATHER NAMED YOU SOPHIA BECAUSE SHE WAS SAID TO BE THE "FEMALE HALF OF GOD'S SOUL"...

Chapter Four

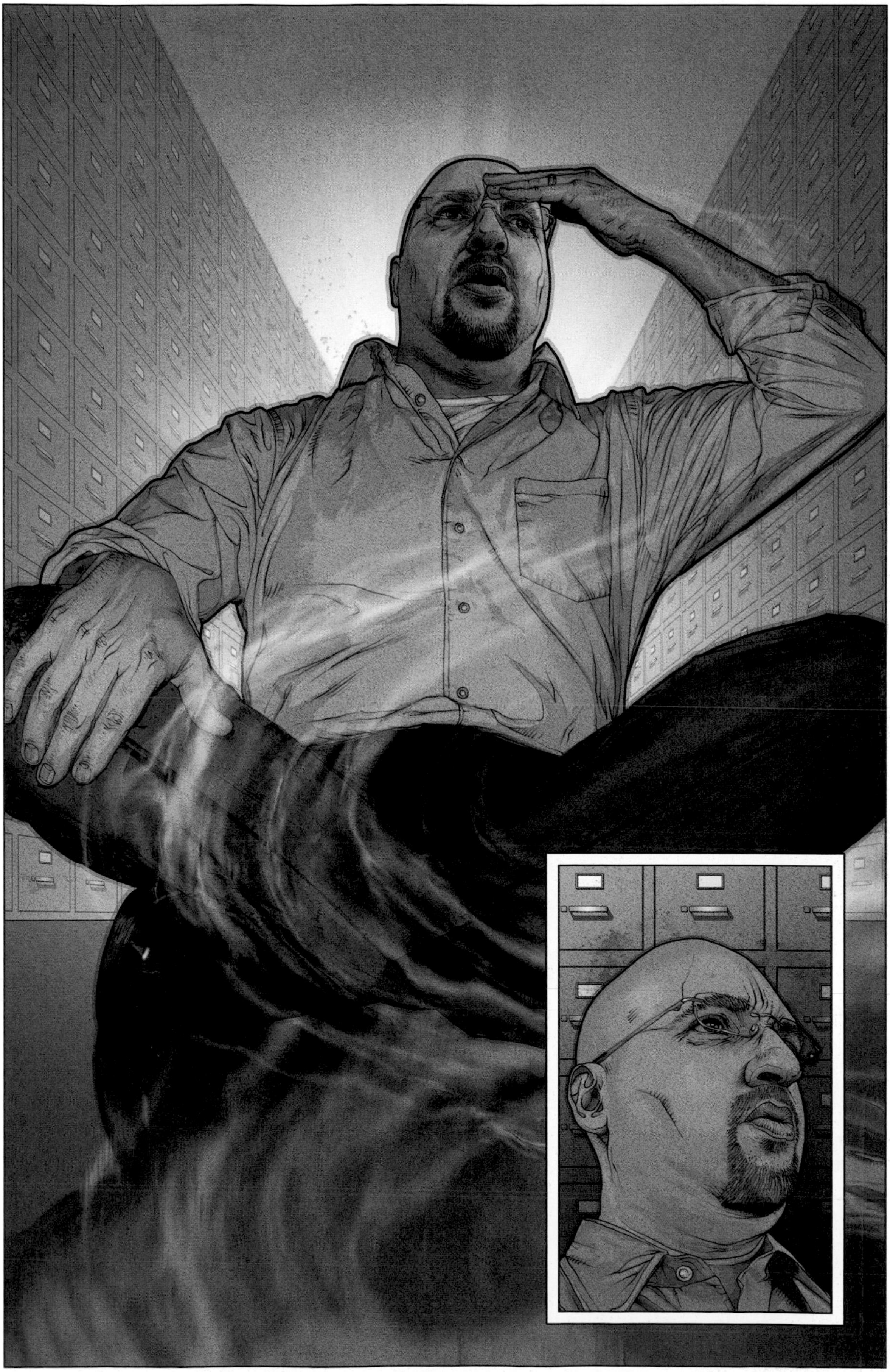

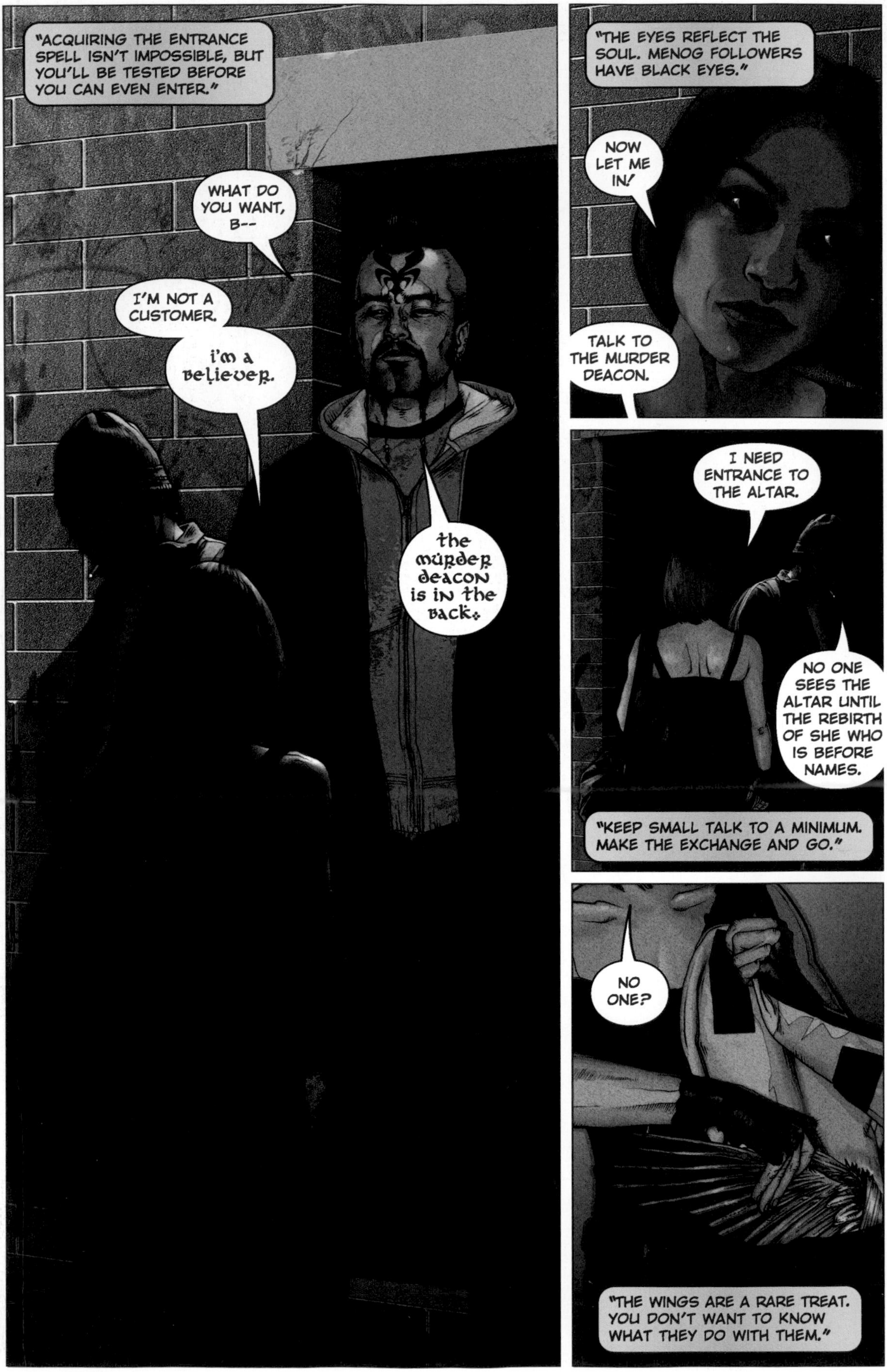
"ACQUIRING THE ENTRANCE SPELL ISN'T IMPOSSIBLE, BUT YOU'LL BE TESTED BEFORE YOU CAN EVEN ENTER."
WHAT DO YOU WANT, B--
I'M NOT A CUSTOMER.
i'm a believer.
the murder deacon is in the back.
"THE EYES REFLECT THE SOUL. MENOG FOLLOWERS HAVE BLACK EYES."
NOW LET ME IN!
TALK TO THE MURDER DEACON.
I NEED ENTRANCE TO THE ALTAR.
NO ONE SEES THE ALTAR UNTIL THE REBIRTH OF SHE WHO IS BEFORE NAMES.
"KEEP SMALL TALK TO A MINIMUM. MAKE THE EXCHANGE AND GO."
NO ONE?
"THE WINGS ARE A RARE TREAT. YOU DON'T WANT TO KNOW WHAT THEY DO WITH THEM."

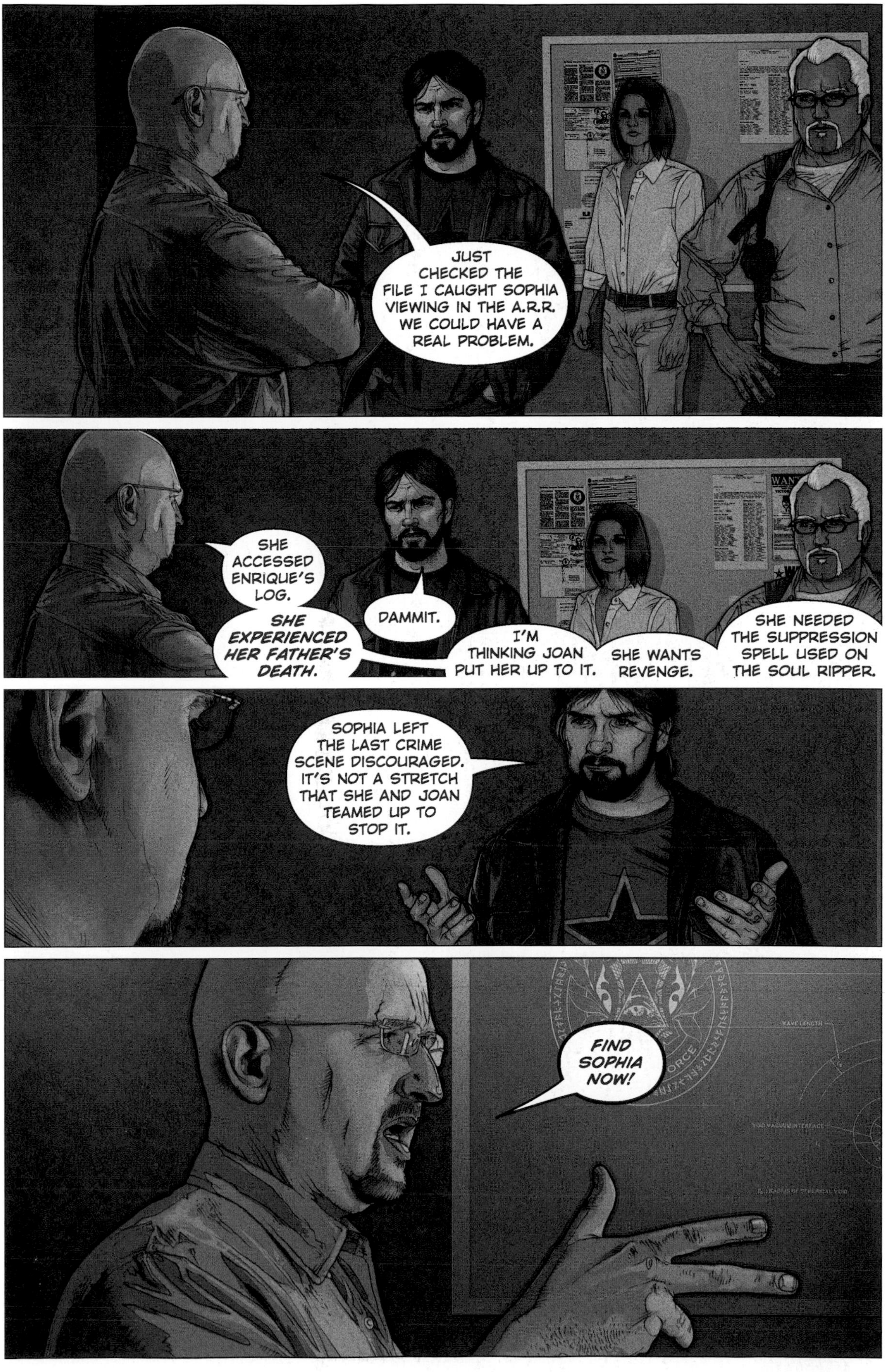
JUST CHECKED THE FILE I CAUGHT SOPHIA VIEWING IN THE A.R.R. WE COULD HAVE A REAL PROBLEM.
SHE ACCESSED ENRIQUE'S LOG.
SHE EXPERIENCED HER FATHER'S DEATH.
DAMMIT.
I'M THINKING JOAN PUT HER UP TO IT.
SHE WANTS REVENGE.
SHE NEEDED THE SUPPRESSION SPELL USED ON THE SOUL RIPPER.
SOPHIA LEFT THE LAST CRIME SCENE DISCOURAGED. IT'S NOT A STRETCH THAT SHE AND JOAN TEAMED UP TO STOP IT.
FIND SOPHIA NOW!

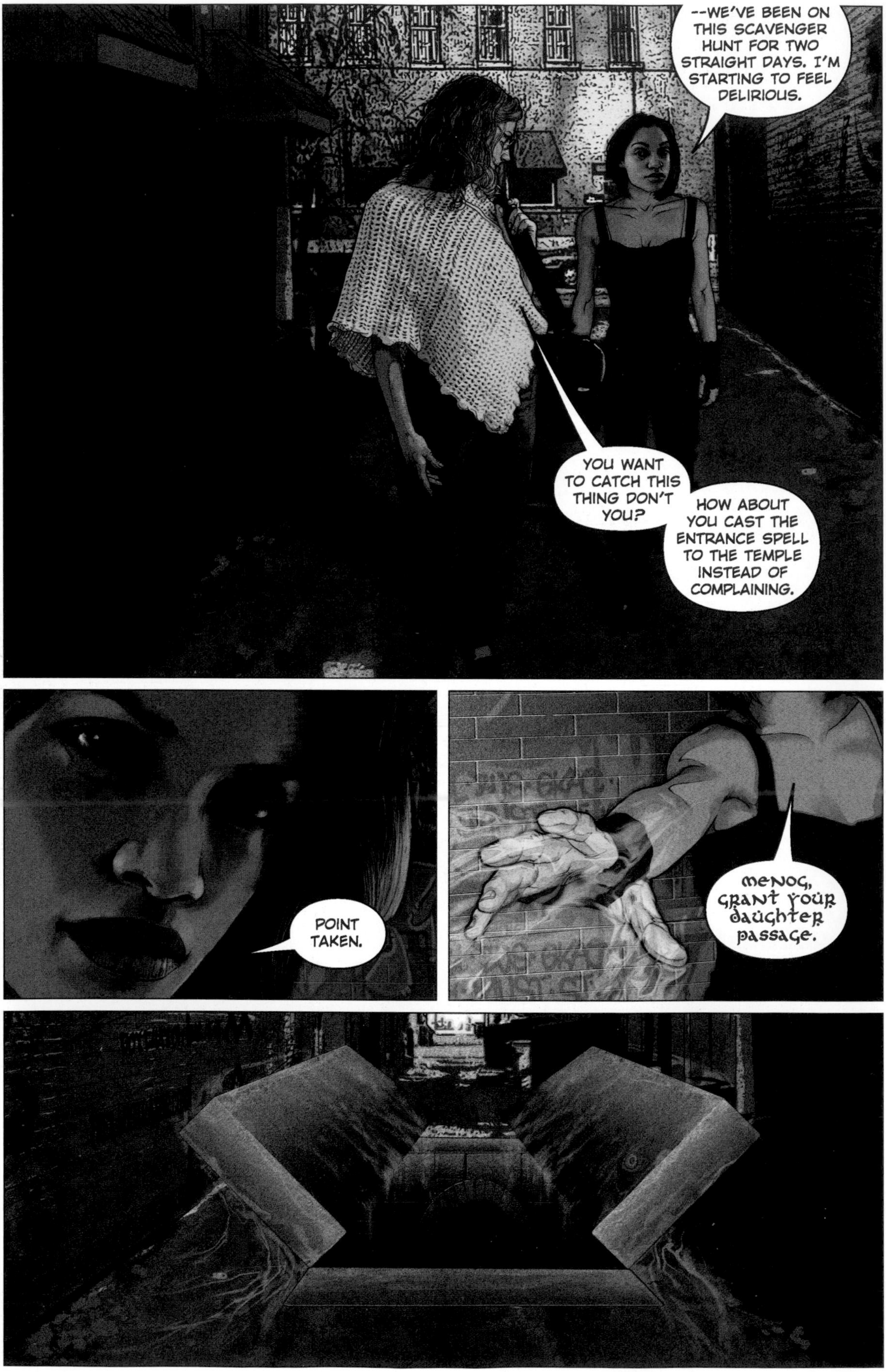
--WE'VE BEEN ON THIS SCAVENGER HUNT FOR TWO STRAIGHT DAYS. I'M STARTING TO FEEL DELIRIOUS.
YOU WANT TO CATCH THIS THING DON'T YOU?
HOW ABOUT YOU CAST THE ENTRANCE SPELL TO THE TEMPLE INSTEAD OF COMPLAINING.
POINT TAKEN.
MENOG, GRANT YOUR DAUGHTER PASSAGE.

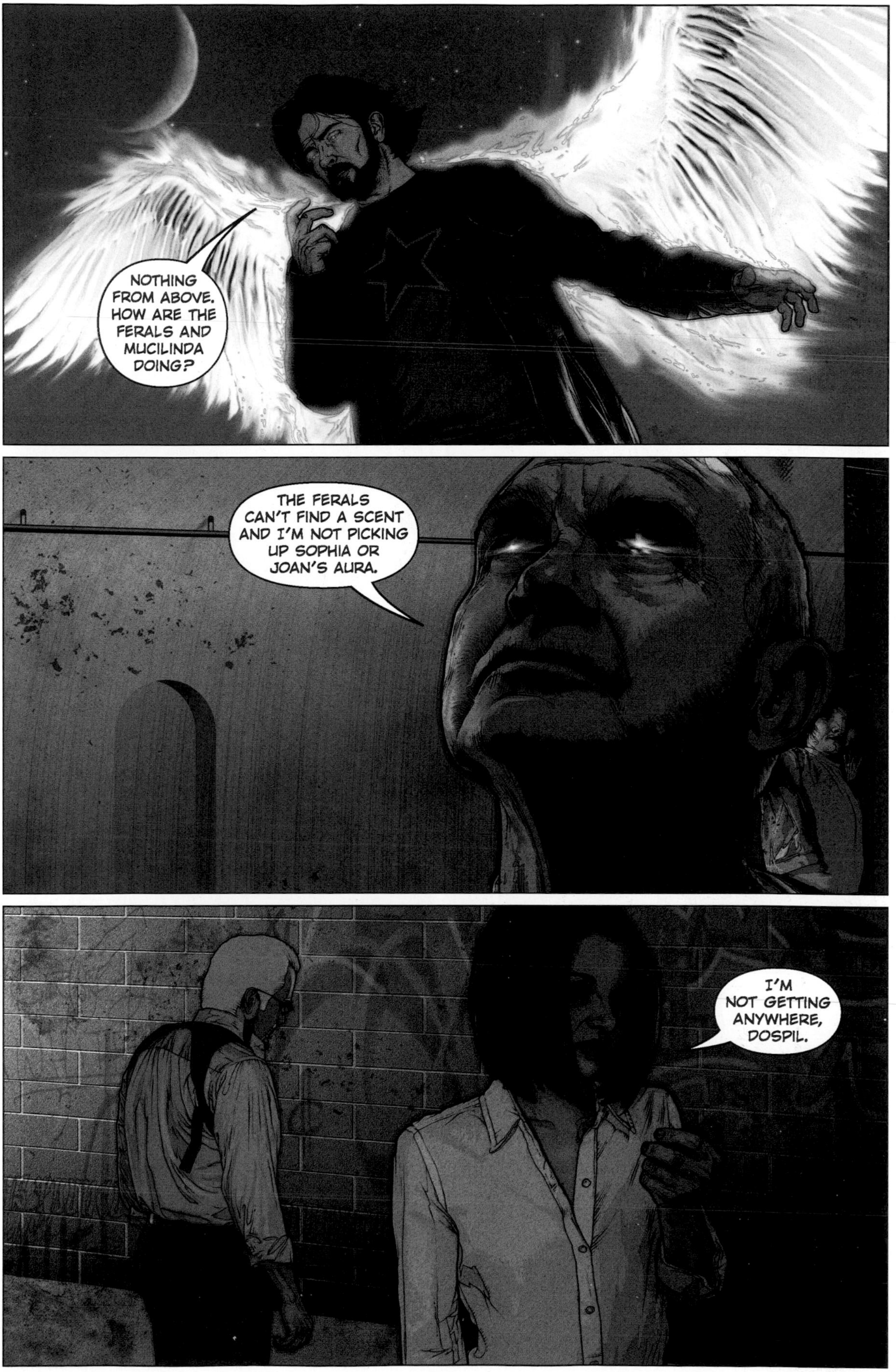
NOTHING FROM ABOVE. HOW ARE THE FERALS AND MUCILINDA DOING?
THE FERALS CAN'T FIND A SCENT AND I'M NOT PICKING UP SOPHIA OR JOAN'S AURA.
I'M NOT GETTING ANYWHERE, DOSPIL.

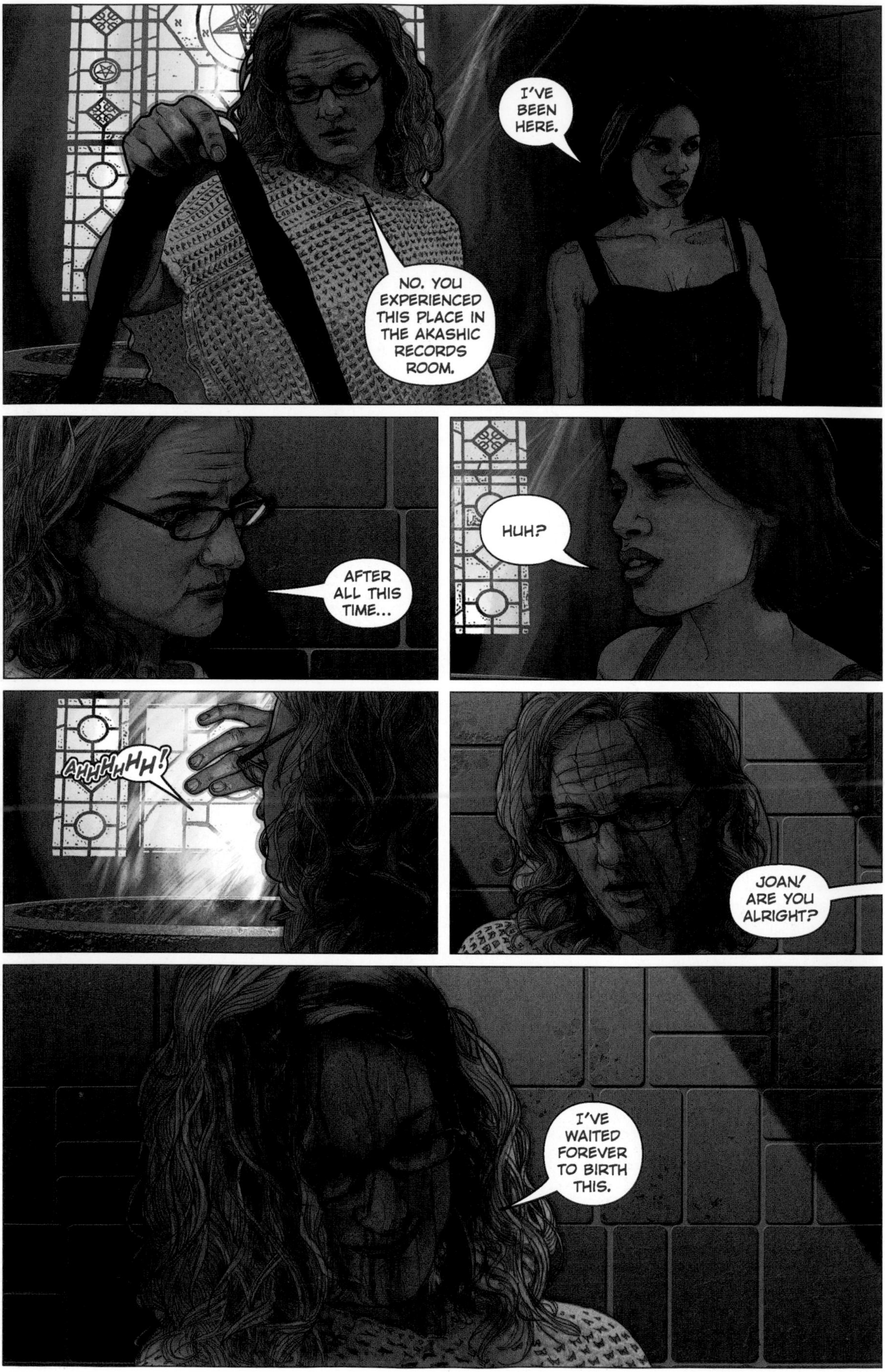
I'VE BEEN HERE.
NO. YOU EXPERIENCED THIS PLACE IN THE AKASHIC RECORDS ROOM.
AFTER ALL THIS TIME...
HUH?
AHHHHHH!
JOAN! ARE YOU ALRIGHT?
I'VE WAITED FOREVER TO BIRTH THIS.

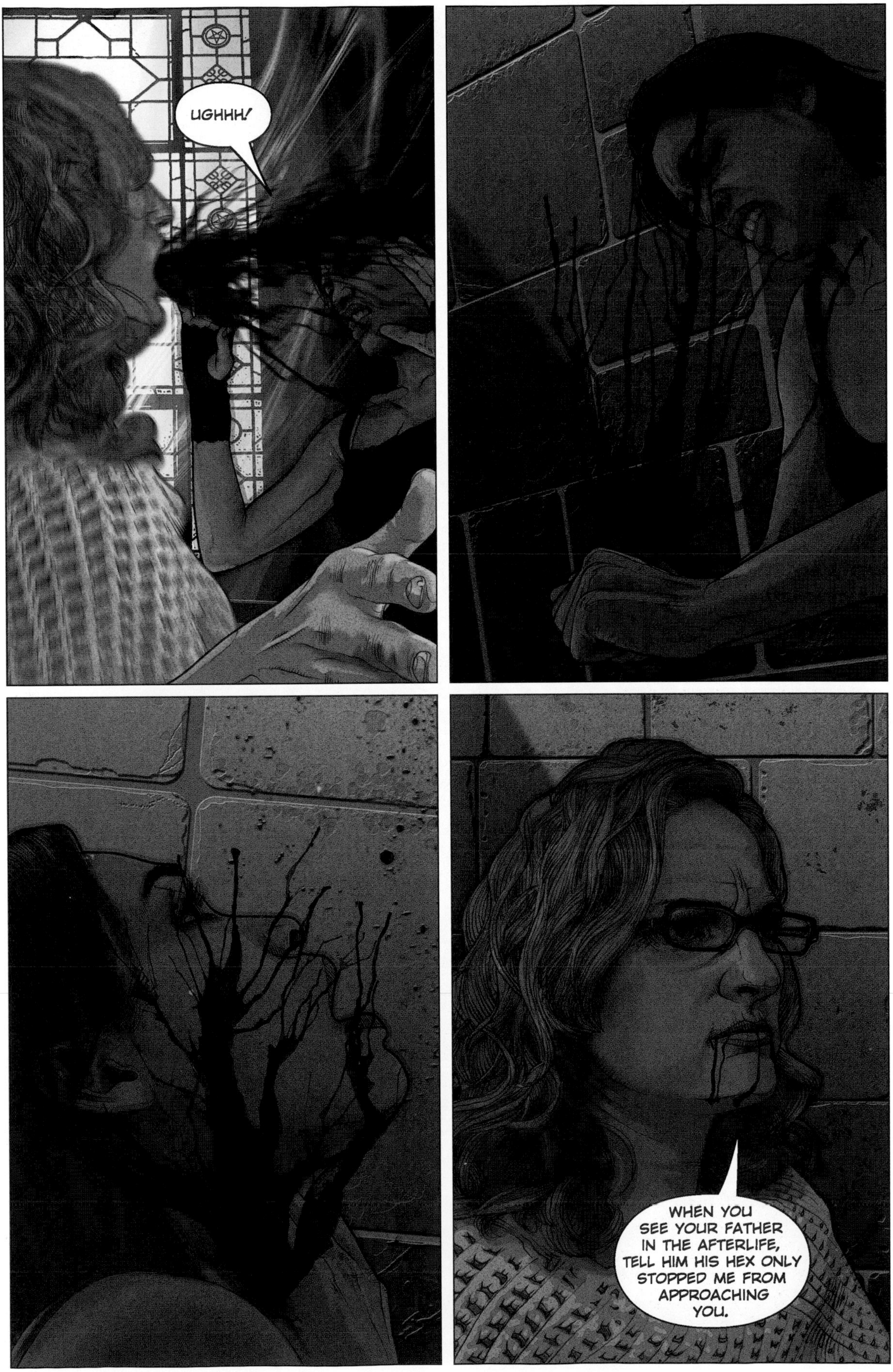
UGHHH!
WHEN YOU SEE YOUR FATHER IN THE AFTERLIFE, TELL HIM HIS HEX ONLY STOPPED ME FROM APPROACHING YOU.

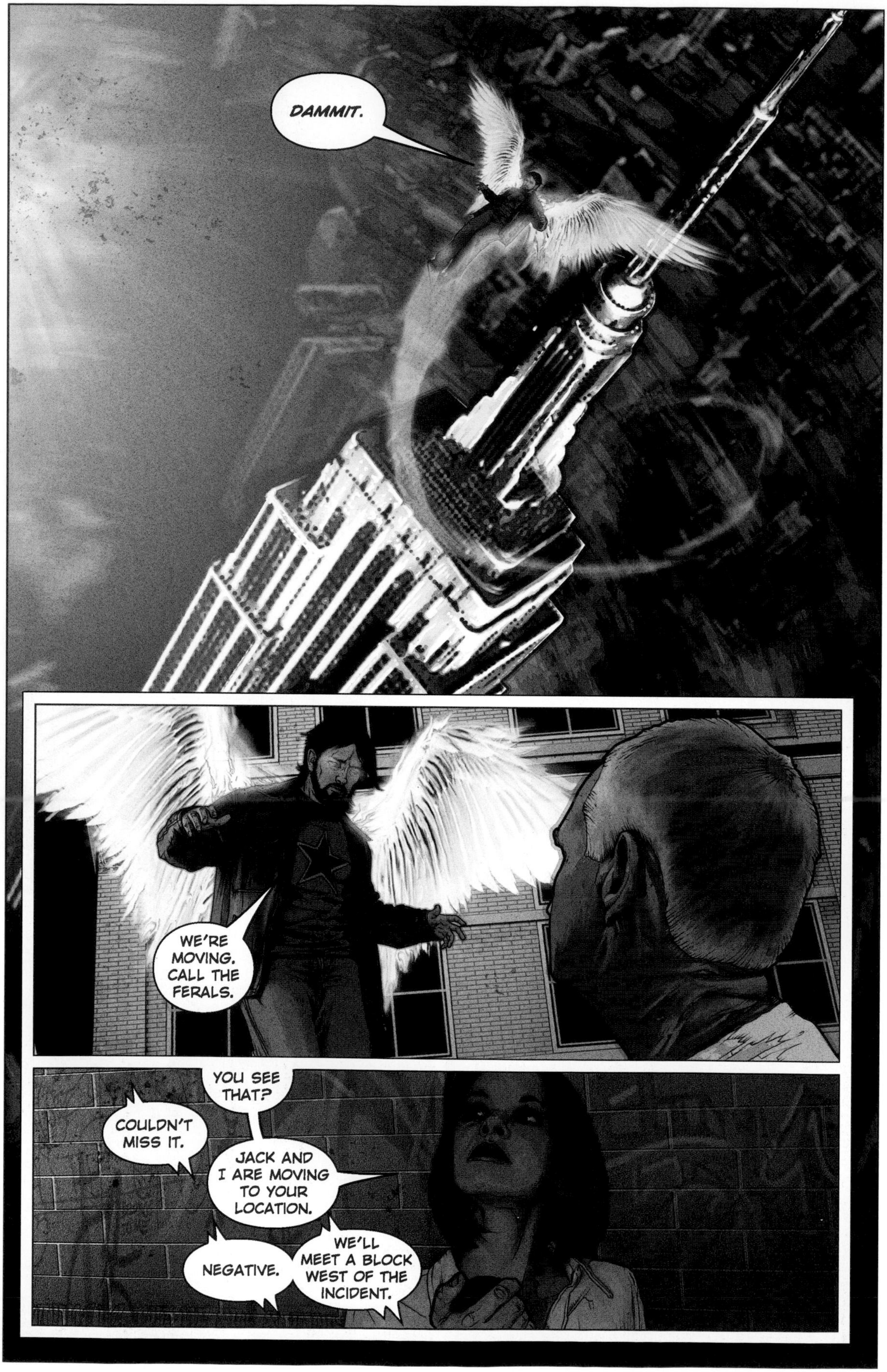
DAMMIT.
WE'RE MOVING. CALL THE FERALS.
YOU SEE THAT?
COULDN'T MISS IT.
JACK AND I ARE MOVING TO YOUR LOCATION.
NEGATIVE.
WE'LL MEET A BLOCK WEST OF THE INCIDENT.

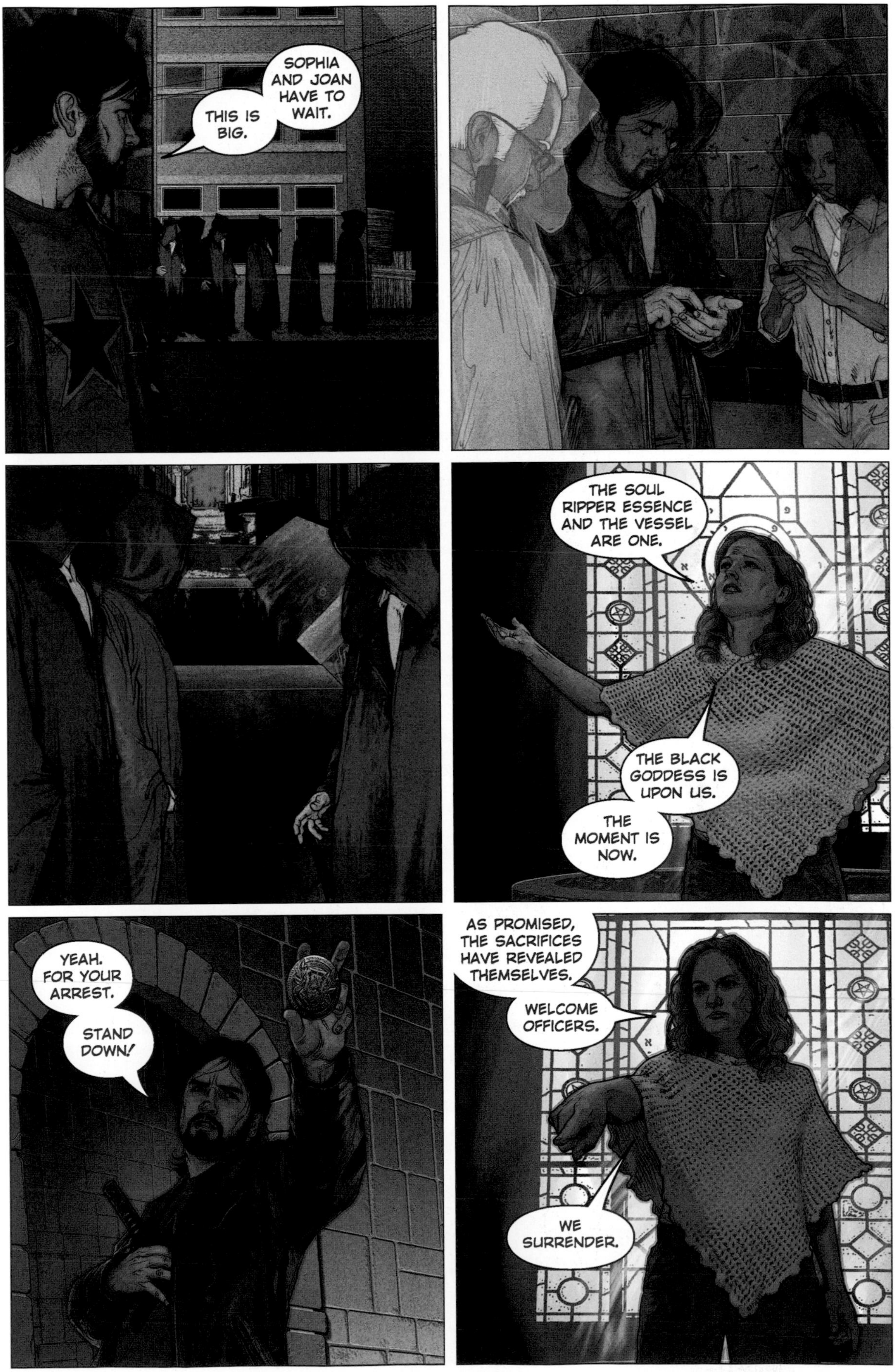
THIS IS BIG.
SOPHIA AND JOAN HAVE TO WAIT.
THE SOUL RIPPER ESSENCE AND THE VESSEL ARE ONE.
THE BLACK GODDESS IS UPON US.
THE MOMENT IS NOW.
YEAH. FOR YOUR ARREST.
STAND DOWN!
AS PROMISED, THE SACRIFICES HAVE REVEALED THEMSELVES.
WELCOME OFFICERS.
WE SURRENDER.

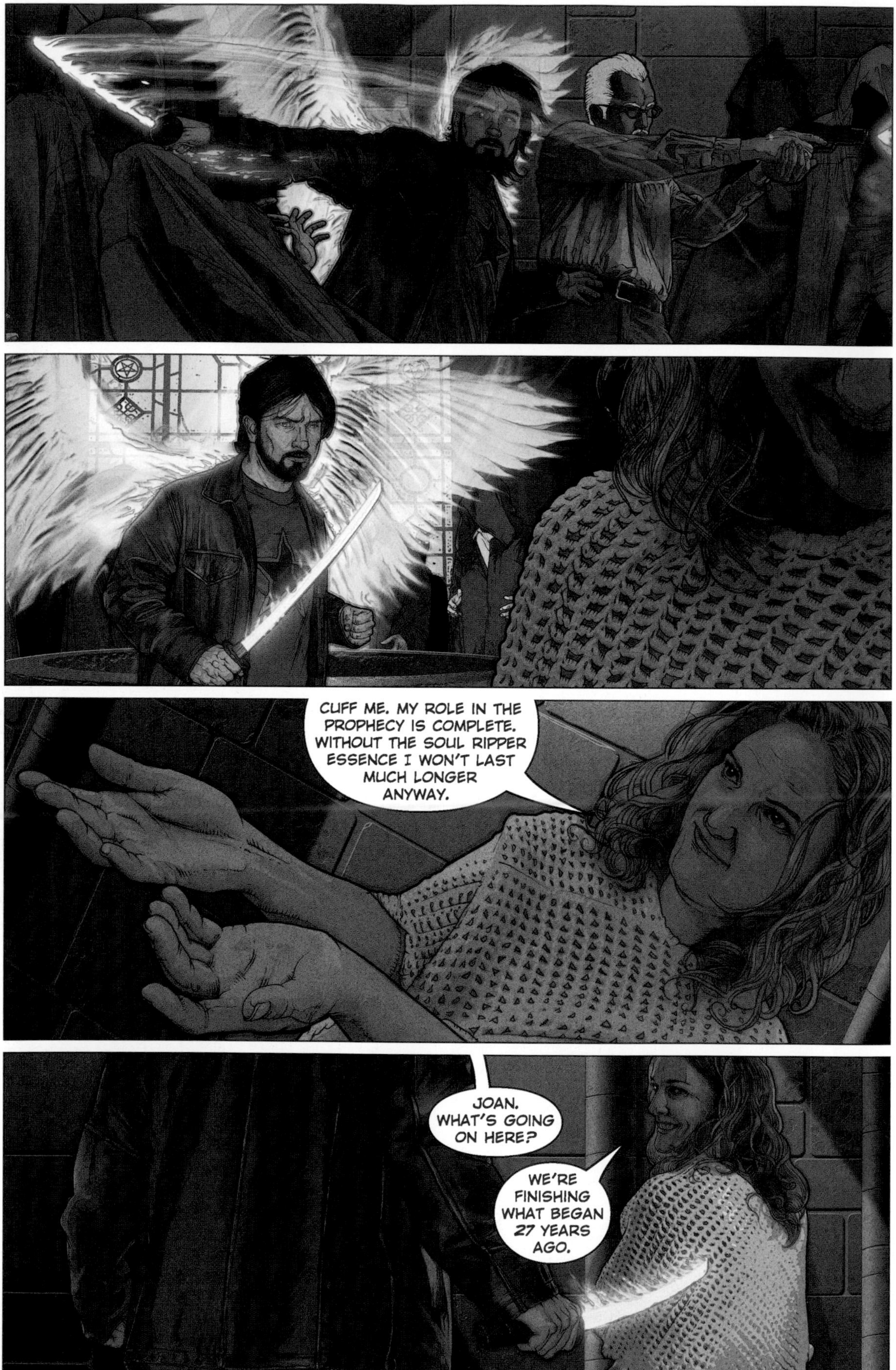
CUFF ME. MY ROLE IN THE PROPHECY IS COMPLETE. WITHOUT THE SOUL RIPPER ESSENCE I WON'T LAST MUCH LONGER ANYWAY.
JOAN. WHAT'S GOING ON HERE?
WE'RE FINISHING WHAT BEGAN 27 YEARS AGO.

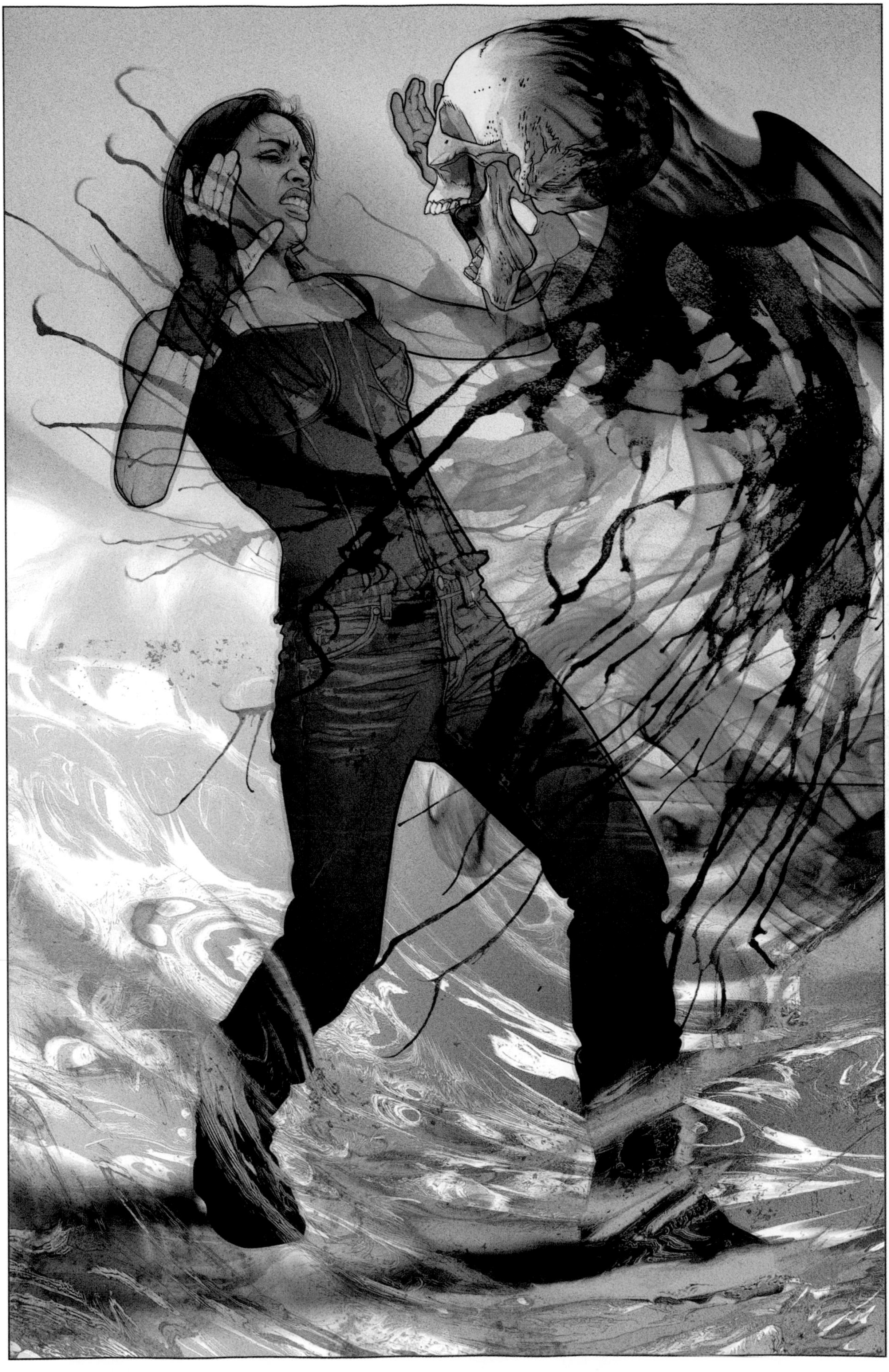

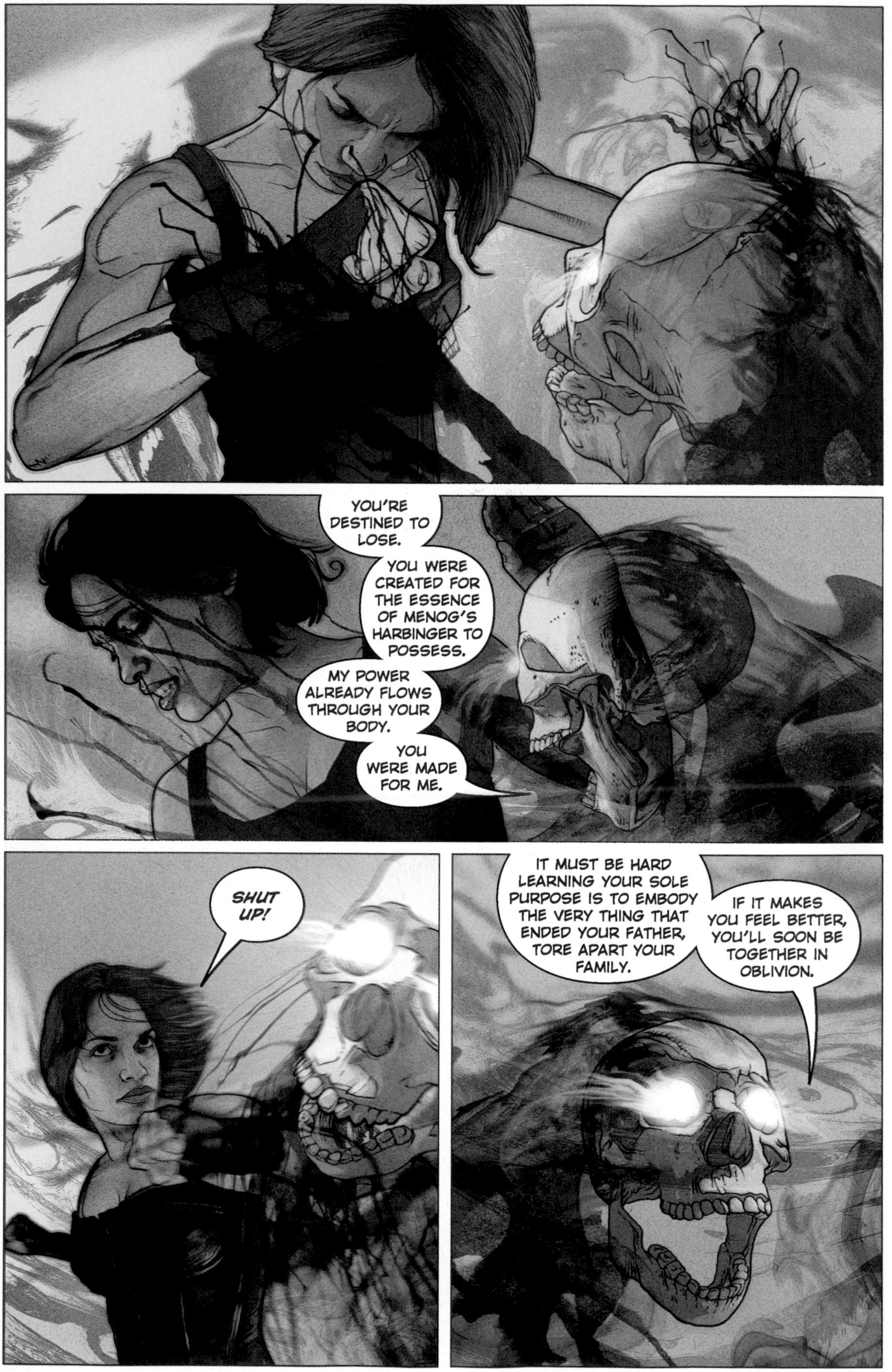
YOU'RE DESTINED TO LOSE.
YOU WERE CREATED FOR THE ESSENCE OF MENOG'S HARBINGER TO POSSESS.
MY POWER ALREADY FLOWS THROUGH YOUR BODY.
YOU WERE MADE FOR ME.
SHUT UP!
IT MUST BE HARD LEARNING YOUR SOLE PURPOSE IS TO EMBODY THE VERY THING THAT ENDED YOUR FATHER, TORE APART YOUR FAMILY.
IF IT MAKES YOU FEEL BETTER, YOU'LL SOON BE TOGETHER IN OBLIVION.

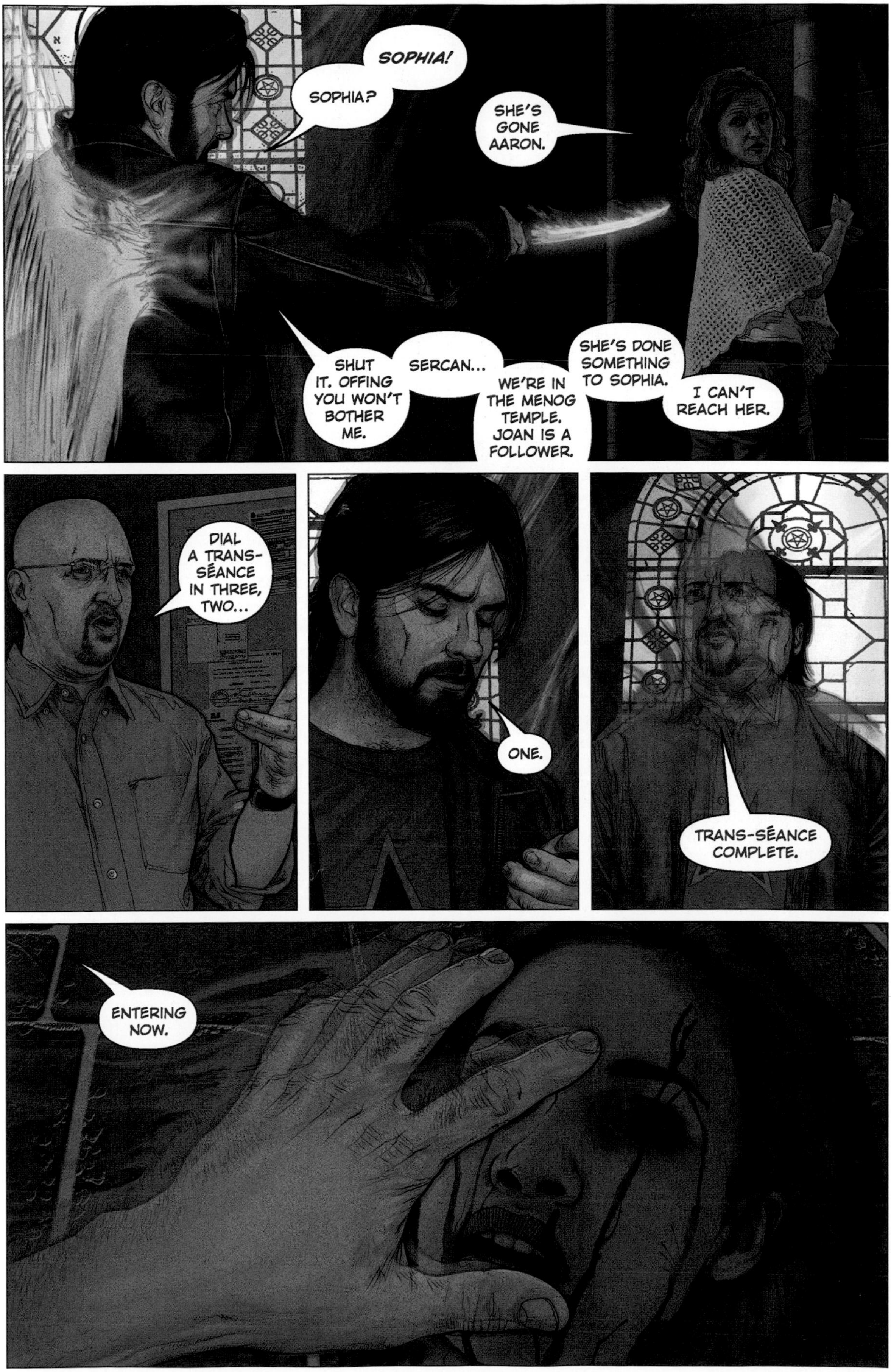
SOPHIA!
SOPHIA?
SHE'S GONE AARON.
SHUT IT. OFFING YOU WON'T BOTHER ME.
SERCAN...
WE'RE IN THE MENOG TEMPLE. JOAN IS A FOLLOWER.
SHE'S DONE SOMETHING TO SOPHIA.
I CAN'T REACH HER.
DIAL A TRANS-SÉANCE IN THREE, TWO...
ONE.
TRANS-SÉANCE COMPLETE.
ENTERING NOW.

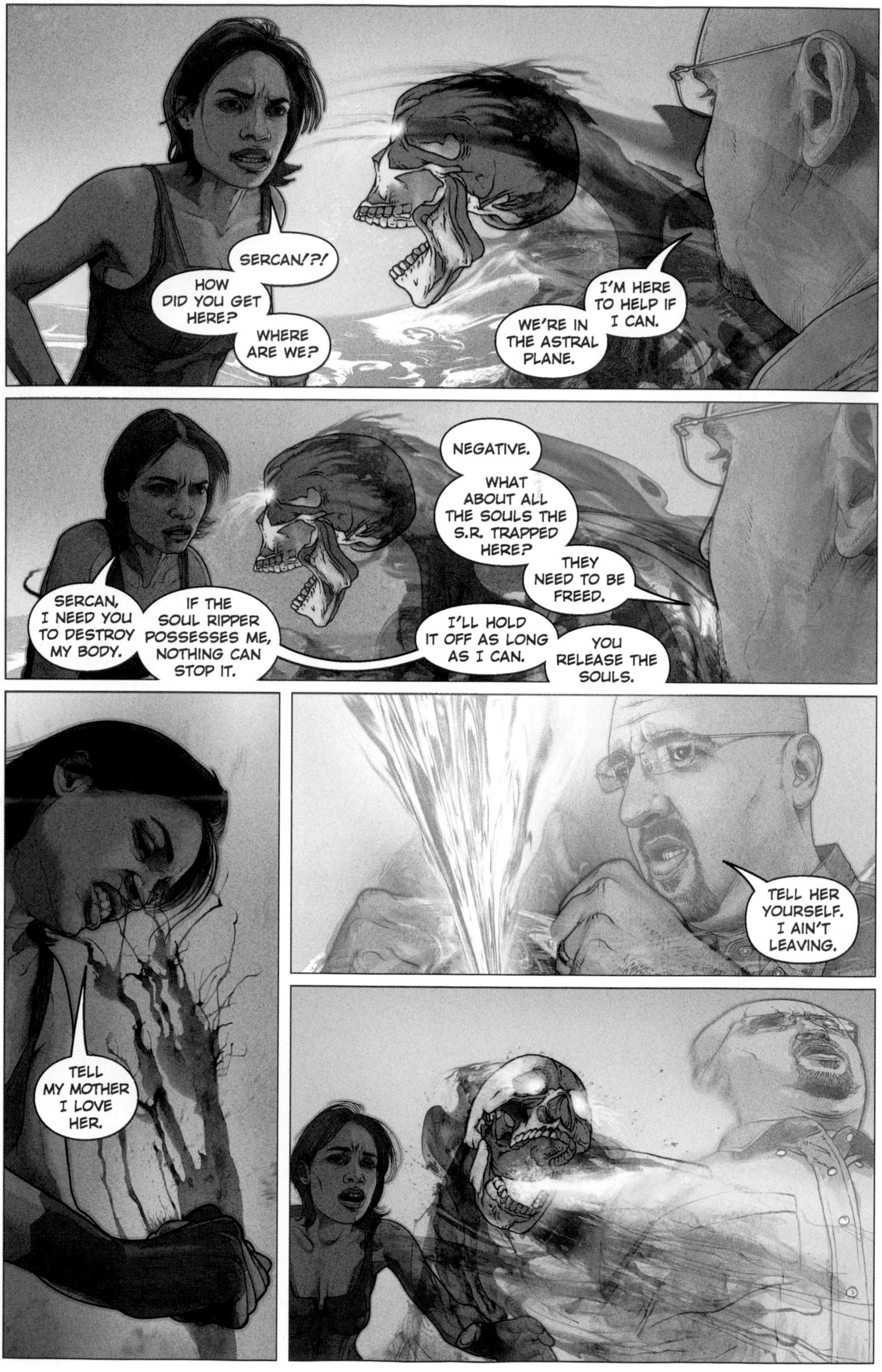
SERCAN!?!
HOW DID YOU GET HERE?
WHERE ARE WE?
I'M HERE TO HELP IF I CAN.
WE'RE IN THE ASTRAL PLANE.
SERCAN, I NEED YOU TO DESTROY MY BODY.
IF THE SOUL RIPPER POSSESSES ME, NOTHING CAN STOP IT.
NEGATIVE.
WHAT ABOUT ALL THE SOULS THE S.R. TRAPPED HERE?
THEY NEED TO BE FREED.
I'LL HOLD IT OFF AS LONG AS I CAN.
YOU RELEASE THE SOULS.
TELL MY MOTHER I LOVE HER.
TELL HER YOURSELF. I AIN'T LEAVING.

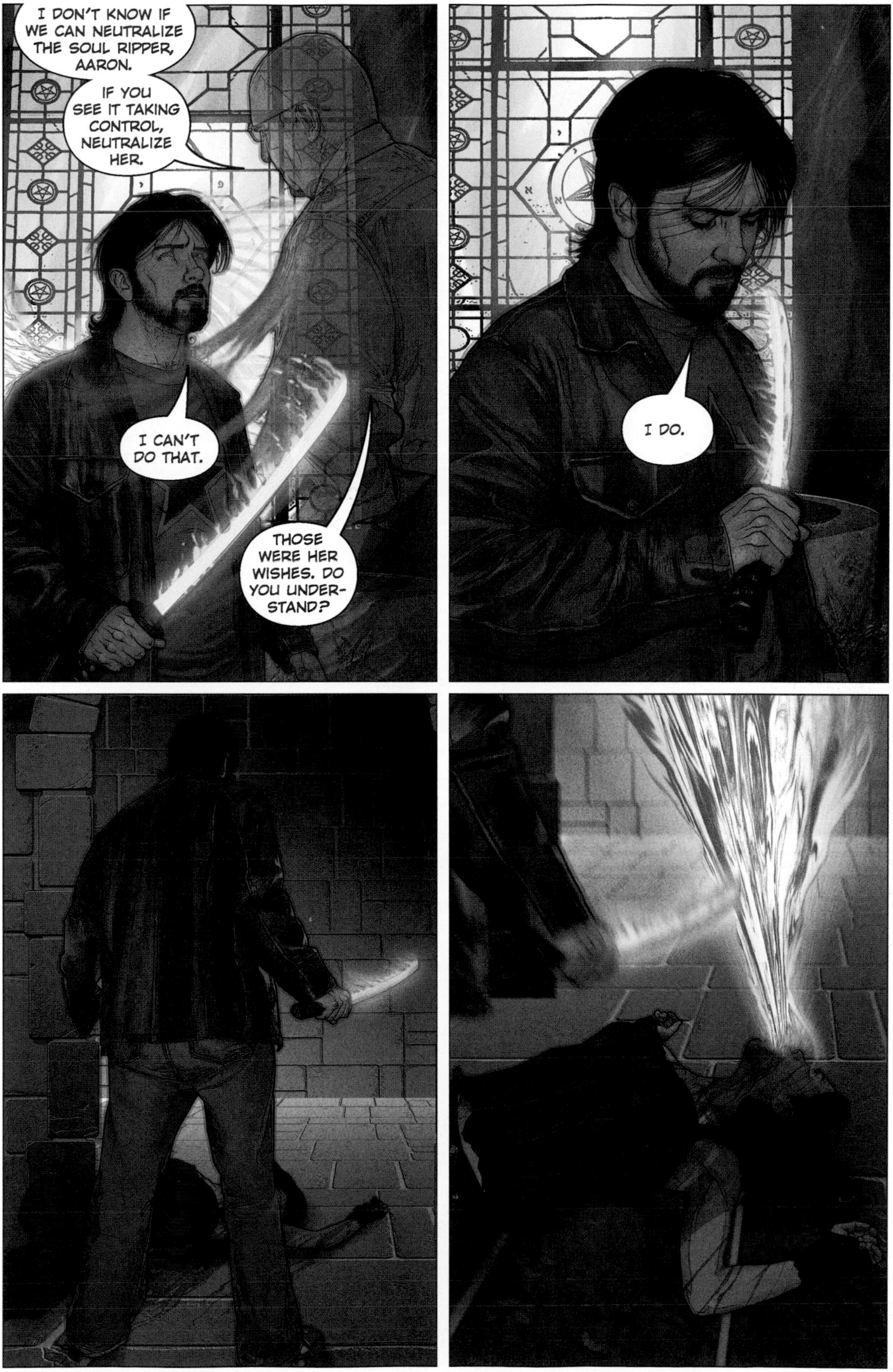
I DON'T KNOW IF WE CAN NEUTRALIZE THE SOUL RIPPER, AARON.
IF YOU SEE IT TAKING CONTROL, NEUTRALIZE HER.
I CAN'T DO THAT.
THOSE WERE HER WISHES. DO YOU UNDER-STAND?
I DO.

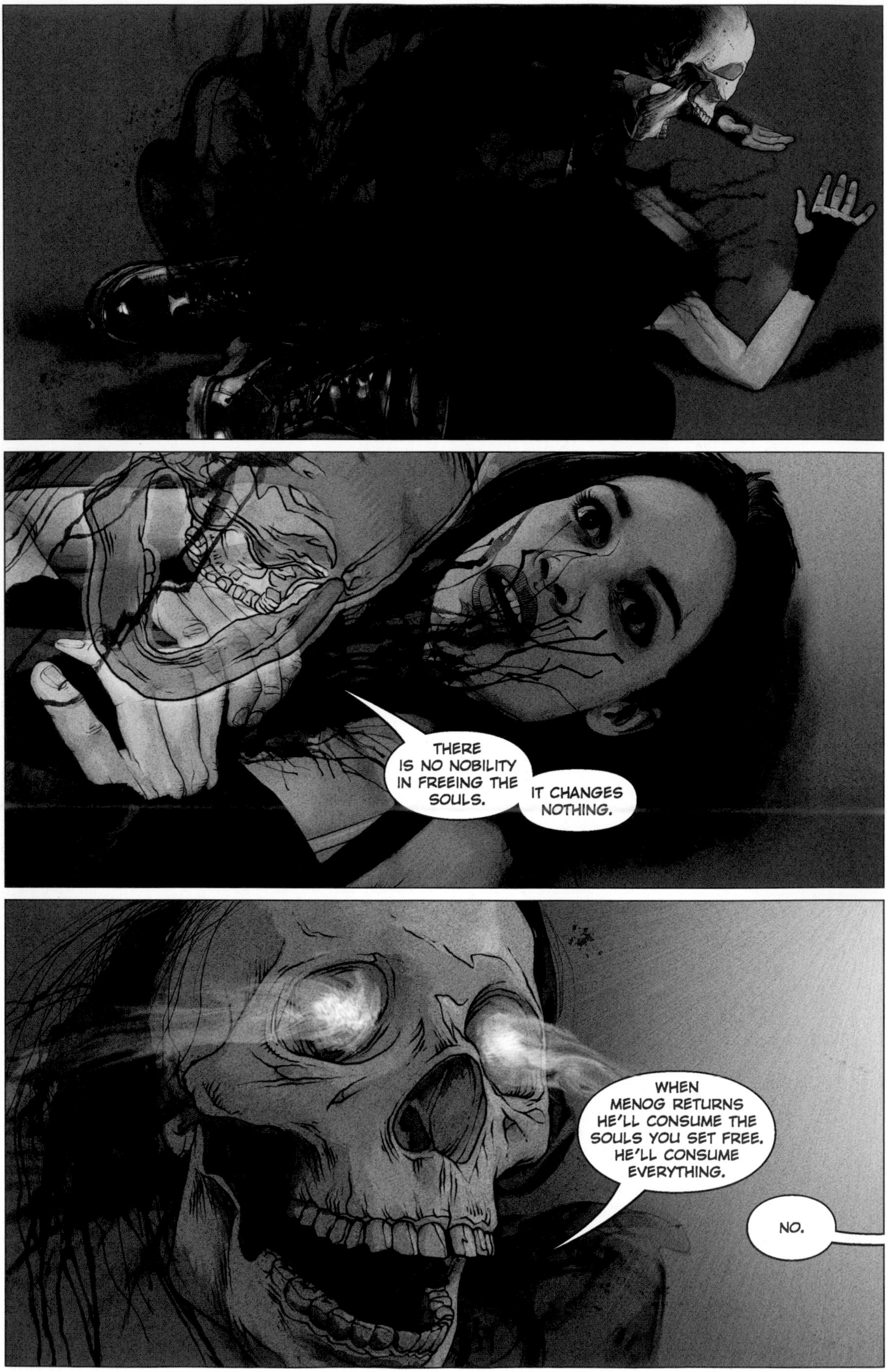
THERE IS NO NOBILITY IN FREEING THE SOULS.
IT CHANGES NOTHING.
WHEN MENOG RETURNS HE'LL CONSUME THE SOULS YOU SET FREE. HE'LL CONSUME EVERYTHING.
NO.

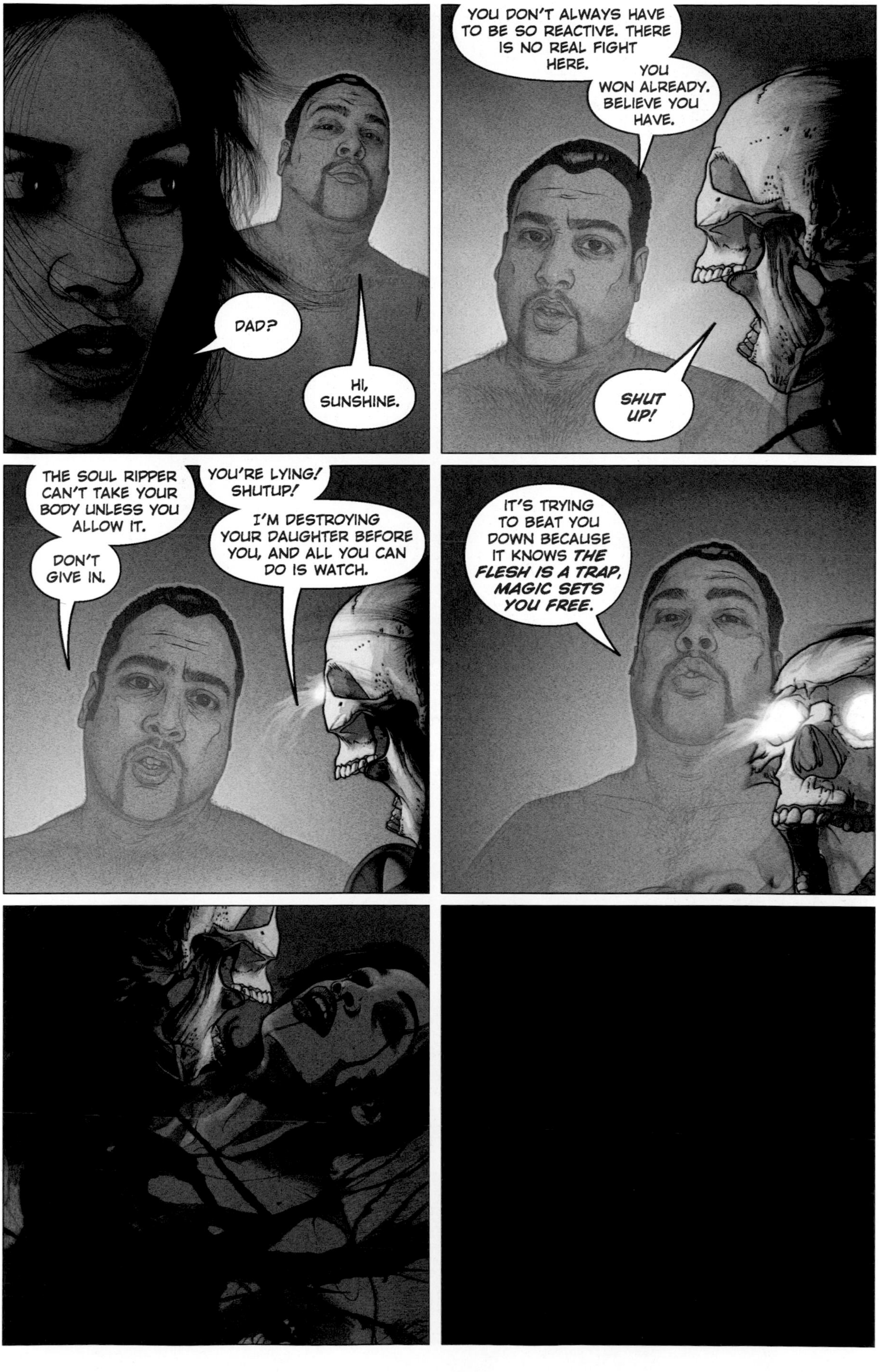
DAD?
HI, SUNSHINE.
YOU DON'T ALWAYS HAVE TO BE SO REACTIVE. THERE IS NO REAL FIGHT HERE.
YOU WON ALREADY. BELIEVE YOU HAVE.
SHUT UP!
THE SOUL RIPPER CAN'T TAKE YOUR BODY UNLESS YOU ALLOW IT.
DON'T GIVE IN.
YOU'RE LYING! SHUTUP!
I'M DESTROYING YOUR DAUGHTER BEFORE YOU, AND ALL YOU CAN DO IS WATCH.
IT'S TRYING TO BEAT YOU DOWN BECAUSE IT KNOWS THE FLESH IS A TRAP, MAGIC SETS YOU FREE.

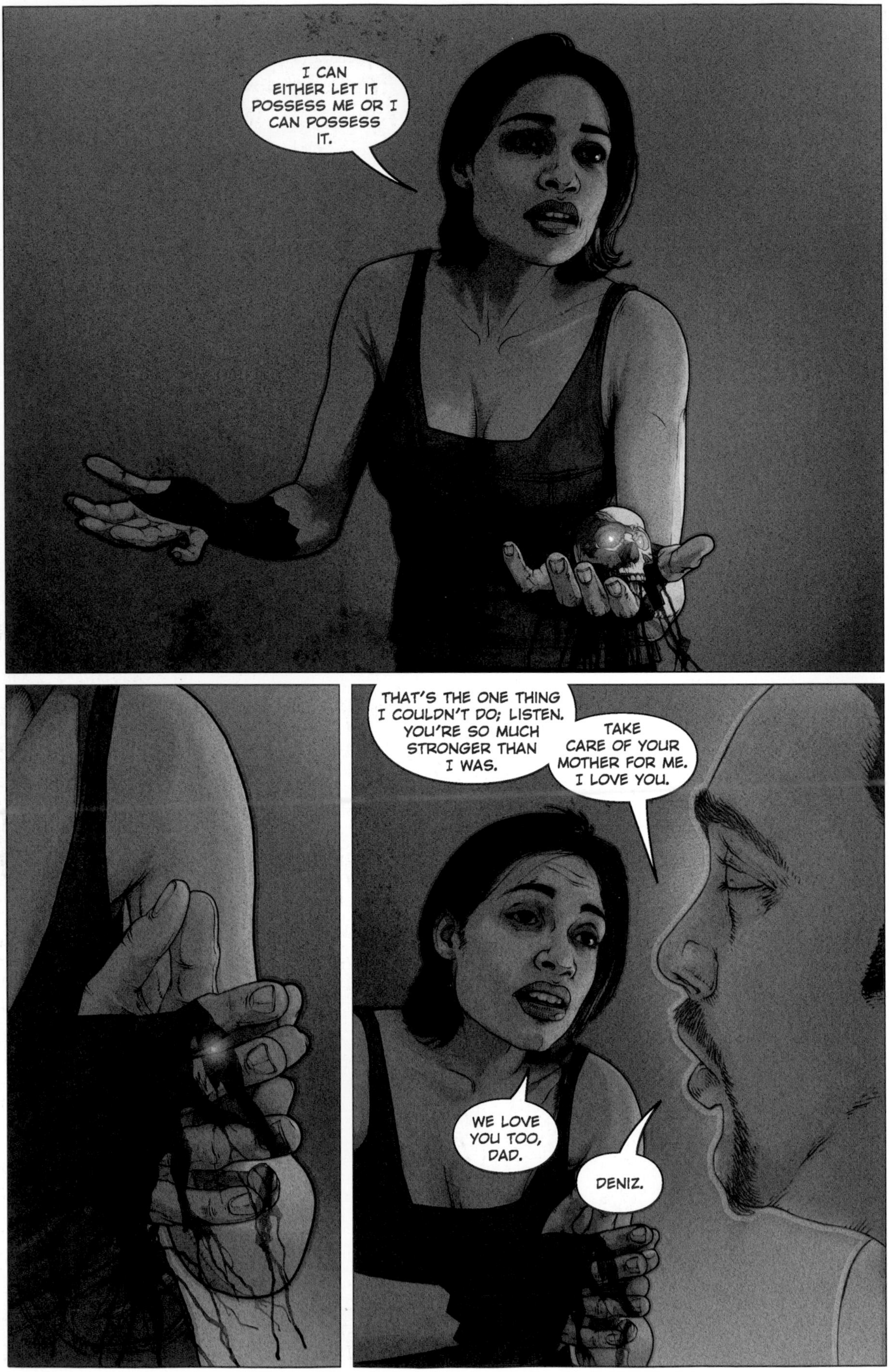
I CAN EITHER LET IT POSSESS ME OR I CAN POSSESS IT.
THAT'S THE ONE THING I COULDN'T DO; LISTEN. YOU'RE SO MUCH STRONGER THAN I WAS.
TAKE CARE OF YOUR MOTHER FOR ME. I LOVE YOU.
WE LOVE YOU TOO, DAD.
DENIZ.

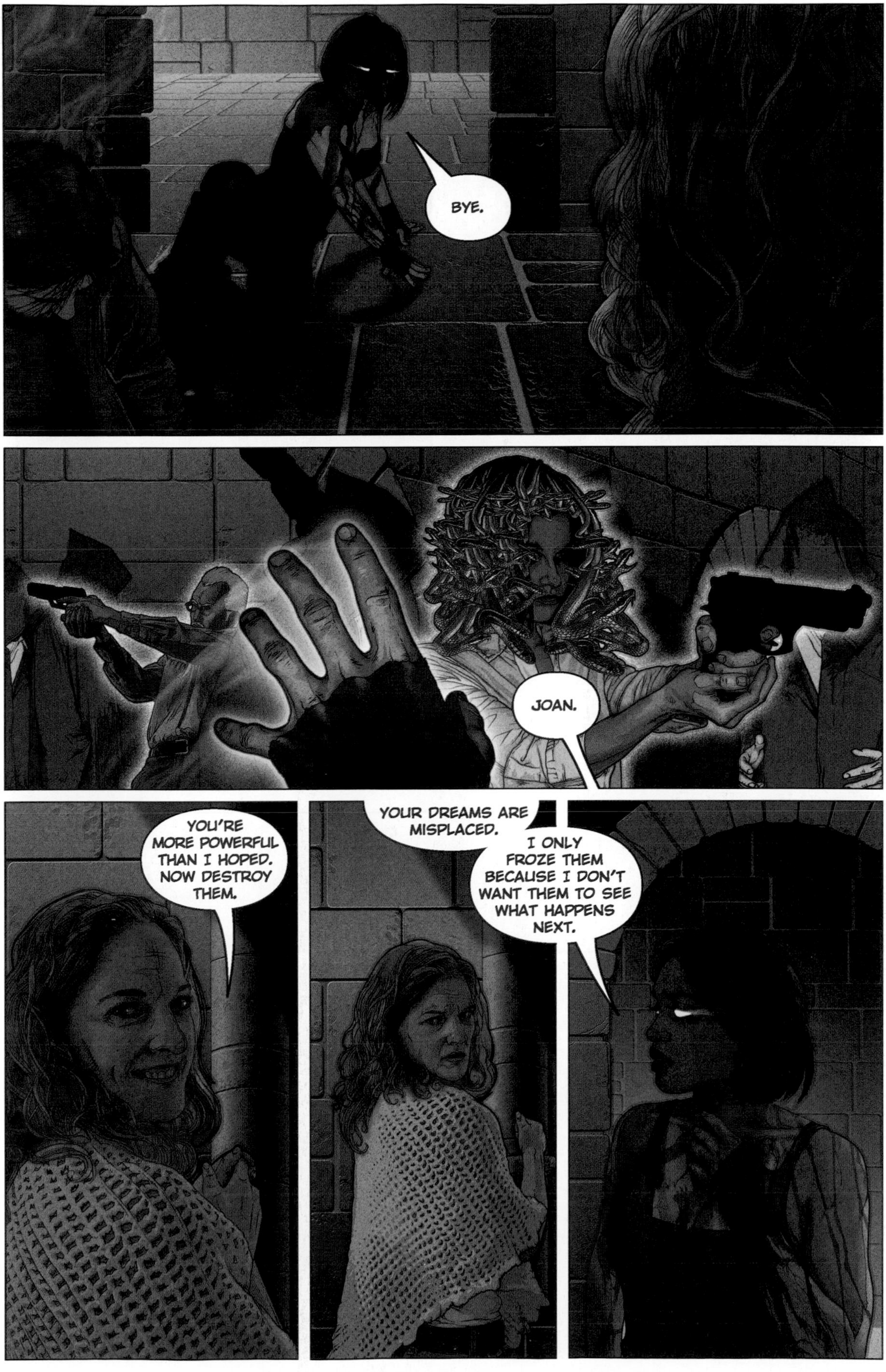
BYE.
JOAN.
YOU'RE MORE POWERFUL THAN I HOPED. NOW DESTROY THEM.
YOUR DREAMS ARE MISPLACED.
I ONLY FROZE THEM BECAUSE I DON'T WANT THEM TO SEE WHAT HAPPENS NEXT.

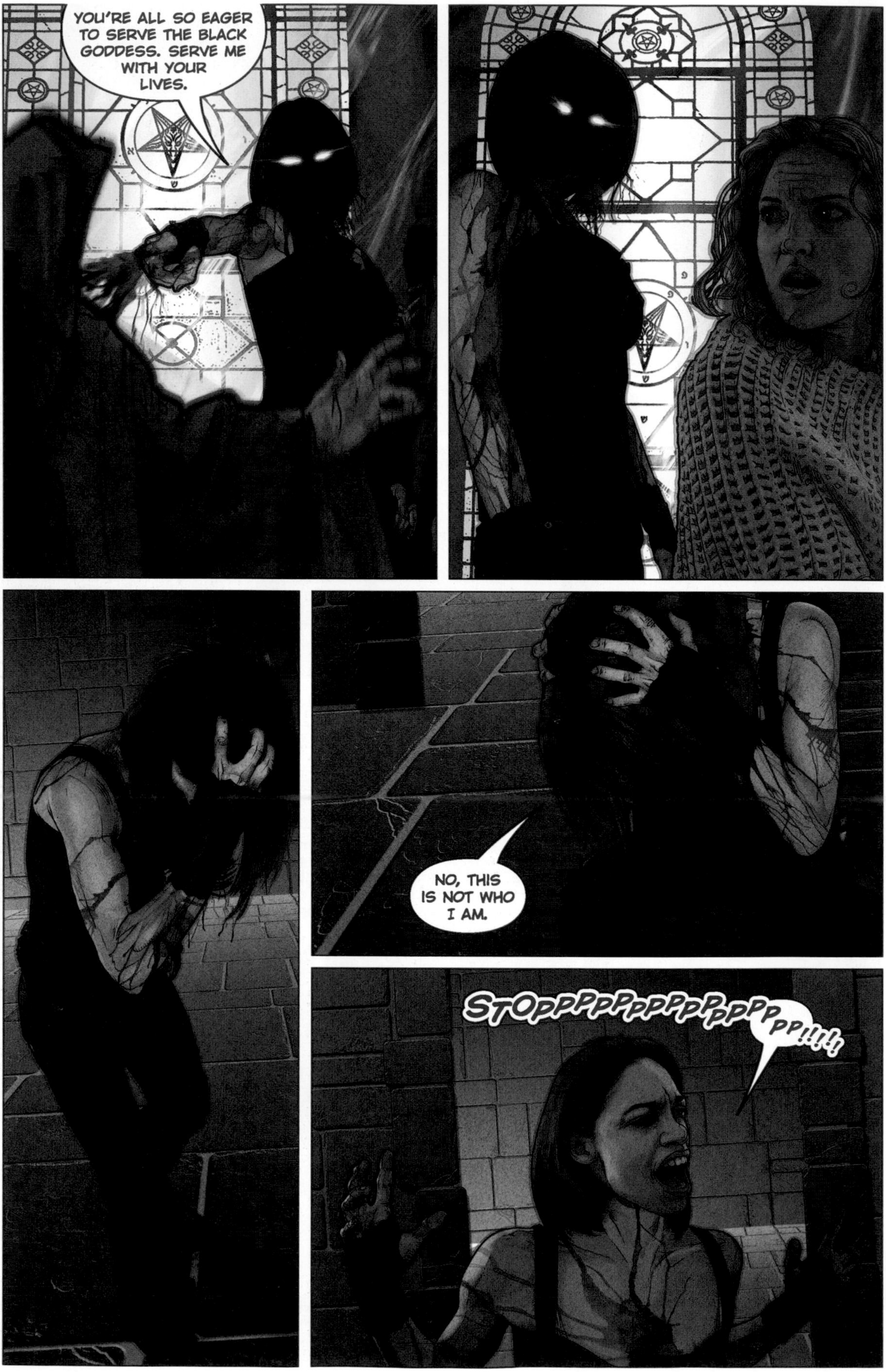
YOU'RE ALL SO EAGER TO SERVE THE BLACK GODDESS. SERVE ME WITH YOUR LIVES.
NO, THIS IS NOT WHO I AM.
STOPPPPPPPPPPPPPP!!!!

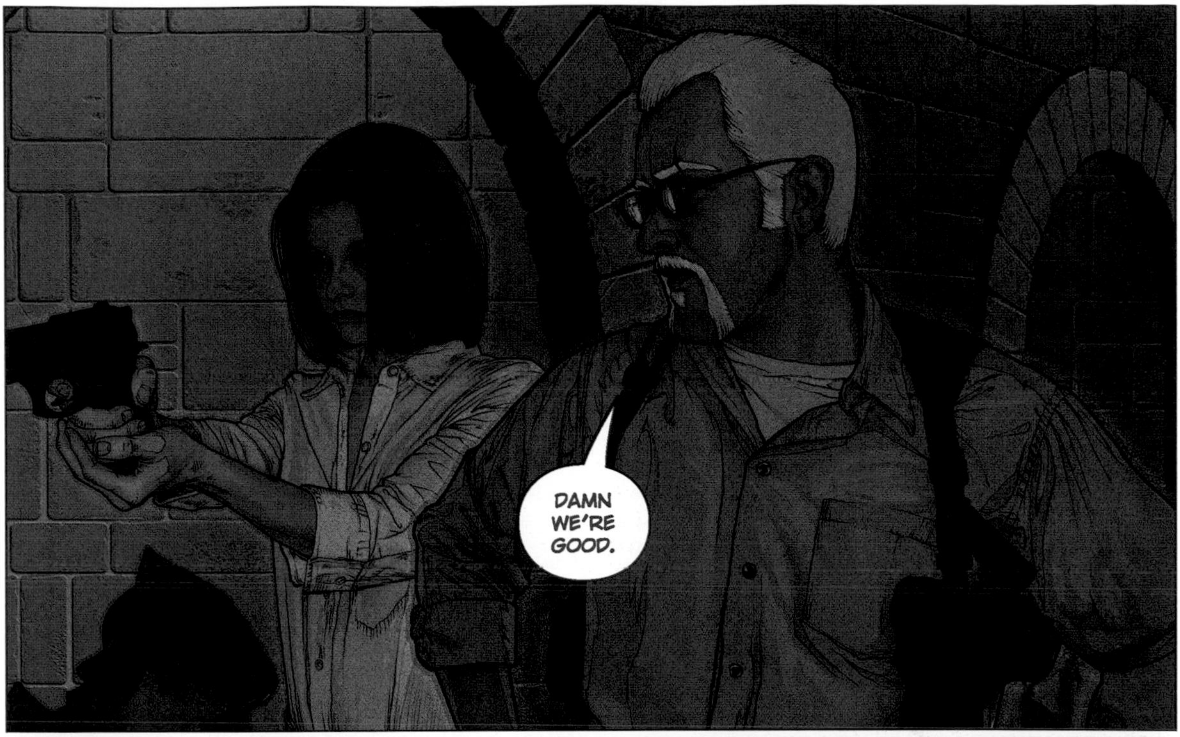
DAMN WE'RE GOOD.

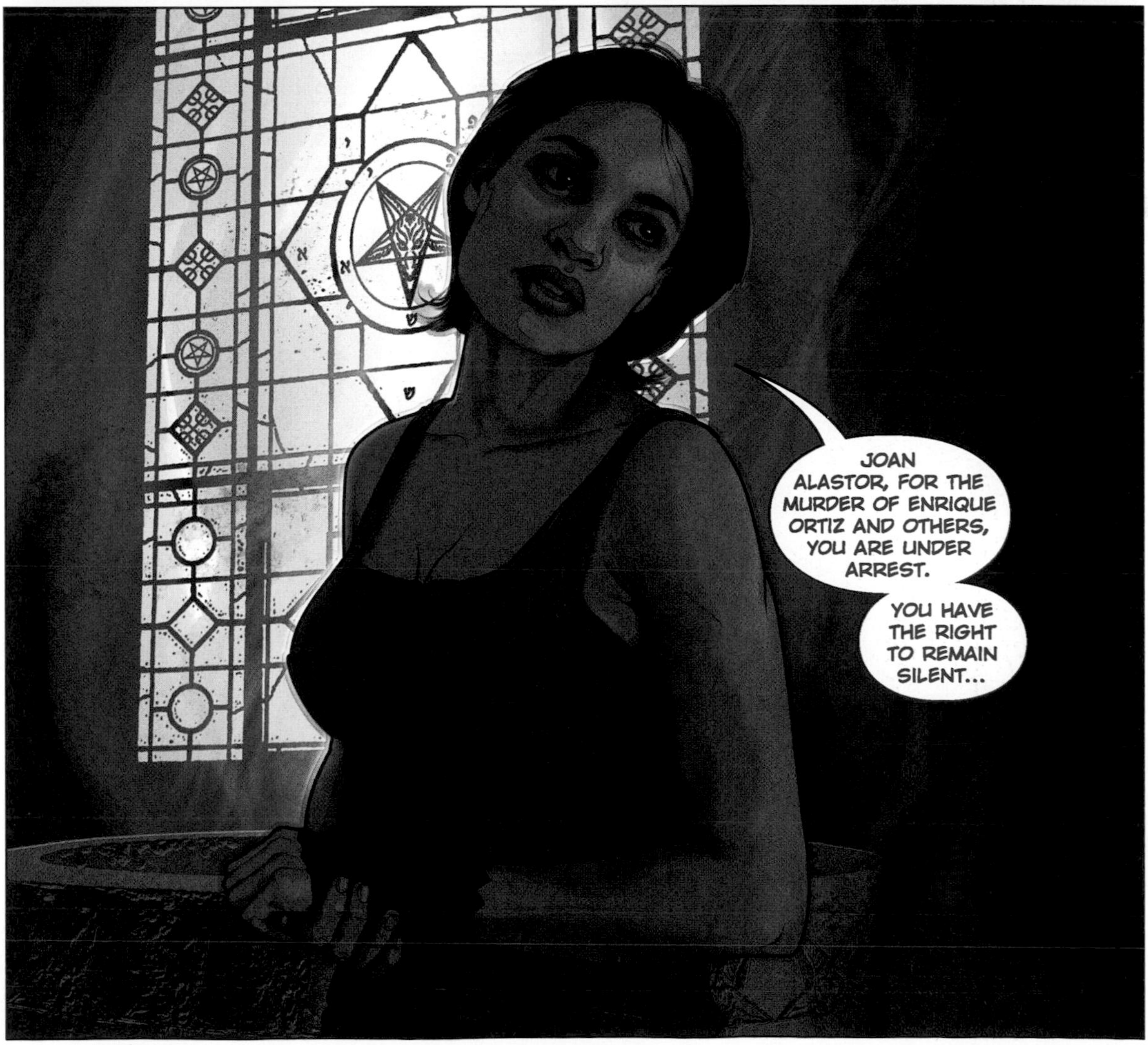
JOAN ALASTOR, FOR THE MURDER OF ENRIQUE ORTIZ AND OTHERS, YOU ARE UNDER ARREST.
YOU HAVE THE RIGHT TO REMAIN SILENT...

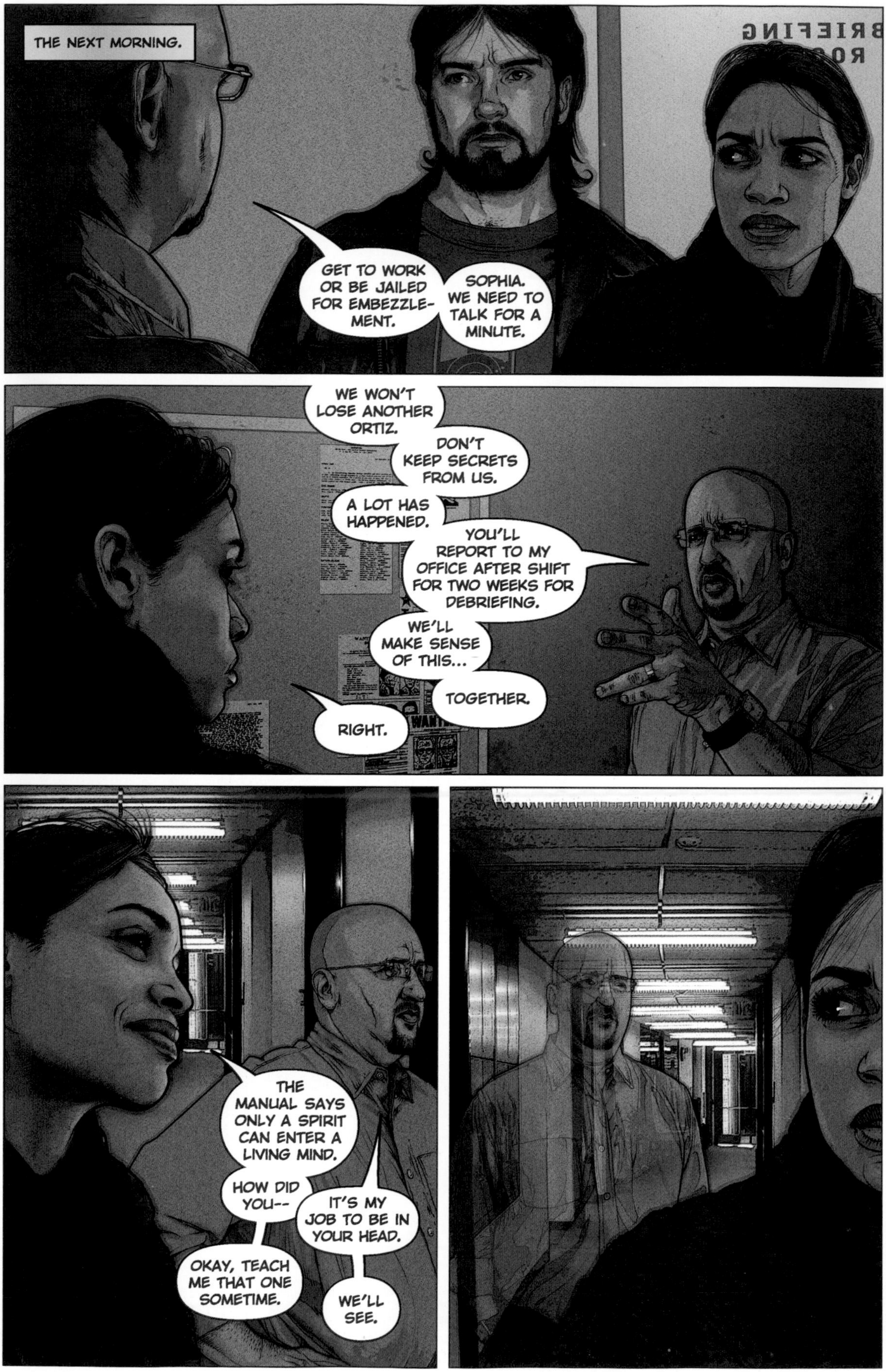
THE NEXT MORNING.
BRIEFING ROO
GET TO WORK OR BE JAILED FOR EMBEZZLE-MENT.
SOPHIA. WE NEED TO TALK FOR A MINUTE.
WE WON'T LOSE ANOTHER ORTIZ.
DON'T KEEP SECRETS FROM US.
A LOT HAS HAPPENED.
YOU'LL REPORT TO MY OFFICE AFTER SHIFT FOR TWO WEEKS FOR DEBRIEFING.
WE'LL MAKE SENSE OF THIS...
TOGETHER.
RIGHT.
THE MANUAL SAYS ONLY A SPIRIT CAN ENTER A LIVING MIND.
HOW DID YOU--
IT'S MY JOB TO BE IN YOUR HEAD.
OKAY, TEACH ME THAT ONE SOMETIME.
WE'LL SEE.

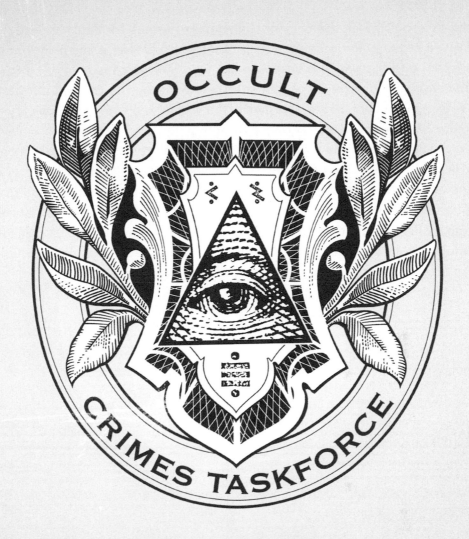

OCCULT CRIMES TASKFORCE

Occult Crimes Taskforce
Officer Training Manual

NOTE: This manual is dedicated to the subject matter experts who met their untimely demises due to supernatural circumstances while compiling the information contained in these pages. Their sacrifices were not in vain. Manhattan is safer. May they rest in peace.

PAMPHLET 602-A
JUNE 1964

WHAT IS MAGIC

In the Emerald Tablet, the ancient philosopher Hermes Trismegistus used the following analogy to describe magic: "That which is seen is like unto that which is unseen, and that which is unseen is like unto that which is seen". The Law of Conservation of Energy states that energy may neither be created nor destroyed. Therefore the sum of all the energies in the system is a constant. Contrary to popular belief our universe is only half of that "system." Energy in our universe is shared with an alternate universe existing parallel from our own. When energy is transmitted between the universes, it is converted acquiring a different set of properties during the process. Energy transmitted back to our world without going through the conversion process is what we refer to as "magic". Unprocessed magical energies are transmitted to our universe via several geographic locales existing in both universes called "Extants." Those skilled in the manipulation of these magical energies can use them to defy our universe's Laws of Reality.

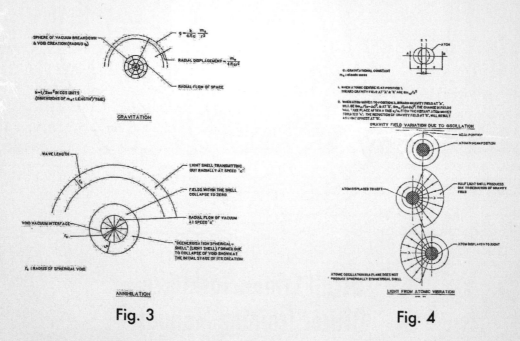

SPHERE OF VACUUM BREAKDOWN & VOID CREATION
RADIAL DISPLACEMENT
RADIAL FLOW OF SPACE
GRAVITATION
WAVE LENGTH
LIGHT SHELL TRANSMITTING OUT RADIALLY AT SPEED 'c'
FIELDS WITHIN THE SHELL COLLAPSE TO ZERO
RADIAL FLOW OF VACUUM AT SPEED 'c'
VOID VACUUM INTERFACE
"DEENERGISATION SPHERICAL-SHELL" (LIGHT SHELL) FORMED DUE TO COLLAPSE OF VOID SHOWN AT THE INITIAL STAGE OF ITS CREATION
RADIUS OF SPHERICAL VOID
ANNIHILATION

Fig. 3

ATOM
GRAVITY FIELD VARIATION DUE TO OSCILLATION
ATOM IN MEAN POSITION
ATOM DISPLACED TO LEFT
HALF LIGHT SHELL PRODUCED DUE TO REDUCTION OF GRAVITY FIELD
ATOM DISPLACED TO RIGHT
ATOMIC OSCILLATION IN A PLANE DOES NOT PRODUCE SPHERICALLY SYMMETRICAL SHELL
LIGHT FROM ATOMIC VIBRATION

Fig. 4

HOW ARE SPELLS CAST?

The famed occultist Aleister Crowley defined "spell casting" as "the science and art of causing change to occur in conformity to will." Magic can easily be manipulating if one understands the properties of magical energy and uses the proper tools to manipulate it. Studies show magic responds to the neural synaptic responses of those who wield it. Rituals, ceremonies and spell casting have less to do with the control of magical energy and more to do with the triggering of particular synaptic responses in the brain of the practitioner. To manipulate magic, two things are needed: a conduit to direct the magical energies conjured and the ability to manipulate magic.

WHO CAN PERFORM MAGIC?

Though magical energies are abundant, only certain individuals can manipulate (i.e. "spell cast") them. Humans with the capability to cast spells are classified as "Tainted." The Tainted Syndrome is a result of exposure to high levels of magic energy radiation or "MERlin" for short (e.g., exposure to elixirs, close proximity to magical emissions.) Greater exposure (bites from Ceteri, victims of high level curses/hexes) can cause vampirism, were-form mutations and zombiism. Most Tainted are unaware they've been exposed to MERlin. If one never attempts to cast spells, their life holds little difference from the uncontaminated. Furthermore, those Tainted who involve themselves in the occult rarely comprehend the reasons their spells are effective while others are not capable of performing magic. Through continued exposure to mystical energies Tainted proficiency in spell casting can increase. So, the more spell casting the Tainted performs, the more capable of performing greater, more powerful spells they become.

WHAT ARE CONDUITS USED TO PERFORM MAGICAL SPELLS?

To cast spells, Tainted conduits, generally referred to as "wands," to collect and direct Magic. Magic can be collected and directed through most organic matter (rocks, wood (Fig. 5), or even a rabbit's foot), though some objects are better for conjuring than others. The process of the collecting magic in a conduit is commonly referred to as "enchanting." When spell casting, for maximum efficiency, a Tainted individual should use matter from the Alternate Universe if possible. Though rare, metal from the Alternate Universe resides in our world as a result of a meteor shower millions of years, presumably, the same meteor shower ending the Prehistoric Age. Metal from the Alternate Universe is called Firon or "Hell Metal." Firon is a silvery, slightly blue metal. It is the strongest, most durable metal known to man, partly because of its atomic structure and partly because its durability increases with enchantment. Firon is simple to enchant. It is of average weight and resembles pewter or silver.

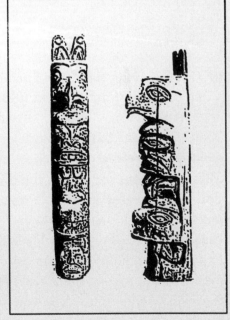

Fig. 5

2

THE OCCULT CRIMES TASKFORCE SHIELD

The Occult Crimes Taskforce Officer Shield is a multi-purpose tool serving as standard police badge; a MERlin meter, measuring magic energy radiation levels; and a charm, protecting officers from hexes, curses and other low-level magical attacks. Unlike other police badges OCT Shields are forged from Firon and can be opened to reveal complex machinery used to aid officers in performing spells quickly by aligning the shield's centerpiece with runes located on the shield's outer edge.

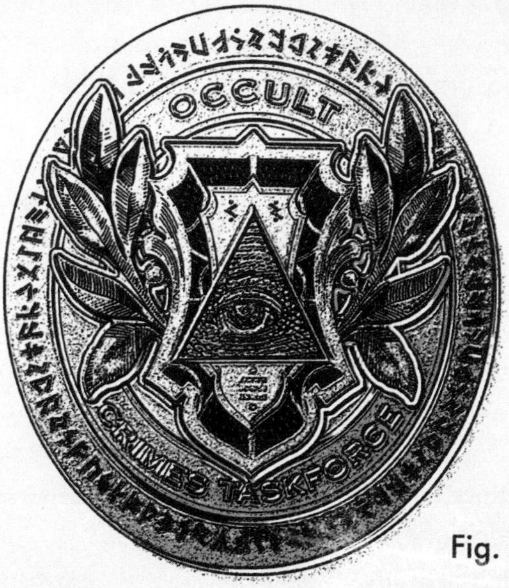
OCCULT
CRIMES TASKFORCE

Fig. 6

NOTE: The Firon supply on Earth is limited, so new shields can only be produced when a new deposit of metal is located. As a result OCT officer roster is static.

The OCT Shield design is modeled after the Antikythera Mechanism, an ancient artifact discovered off the coast of Antikythera, an island northwest of Crete in 1900. In a wrecked vessel, the divers discovered Firon statues, strange weaponry, and tools covered in illegible glyphs. Among their findings was a small, circular mechanism that opened to reveal a series of cogs, sprockets and gears. Carbon dating test showed the mechanism had been manufactured in roughly 80 B.C. Experts initially thought it an astrolabe, an ancient astronomer's tool, but closer examination, proved the Antikythera Mechanism to be a far more complex device, containing a sophisticated system of differential gears. Prior to the mechanism's discovery, gearing of this complexity had not been known to exist until 1575 A.D. Though the mechanism's construction remains a mystery to the general public, it is generally known in magical circles the device was originally manufactured in Atlantis as an educational tool used for teaching children spell casting.

DO BEINGS FROM THE ALTERNATE UNIVERSE RESIDE IN OUR UNIVERSE?

Since the beginning of time, mankind has shared the Earth with Alternate Universe beings or the "Ceteri"(Latin for "others.") Ceteri can be classified in three basic types, each possessing characteristics specific to that class of being:

- Tangible Ceteri are beings who possess a physical body that can be effected on the mortal plane. Since they are not of this world they are generally fatally allergic to common things found in our environment. Sunlight, water, silver, and even garlic in some cases can have negative effects on Tangible Ceteri. They typically possess sentience near or above the average human though most have a hard time comprehending complex technology.

- Viral Ceteri (Fig. 7) are single celled organisms transmitted from Tangible Ceteri to a human host, commonly through bites or intercourse. The Viral Ceteri infects the human host mutating their body. Most humans exposed to magic in this manner mutate to a form similar to the Ceteri who exposed them. Once mutated, the human becomes fatally allergic to the same things as the Ceteri who exposed them. Most Viral Ceteri are single celled organisms and do not possess higher forms of sentience

- Intangible Ceteri, commonly thought to be angels, demons or spirits, do not possess physical bodies however, they have the ability to enter a biological organism and "possess" it. Unlike Tangible and Viral Ceteri, Intangible Ceteri feed on magic and are typically found in areas with a high concentrations of MERlin like places of worship, homes of tainted individuals and Ceteri, or burial grounds.

It is the jobs of the Occult Crimes Taskforce to police Manhattan and ensure the Ceteri do not prey on the citizenry and ensure the Tainted of Manhattan do not abuse magic.

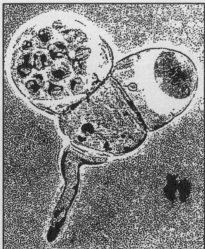

Fig. 7

4

WHAT IS THE OCCULT CRIMES TASKFORCE?

There is an old and forgotten resolution in recesses of the City of New York Annotated Code of Ordinances mandating the creation of a taskforce in the Manhattan Police Department specifically designed to deal with crimes of occult origin.

Formed in the 1800s, the Occult Crimes Taskforce is a covert police unit comprised of the Manhattan Investigators and "Ceteri" who have pledged their existence to the protection of mankind. Together, man and monster have secretly defended Manhattan for over 200 years.

The primary mission of the OCT's is to serve and protect the Manhattan populous from rogue Ceteri, MERlin Contamination and Tainted who exploit magic for personal gain at expense of the citizenry. Contrary to general assumption, the OCT is not a large, sweeping conspiracy. It is a small, elite task force of officers dealing with a problem only they can. The entire operation is no larger then maybe 150 full time officers, investigators and auxiliary personnel.

The OCT precinct is located near the epicenter of the Extant in an area of Manhattan informed Tainted and Ceteri refer to as the "Otherground." Due to the Otherground's proximity to the Extants epicenter, it is a hotbed of magical activity and a haven for Ceteri and Tainted alike. Like Shangri La, Avalon and the Garden of Eden, only Tainted individuals and Ceteri can actually see the Otherground and spells of concealment to prevent the average Tainted person from viewing it.

Fig. 8

IF MANHATTAN WERE AN EXTANT, WHY WOULD ANYONE BUILD A CITY ON THE ISLAND?

Historians claim Peter Minuit (Fig. 9) purchased the Isle of Manhattan in 1626 from Wappinger Indian Tribe for 60 Dutch Guilders or $24. What the historians don't know is why the tribe sold the island for such a low price. The Wappingers had been plagued by demons, ravaged by werewolves and haunted by spirits. Their shamans cast a spell blocking passage from the Alternate Universe, but knew the spell was a temporary solution at best. When Minuit made his offer the Wappingers saw it as an opportunity to avenge themselves for the injustices they suffered at the hands of the early settlers.

Fig. 9

Things remained peaceful on Manhattan for nearly two centuries, but eventually the Wappinger's barrier dissolved and hell broke loose. Those closest to the extant epicenter suffered the worst causalities. Those living farther out saw their lives minimally effected. The OCT was created shortly after the barrier breach as a means of minimizing MERlin contamination and protecting citizens. With the barrier broken and magical energies once again flowing from the extant, the area around the epicenter began to attract magical beings from across the planet.

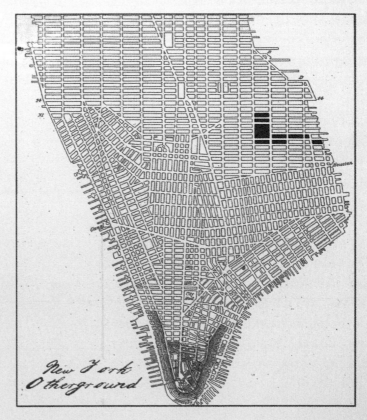

New York
Otherground

6

CHAPTER 2: SPELLS, INCANTATIONS, INVOCATIONS AND ENCHANTMENTS

INTRODUCTION

Genesis Chapter 1, Verse 3: "...And God said let there be light: and there was light."

Since the dawn of existence, the first element of manipulating magical energy has been what is said. Contemporary practitioners of magic define spell casting as the formulaic practice by which the spell caster employs ritual recitation of words to produce desired affects in reality via magical energy. The language of spells relates directly to the desired effect of the conjurer. While basic spells can be created through the use of older languages (the O.C.T. generally trains officers in the use of Latin*) more powerful spells require Metacommunicative Competency, knowledge of root and affix morphemes, and an understanding of the Hidden Letters of the Alphabet.

TALKING THE TALK:

To proficiently recite spells one must first have Metacommunicative Competence, the ability to utilize the four practical means of communication:

Verbal communication: by words or their meaning
Paraverbal communication: loudness of speaking, manner of speaking, use of silence, interruption or interference in conversation
Nonverbal communication: body language
Extra-verbal communication: time, place, context, orientation towards target groups, tactile (feeling by touch) and olfactory (smelling) aspects

With Metacommunicative Competence the aforementioned ways of communication can be used to effectively emphasize root morphemes when reciting incantations. Choice of words, inflection, body language and context all play a vital role in the execution of an incantation, because much like the creation of the world in Genesis, the conjurer is using magic to form something into the world. Improper use of speech could result in a spell not working, or worse, working to an undesired effect.

SPELL CASTING BASICS:

Morphemes are an important part of spell casting because they are the most concise, meaningful linguistic units known to man. There are four types of morphemes: root, affix, stem and clitic, though the construction of spells primarily relates to root and affix morphemes and their functions in relation to communicating the intent to invoke magic effects. A root morpheme is the smallest lingual unit that carries a semantic interpretation. When stripped of affixes, root morphemes are the rawest forms of linguistic data representing the most primal concepts relating to mankind. When these concepts are modified by an affix, the root morpheme represented becomes specific to the situation the user is describing. Though the concept may become more graspable in its more specific form, it loses some of the original power because the new, more specific concept no longer represents as broad of an idea as it did before being modified by the affix.

Ex. The word morph can be used to represent one of various distinct forms of an organism or species, but when modified with the affix "ecto", which means "outside" or "external", the word "ectomorph" is created. "Ectomorph" represents a person with a thin non-muscular body.

While parts of the concepts the root word and affix represent are still present, the combination of the two creates a wholly new concept based on the other two. This is the secret of conjuring spells.

THE HIDDEN ALPHABET:

In the year 1011, at the command of the secret masters behind the White Millenarianism Conspiracy, a writer named Byrhtferð was tasked with ordering the Old English alphabet for "numerological purposes", allowing for the alphabet to be standardized and made uniform, though the true intentions were far more sinister. In his 'reorder' Byrhtferð purposely excluded 23 letters (Fig. 5) from the Alphabet due to their significance in the conjuring of spells.

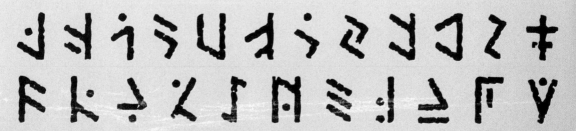

Fig. 5

8

"The Hidden Letters of the Alphabet", are a grouping of letters that combine to create affixes that when modifying root morphemes allow the conjurer to utilize powerful magic. Spells so potent their execution and occurrences are the stuff of legend. Partings of seas, the ability to walk on water, and even resurrection after death are examples of the kind of feats one can perform with these higher magics. As previously stated, words are merely representations of concepts, so by removing the letters used to truly conceptualize certain magical phenomenon, Byrhtferð and the White Millenarianism Conspiracy severely stunted the proliferation of magic in the western world. Millenarianism Conspiracies across the planet have employed similar magic subjugation tactics, but none have been as successful as the exclusion of the 23 letters from the English language.

Most English speakers never even realize the loss of letters, though most problems with self-expression can be traced back to this act, since English users do not possess the proper number of letters to create the words to adequately express how they feel. The White Millenarianism Conspiracy felt this was a small price to pay when compared to the threat wide spread use of high-level magic posed.

As an officer of the Occult Crimes Taskforce, as you accrue time in grade and receive promotions, you are also issued manual updates containing the hidden letters as well as instructions on how to pronounce and employ them to modify root morphemes.

Fig. 6

USING THE OFFICER SHIELD TO CAST SPELLS:

As previously stated in the Manual Introduction, the Occult Crimes Taskforce Officer Shields are forged from the other dimensional metal Firon. Because of its inter-dimensional origins, Firon conducts magical energy in the same way the ferrous metals of Earth conduct electrical currents. Unlike metals of our dimension, Firon gains durability with each successive enchantment; partially absorbing a small portion of the magical energies the conjurer uses. Though the badge increases in durability, it does not increase in weight.

The O.C.T. Shield (Fig. 7) is compromised of three main pieces:
1: The Dial: The outer ring of the O.C.T. Shield is an interchangeable dial engraved with the Forbidden Letters of the Alphabet. As an officer is promoted the dial on his badge becomes more intricate, reflecting the choices he/she has made in creating spells.

2. The Crest/pointer: The officer uses the central piece of the badge to choose the character along the dial they need to perform the incantation they are attempting. The pointer also contains the Extra Sensory Module; officers commonly call this the "third eye". The third eye alerts officers to high levels of magic energy, radiation levels, protects officers from hexes, curses and other low-level magical attacks, and allows officers to perceive matter shrouded by magic and access information normally imperceptible to humans.

3. The Base/ "Cauldron": The base of the badge houses a sophisticated system of differential gears that controls the Shield dialing system and other functions the O.C.T. cannot divulge to entry level investigators. Occult Crimes Taskforce Technical Support refers to the base of the badge as the Cauldron, because the magical exchanges occur there.

The Dial ————————————————

The Crest/pointer ———————————

The Base/ "Cauldron"————————

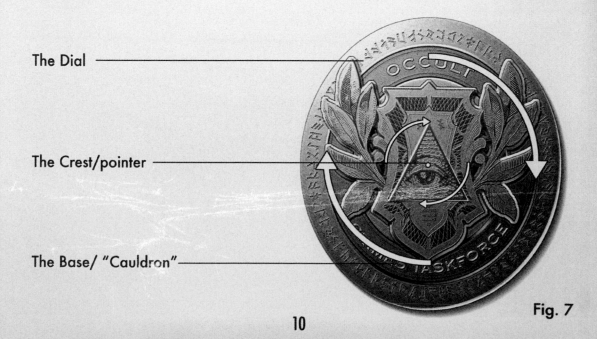

Fig. 7

BASIC STEPS FOR UTILIZING OCCULT CRIMES TASKFORCE SHIELD:

1. Dialing in: Using the crest/pointer, the user spells out the incantation they wish to perform by turning the crest to the corresponding letter on the outer ring of the badge.

OCCULT
CRIMES TASKFORCE

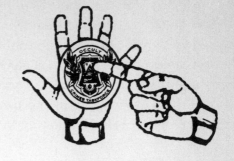

2. Revealing: In a show of ritual symbolism, the officer directs the "eye" of the shield at the intended area for magical occurrence. The action is known as revealing because the user "reveals" to the target the intent to conjure magical energies.

OCCULT

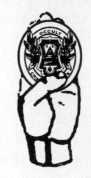

3. Recitation: As the crest/pointer begins to move to the pre-dialed characters on the badge, the user simultaneously recites the spell that was previously dialed into the badge.

OCCULT

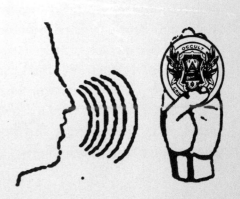

4. Effect: If the above steps are performed properly, magical energy is conjured and a spell is cast.

OCCULT

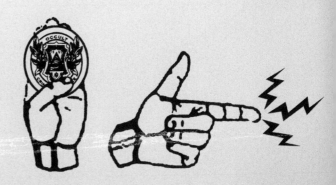

CHAPTER 3: LAWFUL USE OF SPELLCASTING

INTRODUCTION

"Do what thou wilt"
- Thelema Philosophy

"May I do to others as I would that they should do unto me."
- Golden Rule Philosophy

The following chapter is a brief overview of City of New York Administrative Code Article 580.999 Miscellaneous Provisions pertaining to the Magick Civil Code and New York Penal Law Section 66.60 Occult Crime. Officers are encouraged to examine the full legal text governing Occult Civil and Criminal proceedings prior to field duty.

MUUTUS THELEMA
The cornerstone of Occult Civil law is Muutus Thelema or "and ye harm none, do what ye will". Though most magic practitioners, both Tainted and Ceteri, live by the Thelema Philosophy, those practicing magic within the United States of America must also adhere to the Golden Rule when casting spells. Practitioners are freely allowed to perform their crafts and beliefs so long as their practices do not purposely encroach upon the freedoms of others. It is for this reason the O.C.T. exists, to serve and protect untainted, tainted and Ceteri alike from Muutus Thelema Infractions.

CODEX THELEMA
Based on the Hyperborean Codex Maximilianeus Hyperborea Civilis, the Codex Thelema or Magick Civil Code is a systematic assemblage of laws designed to comprehensively manage the core areas of the lives of practitioners of magic in an urban environment. Created June 16, 1827 the code serves to define the extra-normal laws necessary for governing a community of individuals who practice magic. Though some of the laws are outdated, the Code has not been changed as it can only be ratified at specific intervals due to the mystical nature of the concepts the document governs and the citizenry it affects.

There are 888 laws. Listed below is a limited sample:

• If Man or Ceteri curses Earth in his practice, and harms nature, the practitioner will be arrested.

• If Man or Ceteri attempts to create life alone or with another through means of Dark Magick, he will be arrested and have that which was created taken away from him.

• The exercise of Magick civil rights is dependent of the quality of citizen, be he Man or Ceteri, which is only acquired and preserved through conformity to the Codex Thelema.

• The rights of Man or Ceteri shall be lost, 1st, by attempted practice of the Dark Magicks; 2d, by accepting, without the authority of government, arcana or powers of Dark Forces; 3dly, by inclusion into any foul coven which shall require allegiance in opposition with the sanctity of order; 4thly, in short, by any agreement made in a dark Magicks and their masters that might endanger the city of Manhattan.

• Sentences to punishments, the effect of which is to deprive the party condemned of all participation in the Magick civil rights hereafter mentioned, shall imply binding of Magick ability.

• Sentence to banishment to 'That Place Which is Neither' shall imply binding of Magick ability.

• Other perpetual afflictive punishments shall not imply binding of Magick ability, except so far as the law shall have attached that consequence to them.

• Those condemned for necromancy shall, during sentence, or until they shall make appearance, or until their arrest during that period, be deprived of the exercise of Magick Civil Rights.

• When the party under accusation of necromancy shall appear voluntarily during the investigation, to be reckoned from the day of the banishment, or when he shall have been seized and made prisoner during that interval, the judgment shall be entirely reversed; the accused shall be restored to the possession of his property; he shall be tried afresh; and if by the new judgment he is condemned to the same punishment or a different punishment equally drawing after it binding of Magick ability, it shall only take place from the date of the execution of the second judgment.

• In those civil cases in which parties involved are not bound to appear in person, it shall be allowed them to make appearance by means of séance or astral projection.

UNIFORM CODE OF OCCULT POLICE JUSTICE

Though members of the Occult Crimes Taskforce are sworn to uphold Muutus Thelema, they do not possess the Occult Civil Rights of citizens they protect. Instead members of the Occult Crimes Taskforce adhere to the Uniform Code of Occult Police Justice.

On September 15, 1828, the First Hidden Council of Manhattan established 168 Articles of Occult Policing to govern the conduct of the Occult Crimes Taskforce Officers. On October 12, 1875, the Occult Congress enacted 34 Articles of Thelemic Intent (which applied to both the Tainted and the Ceteri), which were not significantly revised until over a century later. The Occult justice system continued to operate under the Articles of Thelemic Intent until May 09, 1939, when the *Uniform Code of Occult Police Justice* went into effect. UCOPJ was signed into law by President Franklin D. Roosevelt, and became effective on June 16, 1939. The word "Uniform" in the Code's title refers to the congressional intent to make Occult Justice uniform or consistent among the Tainted and Ceteri. The UCOPJ encompasses both the Articles of Occult Policing and the Articles of Thelemic Intent while adding new laws based on precedents made after ATI was enacted.

O.C.T. INVESTIGATOR CORE VALUE

The core of the Uniform Code of Occult Police Justice is the Thelema Restrictus Oath which each investigator is required to take upon being inducted into the O.C.T.

Though practicing magic is considered an innate right of those capable of performing magical feats, Occult Crimes Taskforce Investigators are placed in an ethical quandary when faced with the dilemma of using magic for personal gain. To encourage trust from the citizenry, the O.C.T. Hermetic Chiefs created the Themela Restrictus Oath. Occult Crimes Taskforce Members are forbidden to use their magical talents or government conjuring paraphernalia for personal gain.

THE THEMELA RESTRICTUS OATH

I (state name) swear by 'That Which Created What is Above, Below and Aside' and I take to witness all the gods, all the goddesses, to keep according to my ability and my judgment, the following Oath:

To consider dear to me as my parents him who revealed to me this Truth; to live in secret with Untainted and if necessary to share my talents with him; To look upon his children as my own brethren, to teach them this Truth if need be without fee or written promise; to impart to my sons and the sons of the Mage who taught me and the disciples who have sworn themselves to the principles of the profession, but to these alone the precept and the instruction.

I will conjure Magicks for the good of my fellow citizens according to my capability and my judgment and never do harm to anyone unjustly.

To please no one true will I never needlessly perform a deadly Magick nor perform Magicks which may alter the course of destiny.

Nor will I grant the untainted possession of harmful or potentially harmful Magicks.

But I will preserve the purity of life and Magick.

I will not cut of flesh, for through this act Dark Magicks manifest; I will leave this operation to be performed by those deemed capable by the Hermetic Chiefs.

In every circumstance where I approach I will enter only for the good of the citizenry, keeping myself far from all intentional ill-doing and all seduction and especially from the lustful pleasures of Dark Magicks.

All that may come to my knowledge in the practice of the Truth or in daily occurrence of my sacred duty, which ought not to be spread abroad, I will keep secret and will never reveal.

If I keep this oath faithfully, may I enjoy my life and practice the Truth, respected by all Men and Ceteri and in all times; but if I swerve from it or violate it, may the reverse be my lot three fold.

CHAPTER 4: CONJURING ARTS AND POLICE SPELL TACTICS

OVERVIEW

"Conjuring is the Science of understanding oneself and one's conditions. It is the Art of applying that understanding in action."
- Aleister Crowley

With a basic understanding of the origins of true magic, the mechanics of constructing and executing spells one can evaluate the canonical spells employed by OCT officers in the line of duty.

A functional mastery of magic is one of the most important tools in an Occult Crimes Taskforce Investigator's arsenal. Canonical Spells, Incantations, Invocations and Enchantments are divided into the following subcategories: defensive, offensive, concealment and communicative.

In fulfillment of their Thelema Restrictus Oath officers are encouraged to mainly use defensive magic, but when a perpetrator breaches basic Muutus Thelema and the officer is forced to defend themselves offensive magicks are permitted, but only with extreme caution.

NOTE: As an officer accrues time in grade and receives promotions, manual updates with more complex spells will be issued. Access to spells is determined by the number of Hidden Letters of the Alphabet located on the outer dial of an officer's badge. As an officer is promoted their dial is replaced with a different dials possessing more letters providing for a greater number of spell combinations.

The entries below cover the basic spell combinations readily available to officers possessing a Stage 1 Dial. One should bear in mind a newly recruited officer is not a master conjurer. The goal of the new officer is primarily is to cast competent spells, not to create vast incantations. Thus, one should not expect to fully use magic in its infinite power when initially employing magic in the line of duty. One might speculate about the possible combinations of the Stage 1 Dial, but one should not expect their personal spell combinations to have the same results as preordained spells. This is not meant to discourage the enjoyment derived from formulating original spells, but to caution the newly recruited officer to remember the spells listed below are tested, efficient and effective methods for utilizing magic in the line of duty.

DEFENSIVE SPELLS

INTRODUCTION

Defensive magicks are described as incantations used for barring a perpetrator from conjuring magicks to the detriment of themselves, bystanders or public/private property. Defensive magick also describes the series of spells employed by officers to protect themselves from harm. The term may also refer to the tactics involved in "defense", or a sub-division of officers within a larger team whose primary responsibility is take the defensive position in large scale tactical exercises.

AD PROTESTOR
PRONUNCIATION: ad PRO-test-OR
DESCRIPTION: Spell which encases conjurer or target in a thin translucent membrane made of magic.
BADGE COMBINATION: SHELL
NOTES: Though the Ad Protestor Spell does provide some form of protection against concussive attacks it is not without its weaknesses. The spell provides for air to pass through the shell membrane and subsequently leaves the user vulnerable to gaseous attacks.

ANIMADVERTO PER
PRONUNCIATION: an-IMA-ad-VER-to PER
DESCRIPTION: Spell which causes the conjurer to become temporarily intangible.
BADGE COMBINATION: see through
NOTES: Though the Animadverto Per Spell does provide some form of protection against concussive attacks by making them temporarily intangible, the spell is limited by the length of time the conjurer can hold their breath. One cannot breathe oxygen while intangible.

HAUD ANIMADVERTO
PRONUNCIATION: HA-d an-IMA-ad-VER-to
DESCRIPTION: Spell which causes the conjurer to become temporarily visually undetectable.
BADGE COMBINATION: SHELL
NOTES: NA

OFFENSIVE SPELLS

INTRODUCTION

Offensive magicks are described as incantations used for attacking or forcibly engaging a perpetrator for the purpose of subduing them. The term may also refer to the tactics involved in "offense", or a sub-division of officers within a larger team whose primary responsibility is to take the offensive position in large scale tactical exercises.

CONJUNCTIS VIRBUS INCURSIO
PRONUNCIATION: con-JUNK-tis VIR-bus IN-cur-SI-o
DESCRIPTION: Spell which causes channeled magical energy to be redirected through an enchanted firearm.
BADGE COMBINATION: BLAST
NOTES: Though effective, this spell must be used with caution as it causes high amounts of collateral damage and drains the average of magical energy leaving them fatigued.

A POSSE AD ESSE AD HOC AD REM
PRONUNCIATION: a-POSS-e AD-esse-AD-hoc-AD-rem
DESCRIPTION: Spell which causes magical energy to be channeled through the conjurer's body and redirected at a target.
BADGE COMBINATION: CHANNEL
NOTES: Though effective, this spell must be used with caution as it converts the conjurer's body into a conduit for raw magical energy. Serving as a conduit for raw magical energies can prematurely degrade the human cellular structure.

OSTENDO SUM
PRONUNCIATION: os-TEN-do sum
DESCRIPTION: Spell which repels an offensive magical attack back at the attacker.
BADGE COMBINATION: SHELL
NOTES: Though the Ostendo Sum does provide reliable protection against standard mystical concussive attacks by re-directing an offensive magical spell back to its place of origin the spell can be overridden by a powerful offensive magical attack. If overridden the spell will be broken and the conjurer will incur damage from the attack spell.

CONCEALMENT SPELLS

INTRODUCTION

Concealment spells are employed by officers for the purpose of obscuring an object from view or rendering it inconspicuous. Camouflage and deception are the two iterations of the spell. The objective of the concealment spell is often to keep the presence of an officer secret or divert the perpetrator(s) attention from the actual location of the officer.

A CAPITE AD CALCEM MIRROR (INSERT NAME HERE)
PRONUNCIATION: a CAP-it-A AD-cal-SEM
DESCRIPTION: Spell which causes conjurer to shift shapes (NOTE: shape shifting differs from shape changing) to reflect the outward appearance of another person.
BADGE COMBINATION: MYSTIQUE
NOTES: The A Capite Ad Calcem Mirror Spell allows an officer to mimic the appearance of an individual but not their voice.

PALLIUM
PRONUNCIATION: pa-LI-um
DESCRIPTION: Spell used to shroud the true appearance of an individual or items they hold.
BADGE COMBINATION: CLOAK
NOTES: The Pallium Spell is commonly used by Ceteri to assume a near human guise. It is also employed by officers to mask the appearance of objects they might need for a mission that could call attention to them if visible in public.

GEMINUS
PRONUNCIATION: gem-MIN-us
DESCRIPTION: Spell used to confuse an individual by creating multiple copies of the conjurer.
BADGE COMBINATION: DOUBLE
NOTES: The Geminus Spell is typically used to give officers a strategic advantage over perpetrators by confusing them with multiple visages of the officer. By creating illusionary duplicates an officer gains the element of surprise and means to prematurely tire a perpetrator by making them expend excessive amounts of energy in misdirected attacks.

COMMUNICATIVE SPELLS

INTRODUCTION

Communication Spells are used in the process of relaying information between officers over vast distances. Most cases magic-mediated communicative interactions can be conjured in three distinct forms: co-possession, signal, and illusionary.

TRANS-SÉANCE
PRONUNCIATION: None Applicable
DESCRIPTION: Spell which causes co-conjurer to temporarily become possessed by a co-conjurer.
BADGE COMBINATION: OCCUPY
NOTES: The Trans-Séance Spell is especially useful for newly recruited officers as it allows them to temporarily utilize the skills of more experienced officers in real time, in the field.

A POSSE AD ESSE HOC TRADITUM REINFORCEMENTS
PRONUNCIATION: a POSS-e AD esse HOC trad-DIT-um
DESCRIPTION: Spell relays a distress message and location officer location to Occult Crimes Taskforce Special Weapons and Tactics Division
BADGE COMBINATION: BLAST
NOTES: Upon successfully completing the A Posse Ad Esse Hoc Traditum Reinforcement Spell the OCT SWAT Team will arrive onsite within 3 minutes unless there is an incantation in the vicinity blocking mystical teleportation.

SECUNDUM STATUA
PRONUNCIATION: se-CUN-dum stat-TUA
DESCRIPTION: The spell allows an officer to temporarily record and project their image to another officer for the purpose of relaying information.
BADGE COMBINATION: IMAGED
NOTES: The Secundum Statua Spell is commonly used by officers as a means of leaving messages for other officers at crime scenes or dangerous environments. The messages are detected and can be accessed by other officers using the OCT Officer Shield.

CHAPTER 10: THE AKASHIC RECORDS ROOM

INTRODUCTION

The Akashic Records Room serves as an open-entry "backdoor" portal into the universe's oldest, most comprehensive information store. The access terminal is housed in the Occult Crimes Taskforce Precinct. The Records Room allows an officer to make inquiries based on information gathered in investigations and quickly acquire additional intelligence to further their cases.

EX. An investigator trying to uncover the identity of a burglar could not ask the Akashic Record Room "who committed the burglary" but he could ask questions pertaining to the specific whereabouts of suspects at the time of the crime.

HISTORY

Though the exact origins of the Akashic Records remain unknown, it is known the Record resides in the Ether, on a non-corporeal plane of existence outside the Natural World and the Dimension Beyond. For Centuries mystics of ancient cultures, including the Atlanteans, Egyptians, Phoenicians, Indians, Tibetans, Shangri-Lans, Aborigines, Chinese, Hebrews, Druids and Mayans have accessed the Record.

The Akashic Record is an omniscient database of all existence. The Records encompass all events and responses of all consciousnesses, in all realities. Subsequently every life form contributes to the record and is capable of accessing the Record through the use of magic or science. To gain access one must enter a state known as "the Witness".

ENTERING THE WITNESS STATE
NOTE: Access to the Akashic Record Room is limited to Second Year and above Investigators.

WARNING: The Akashic Records Room must be used with extreme caution. A finite consciousness can be overwhelmed by the infinite information stores of the Akashic Record Room if one does not properly pose questions. While accessing the Akashic Records both the events and responses are perceived comparable to an enhanced cinematic experience. Posing too many questions or posing questions in short intervals could result in sensory overload.

STEP 1. Place the Occult Crimes Taskforce Shield on the forehead using the pointer and index finger of the right hand. The eye of the Shield acts as a conduit/ "third eye" allowing the investigator to perceive the information streaming from the Record.

STEP 2. To enter the preconscious state necessary to access the Records one must quiet the mind. This can easily be achieved by envisioning of a calming memory or focusing on a pre-established mental construct.

NOTE: The O.C.T. Psychic Department recommends envisioning a white Isosceles triangle.

Step 3. Sitting comfortably but upright on a meditation pillow in the center of the Records room, feel your weight on the cushion and relax into it. Inhale the ether breathing in and out through your nose, taking a few deep breaths to allow the ether to settle in your lungs. Let your awareness gather at a point at the base of your spine; realize it as a point of energy. Notice the expanding awareness you experience.

STEP 4. Move your expanding awareness to your crown of your head; feel your awareness naturally move towards your forehead where the Shield rests. Notice what sensations you feel. Feel these two points align, connected by a line of energy, permeating from inside the skull. Allow energy to move freely between these two points.

STEP 5. Let your awareness come to rest at the origin of the energy, at the base of your skull.

STEP 6. From the origin point, envision the line of light extending upwards through the badge, into the Akashic Record. Breathing out, let your inquiries travel into the Record.

STEP 7. Breathing in, accept the sensory data entering your mind. Allow it to fill your whole body from the feet up to the crown of your head, bringing a feeling of an alternative being or existence. Return your awareness and your breathing to the center of your being.

STEP 8. Allow the alternative experiences to transpire in their pre-ordained sequence. Notice the events occurring around you and take mental notes of the things you see.

STEP 9. As the sequence ends, allow your regular awareness to realign. Once your regular awareness is re-engaged, document the information you perceived in the Akashic Records Room.

CHAPTER 5: THE BLACKLINE

INTRODUCTION

The Blackline describes the phenomenon where a ghostly apparition of a subway train with six cars suddenly appears in New York Subway Stations at high speeds and disappears from subway platforms. The train is operated by a phantom conductor who screams out the window of the train as it barrels down the tracks.

The Blackline Subway Car has been sighted in abandoned tunnels by subway workers. Others have seen it passing through stations at blinding speeds after midnight. Some even claim the Blackline picks up passengers, who disappear into the train only to "get off" in Hell. The interior of the train is described as being empty, or containing monstrous passengers.

Some stories connect the Blackline with the abandoned Sedgewick Ave. Station. Sedgewick has a reputation for being haunted. The old saying goes: "Only the dead get off at Sedgewick." The legends of the Blackline can be compared to those of the Flying Dutchman.

LEGEND

Conductor Anthony Harris was a staunch train operator who once proclaimed that not even the Devil himself would stop him from ensuring his passengers arrived on time. The story goes: in 1932, during rush hour, on the way to Sedgwick Avenue Station, a series of rail accidents altered Harris's schedule making him potentially late. Harris walked the train, swearing to the passengers and screaming at Lucipher that he would get his passengers to their stations on time, no matter what might happen. The train was told to slow down, but Harris barreled into the station though there was already a docked train inside. Just before colliding with the stationed train the Devil spoke to him, proposing Harris sell or trade his soul for the timely arrival of his passengers. Harris replied: 'May I be eternally damned if I do, though I should ride these rails till the Day of Judgment if my passengers arrive at their destinations.' And to be sure, though his passengers made it, he never did go into that station. For it is believed that he continues to travel about the rails still, and will do so long enough. This train is never seen but with terrible winds and horrible screams along with it.

USES OF THE BLACKLINE

The Blackline allows the Occult Crimes Taskforce Officers near instantaneous transport throughout New York City. The subway cars serve as a mobile forensics lab, medical car, armory and additional car for reinforcements when needed.

SHASTEEN, TONY

OCCULT CRIMES TASKFORCE

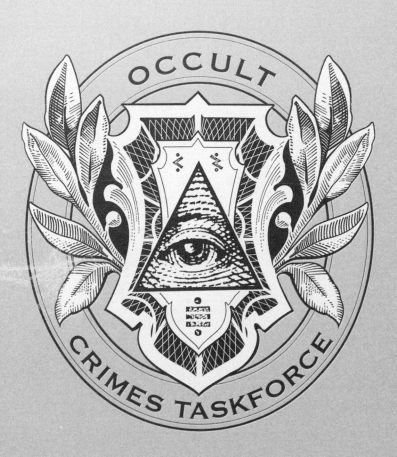

Occult Crimes Taskforce Illustration File

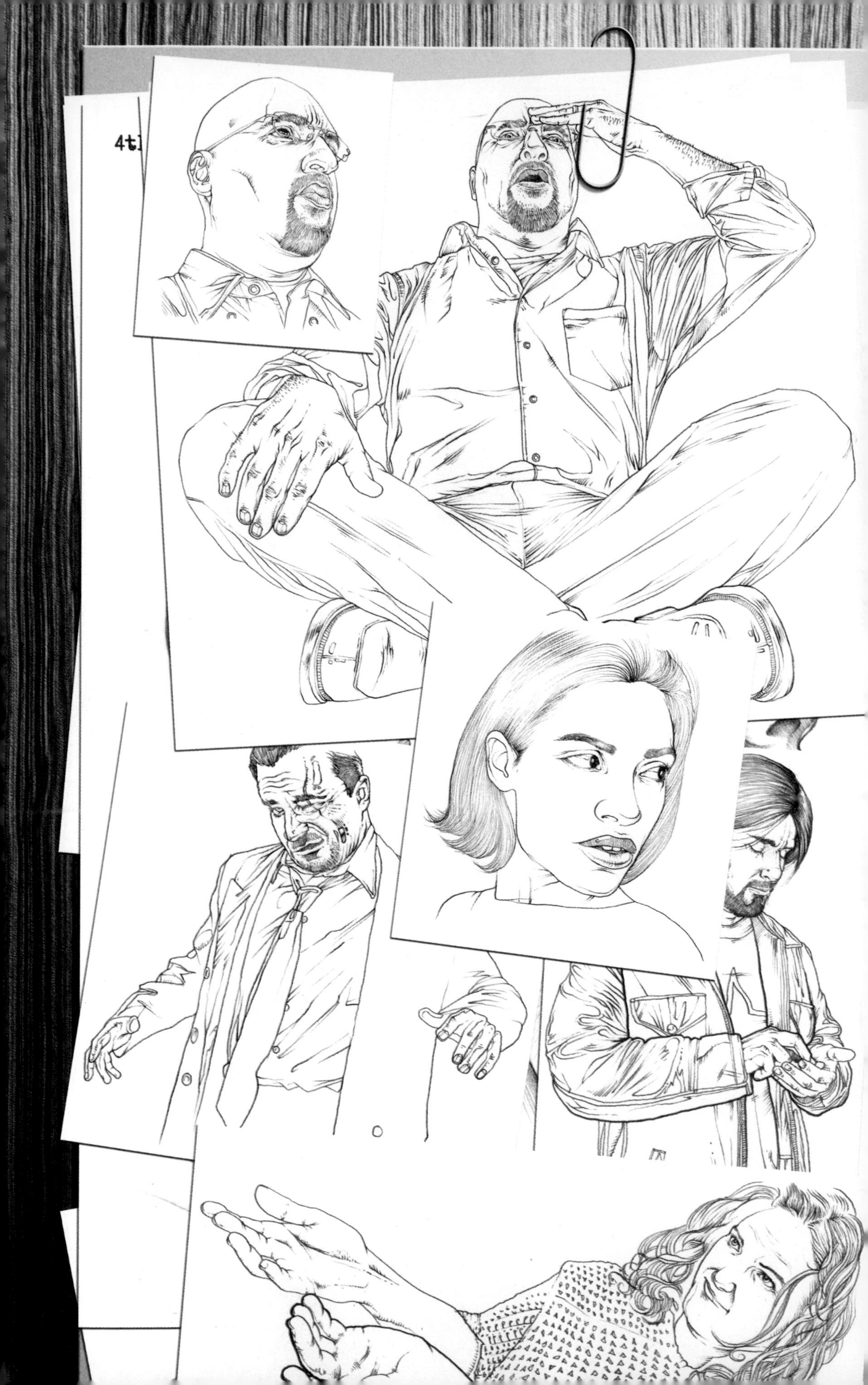

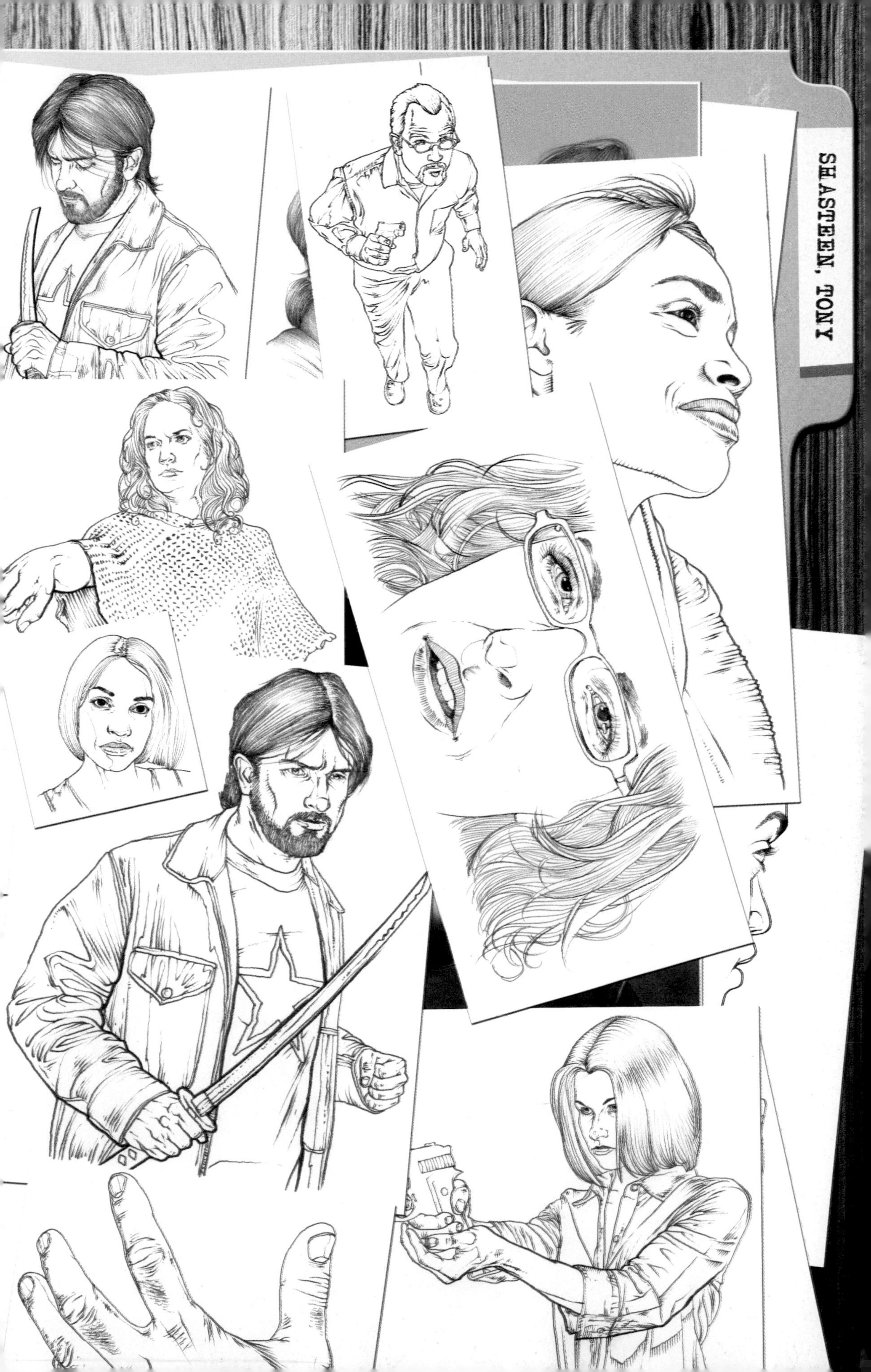
SHASTEEN, TONY

4th cover pencils

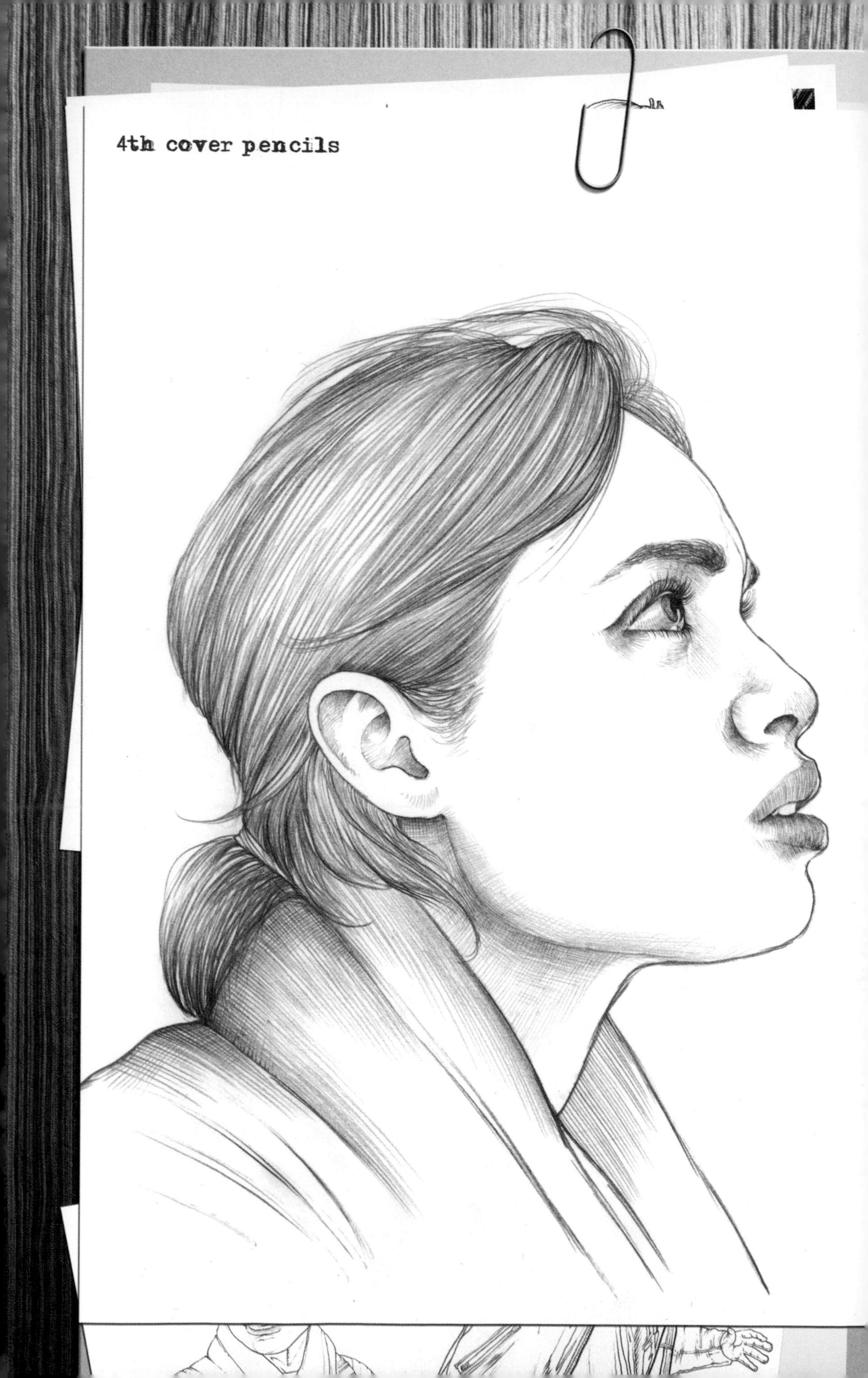

cover process

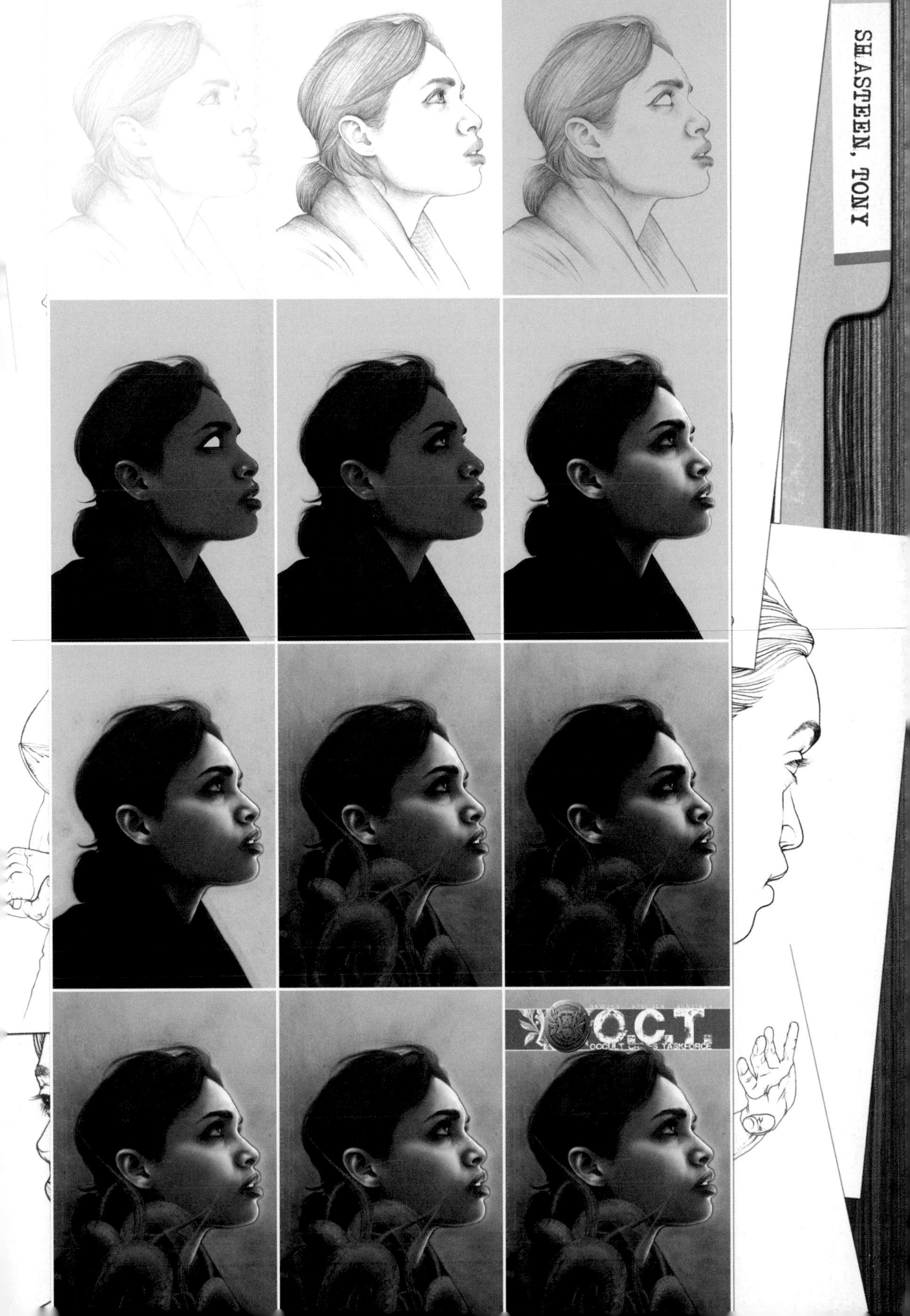

SHASTEEN, TONY

O.C.T
OCCULT CRIMES TASKFORCE

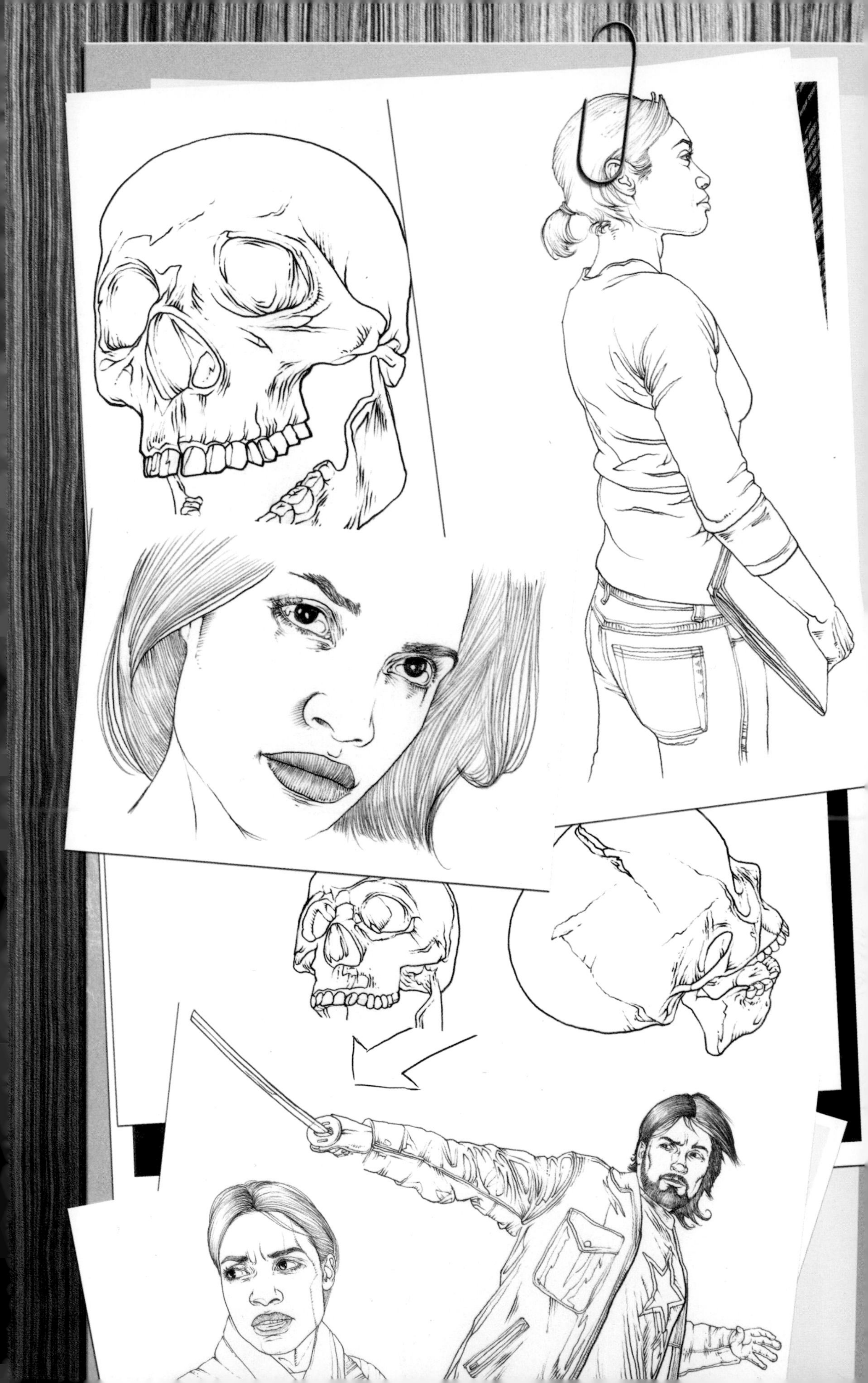

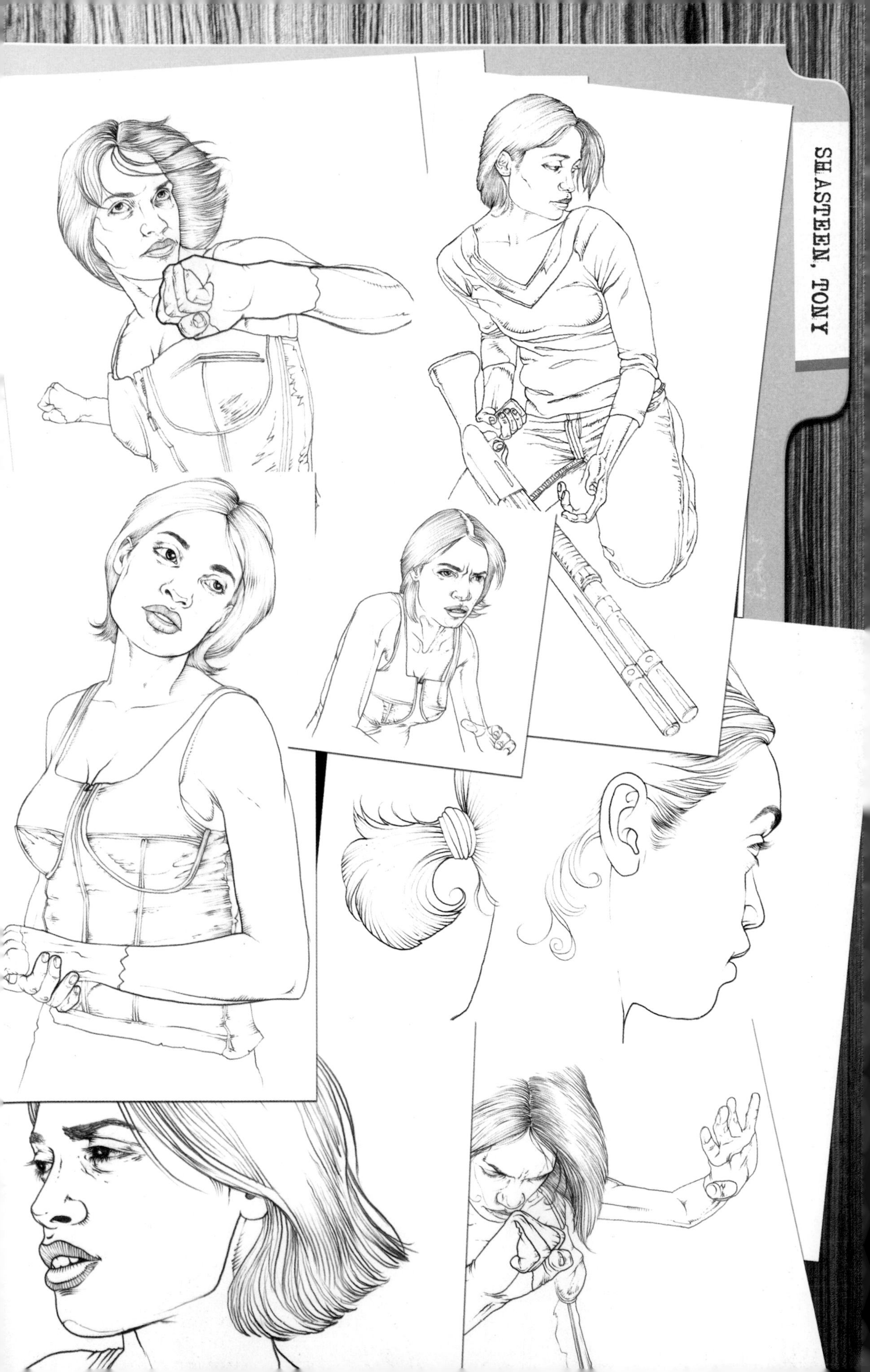
SHASTEEN, TONY

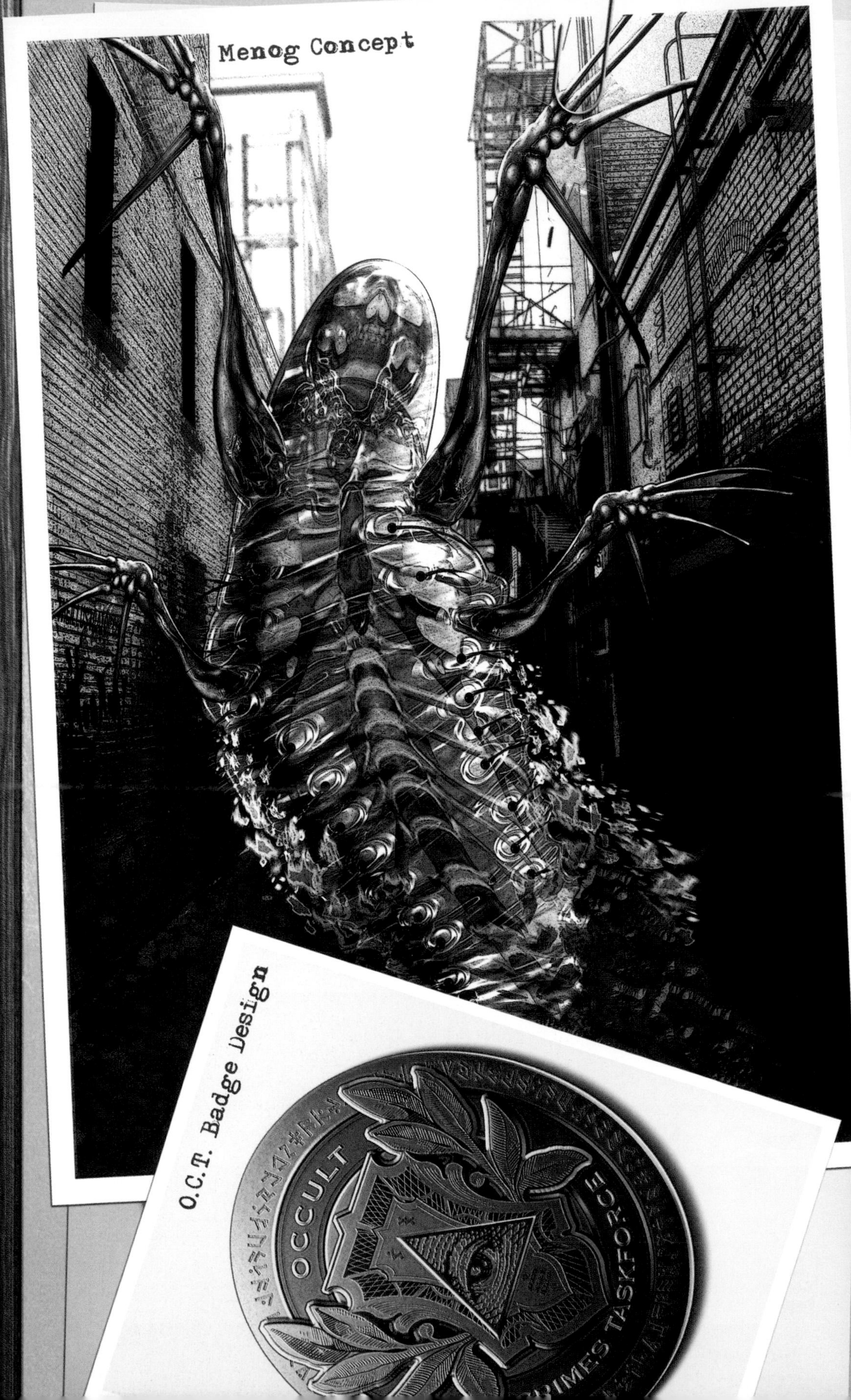
Menog Concept
O.C.T. Badge Design
OCCULT
CRIMES TASKFORCE

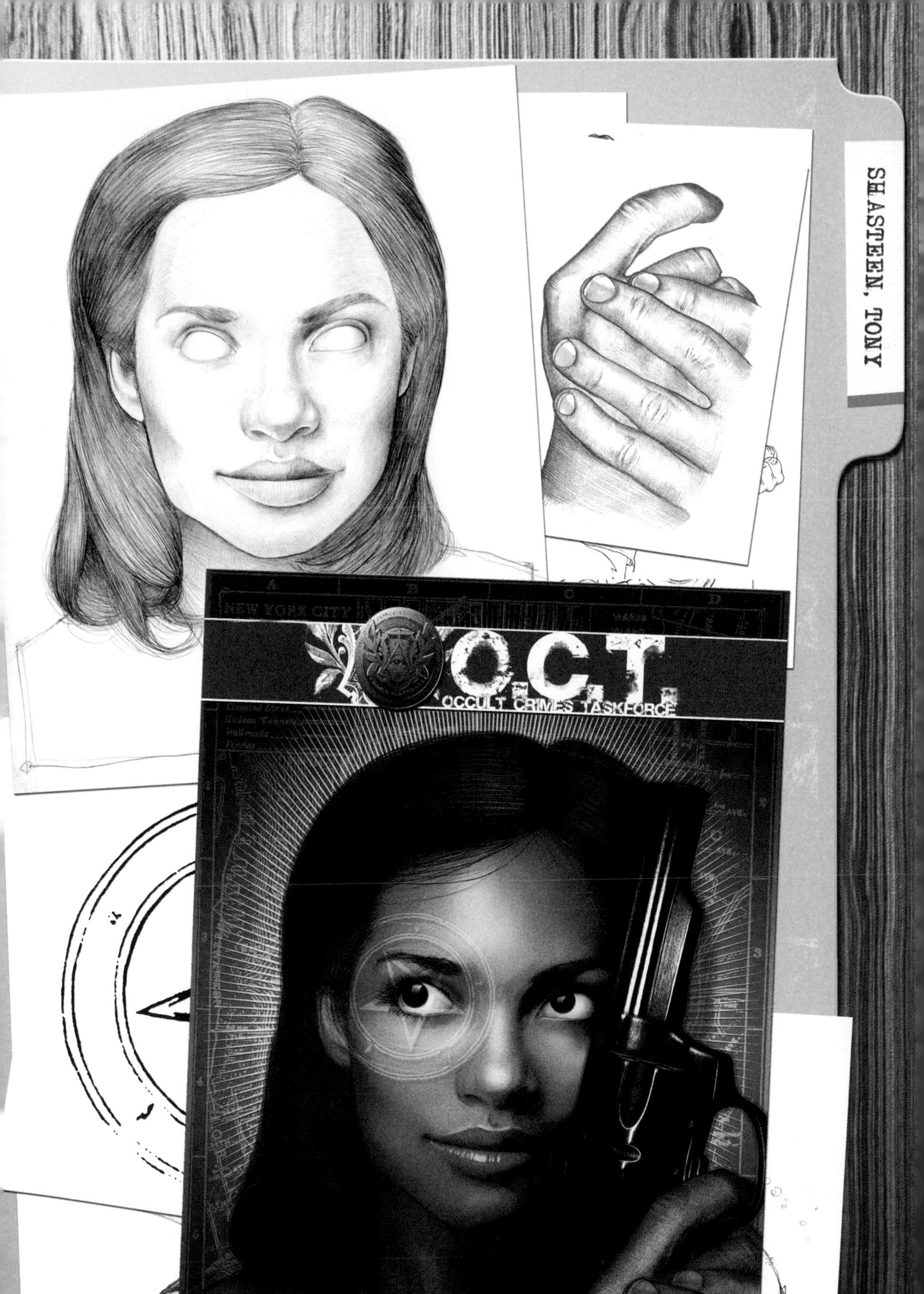
SHASTEEN, TONY
NEW YORK CITY
O.C.T.
OCCULT CRIMES TASKFORCE

This was the original cover we used for the pitch. We decided it didn t grab the reader as much as it should for the first issue. – TS

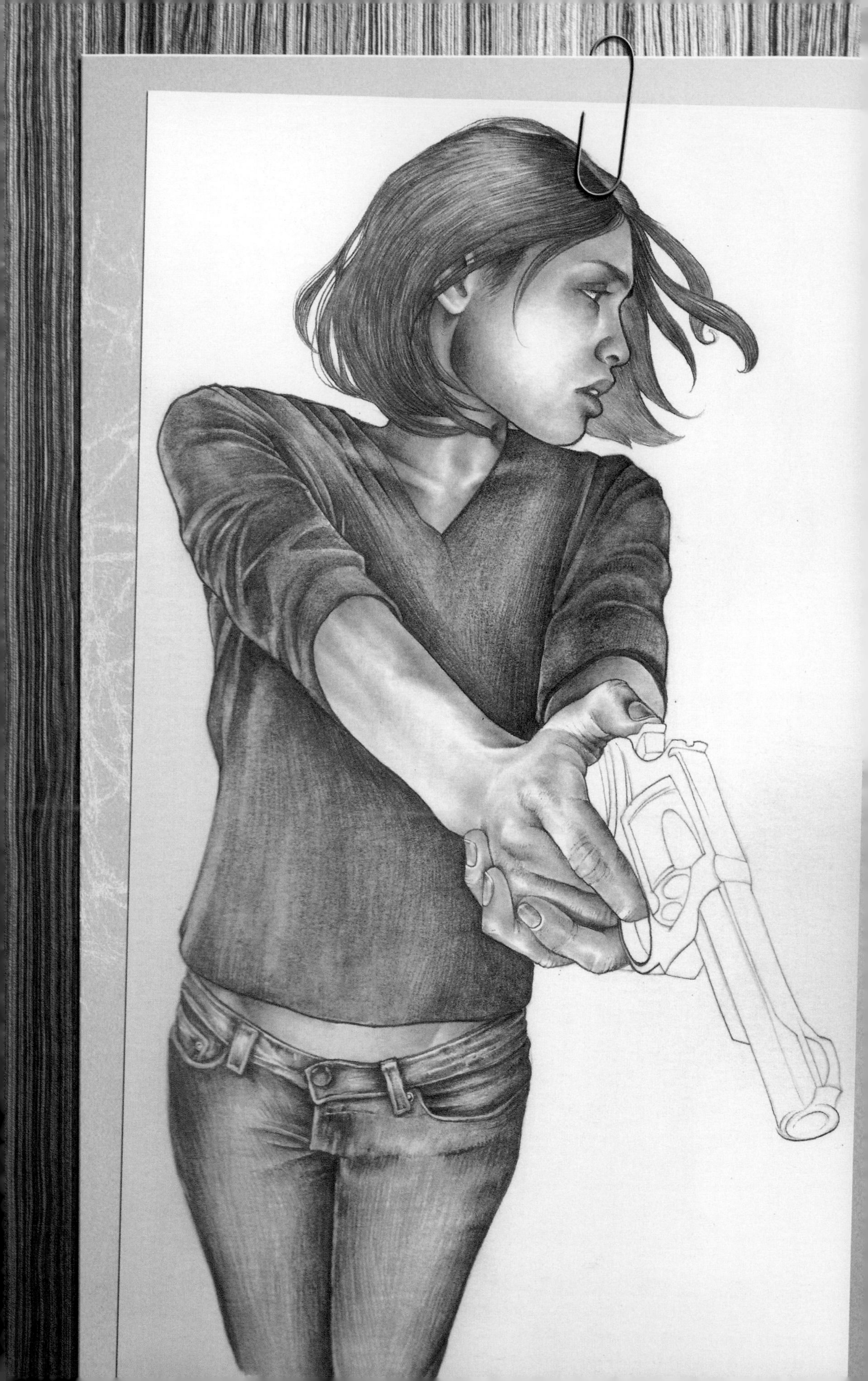

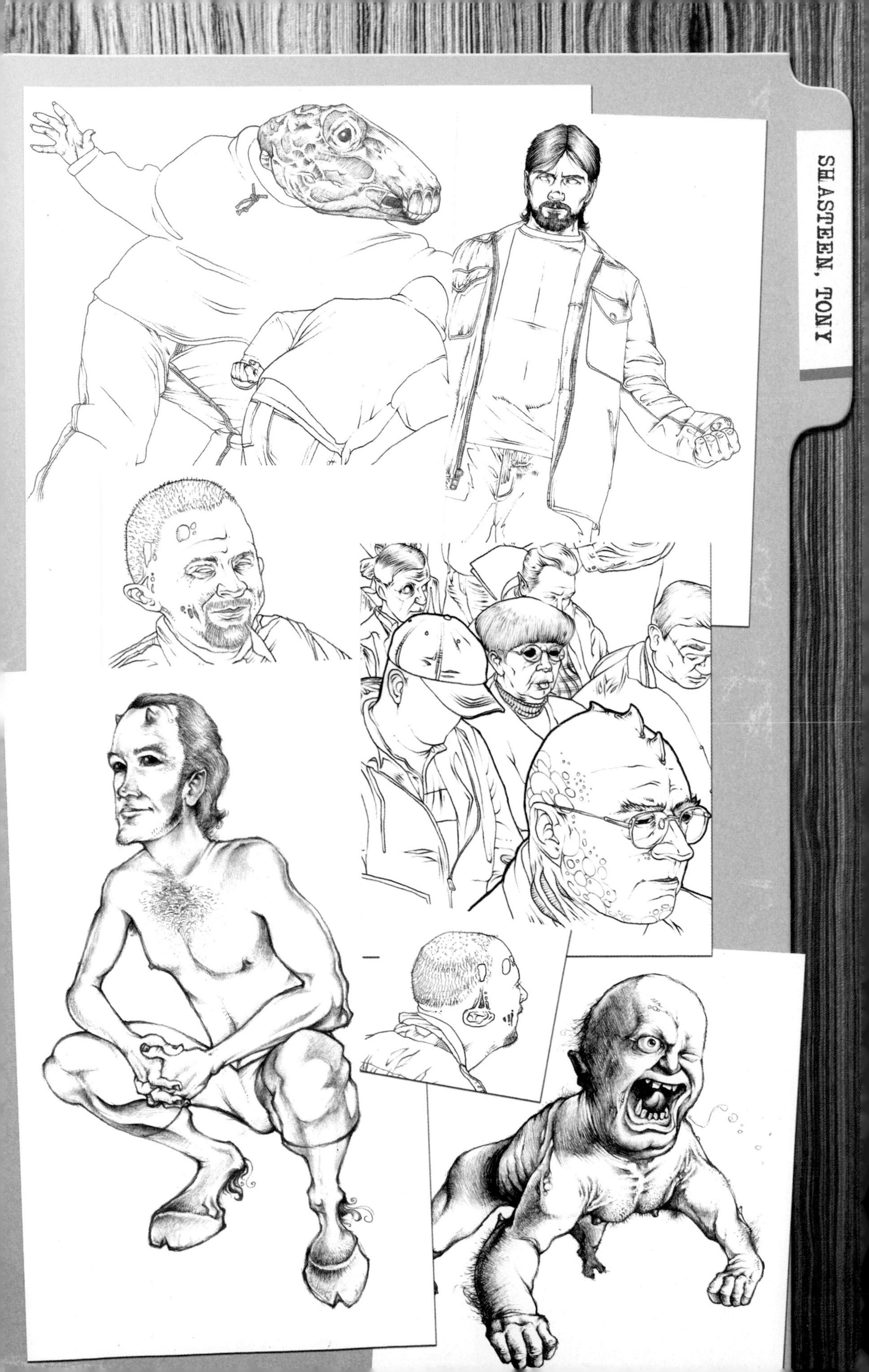
SHASTEEN, TONY

COVER GALLERY

Quick thumbnail sketches for cover concepts.

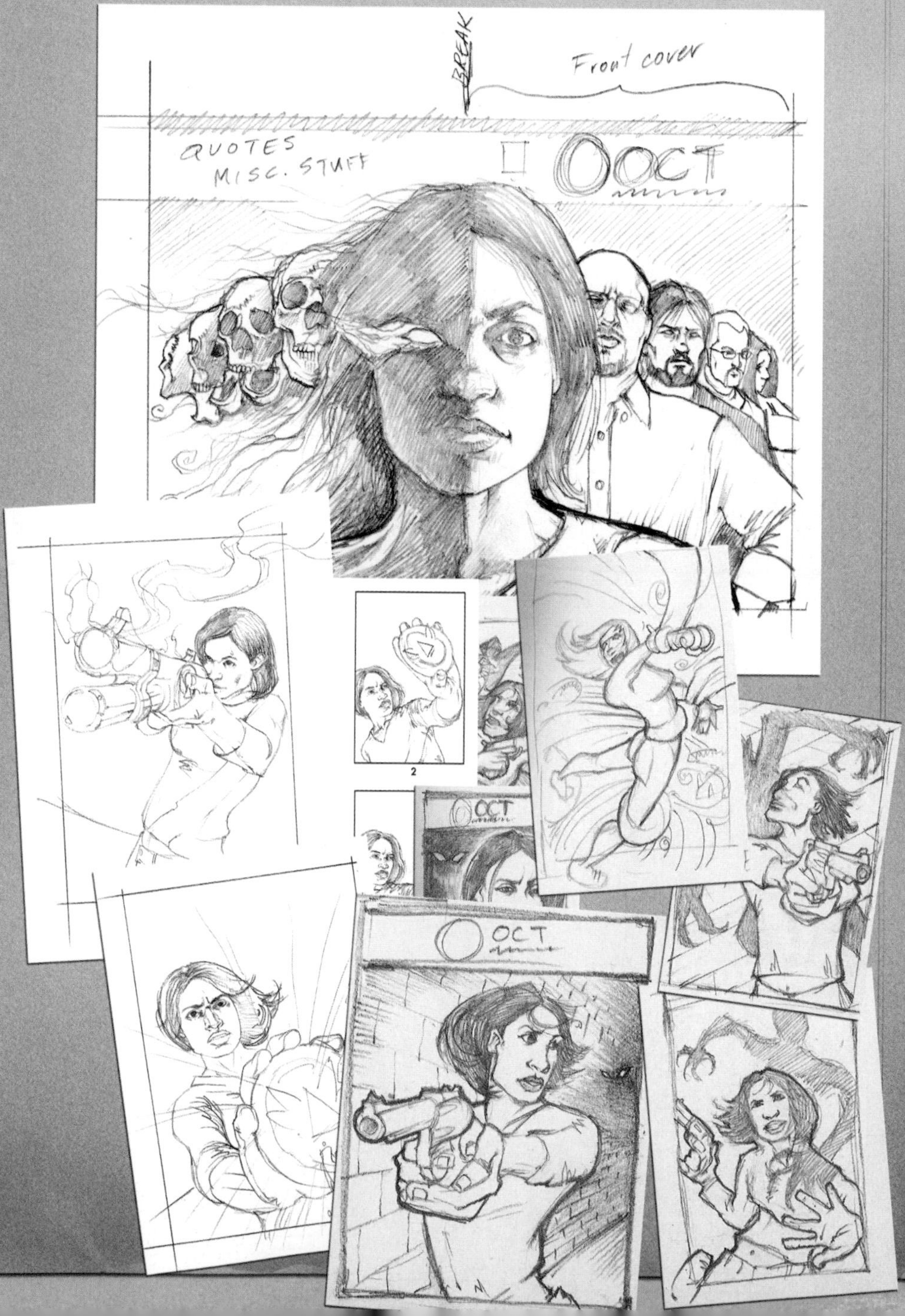
BREAK
Front cover
QUOTES
MISC. STUFF
OCT
2
OCT
OCT

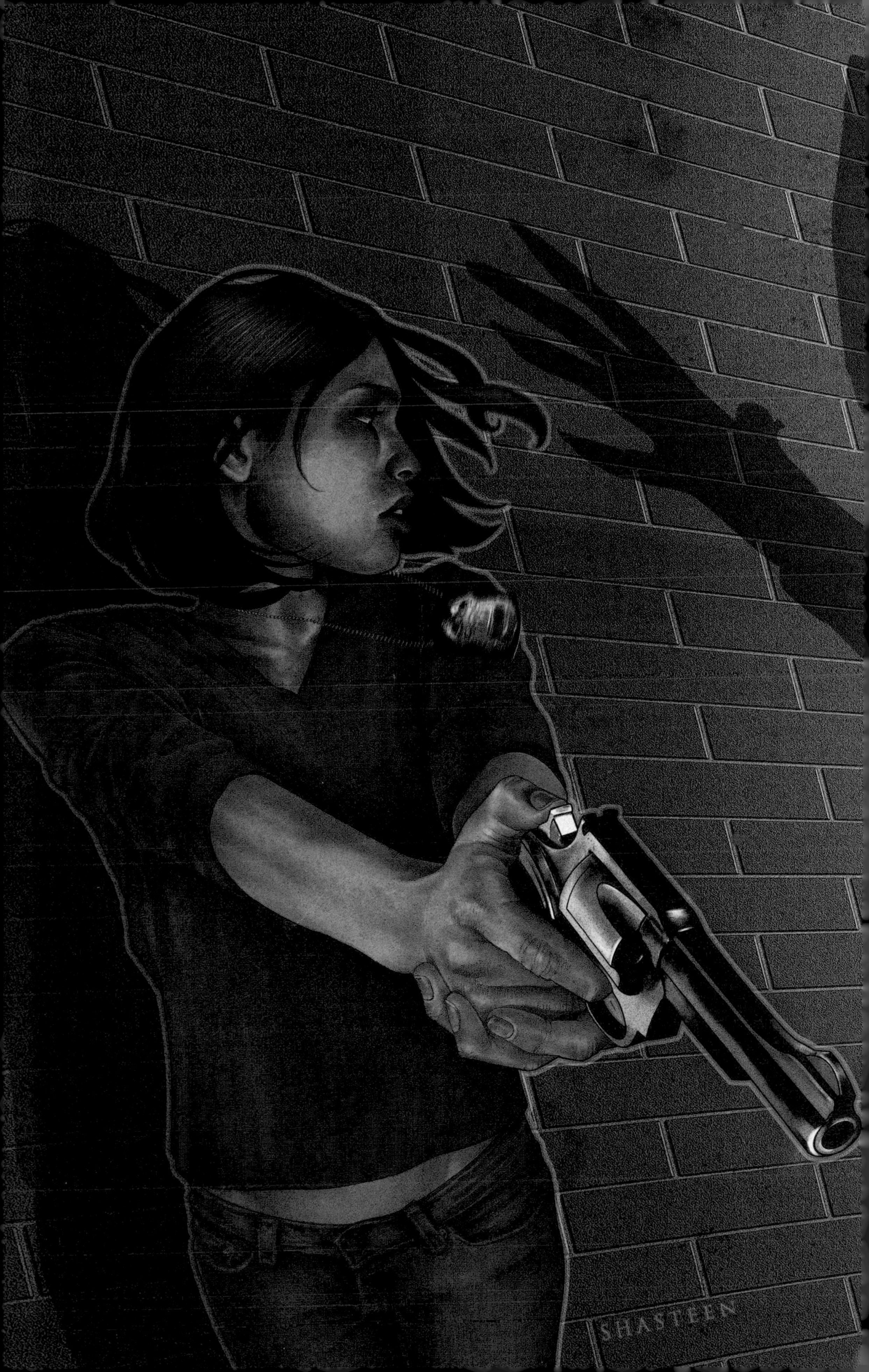
SHASTEEN

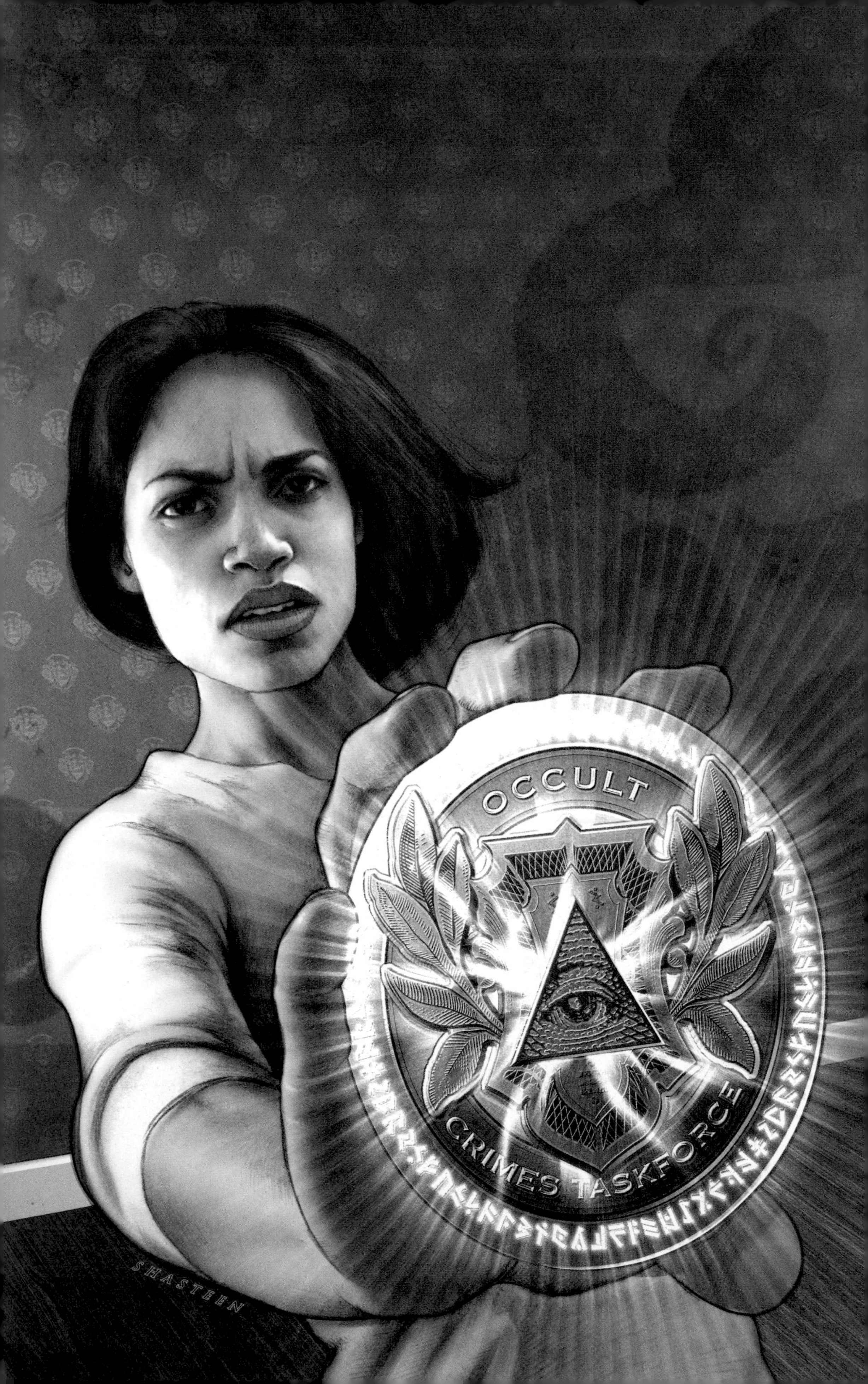
OCCULT
CRIMES TASKFORCE
SHASTEEN

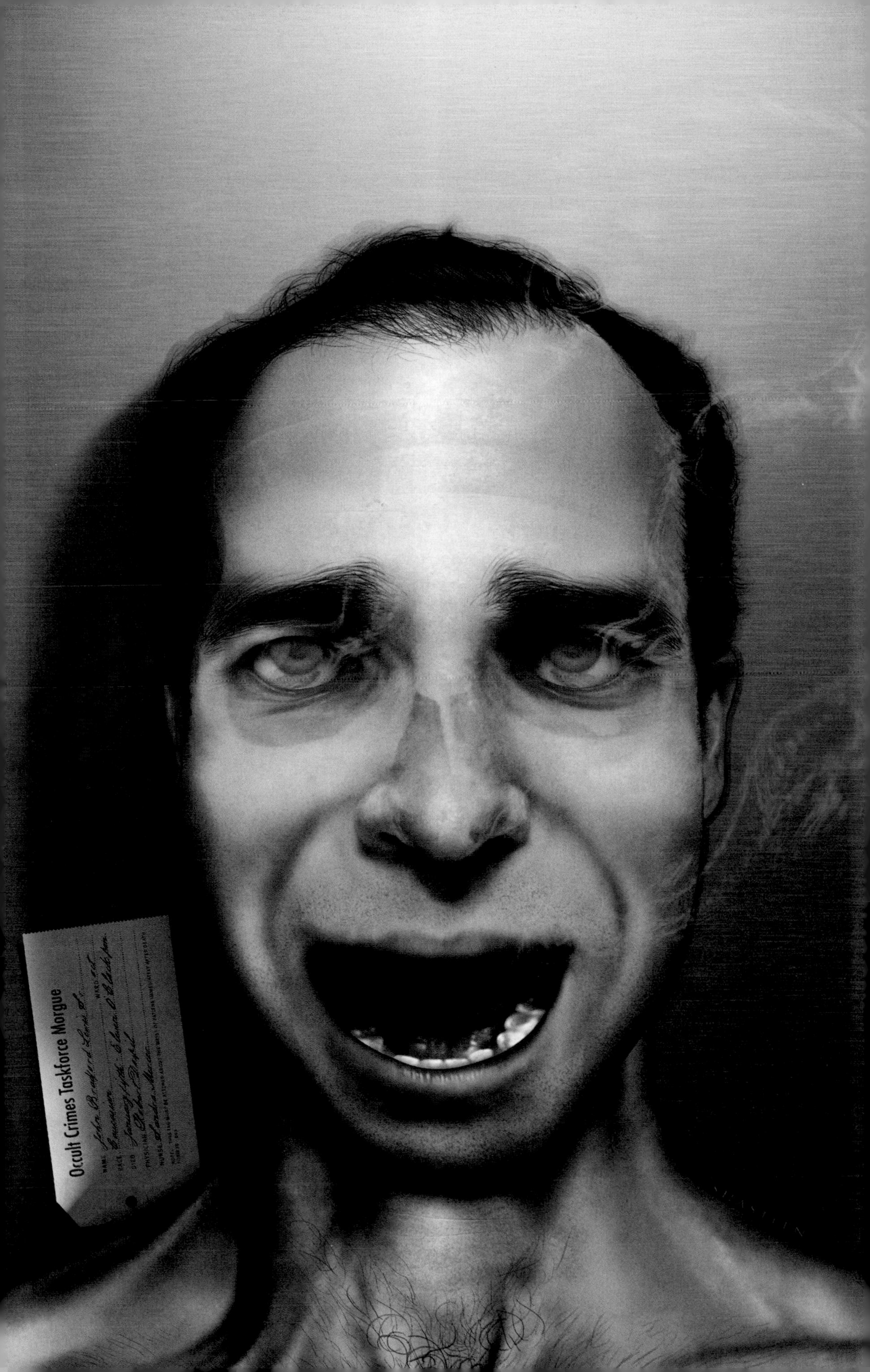
Occult Crimes Taskforce Morgue

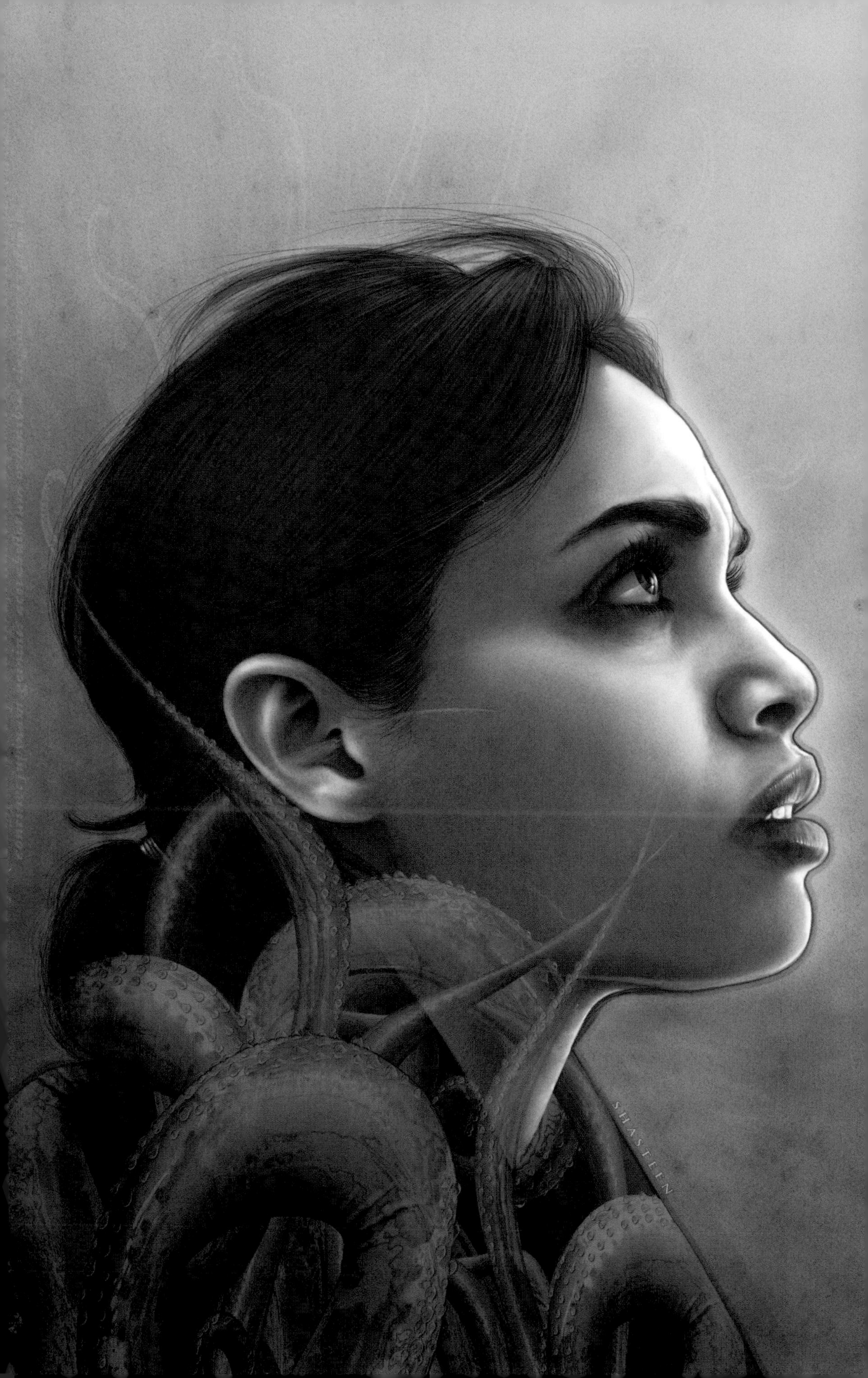
SHASTEEN

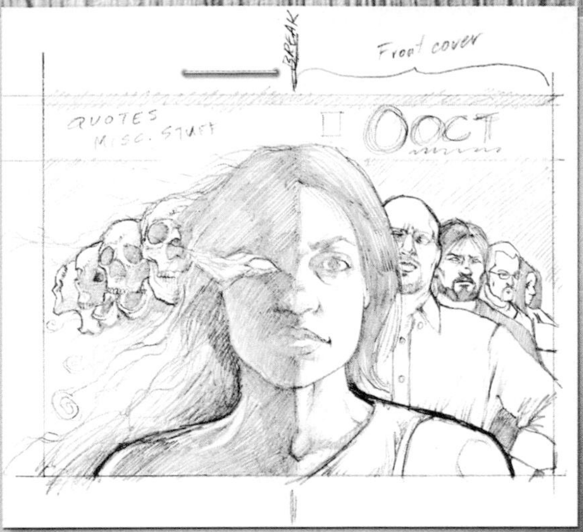
BREAK
Front cover
QUOTES
MISC. STUFF
OOCT

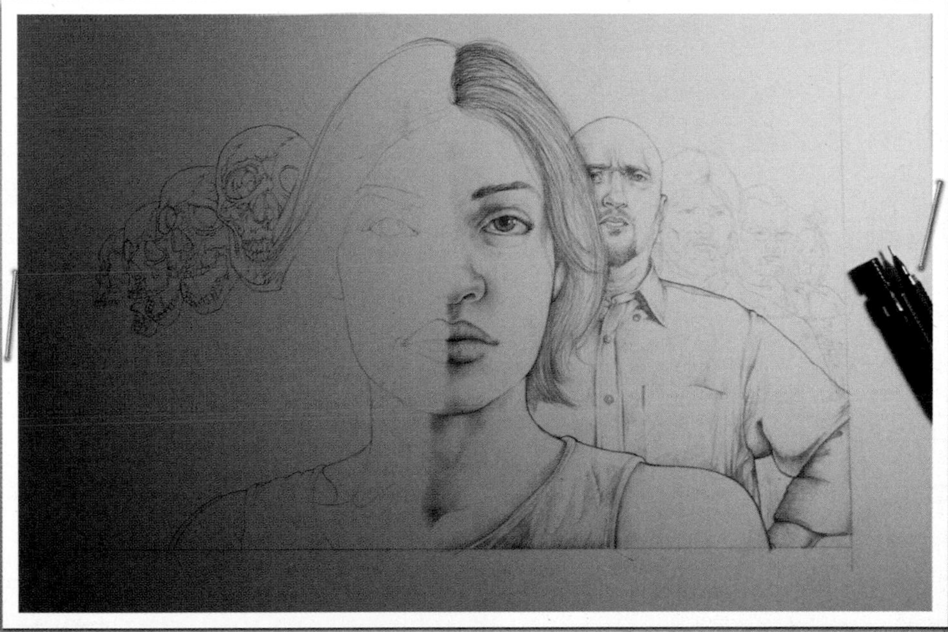

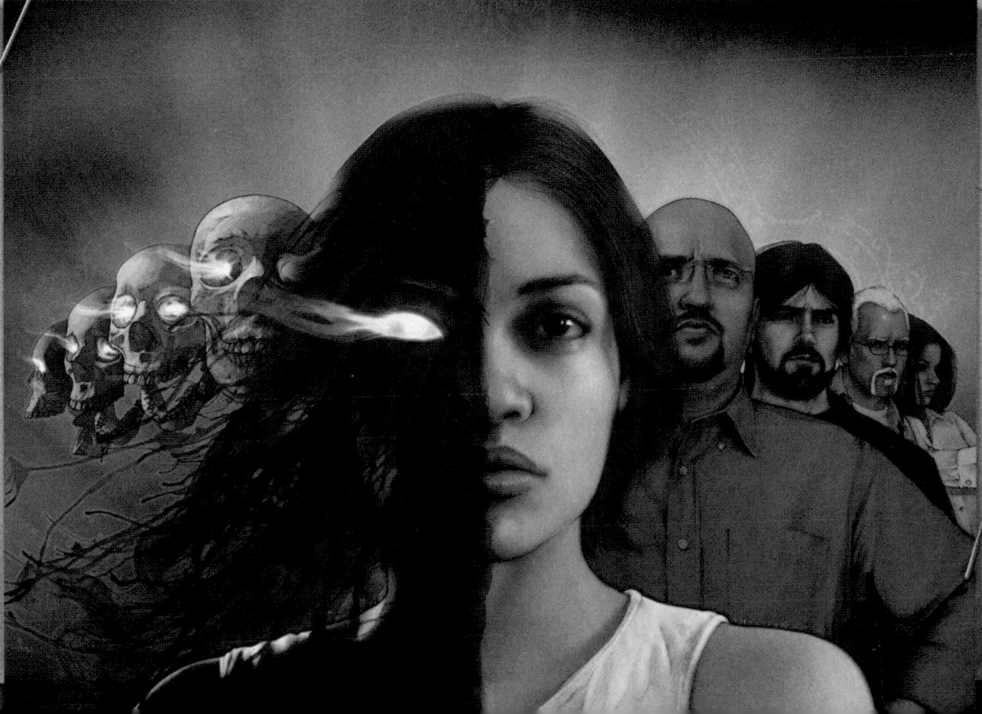

the Ride™

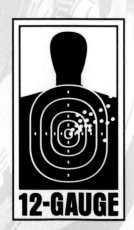

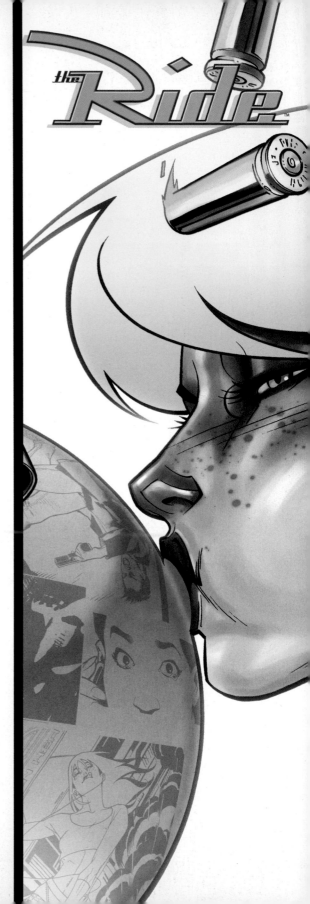

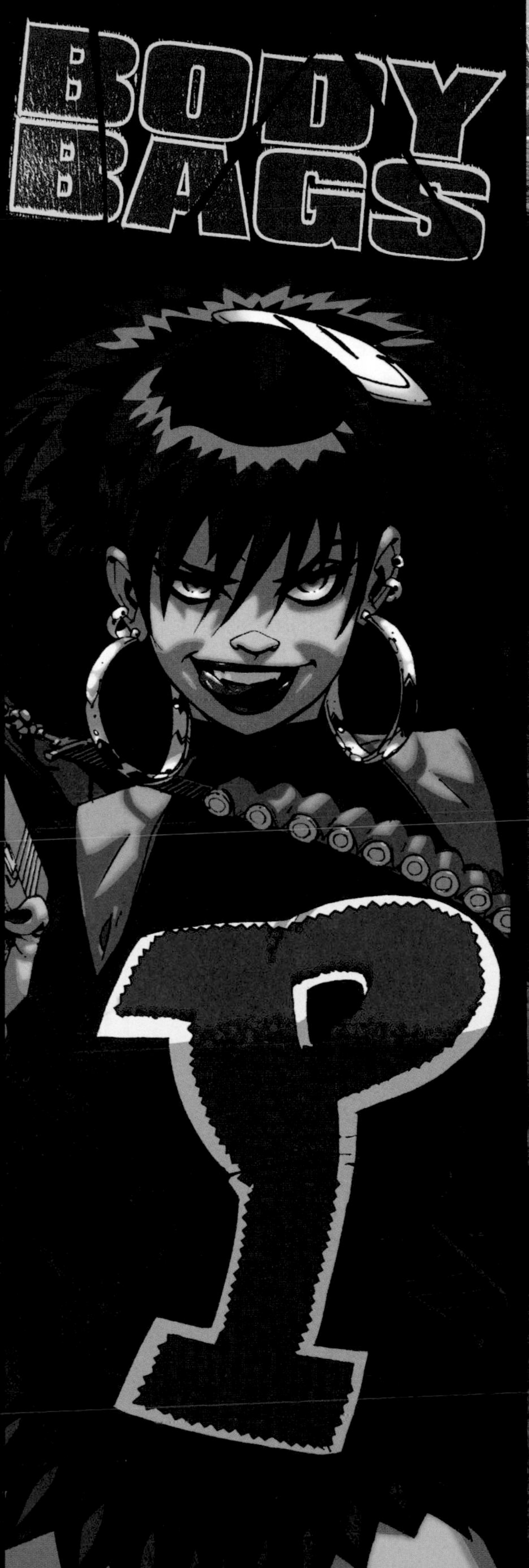
BODY
BAGS

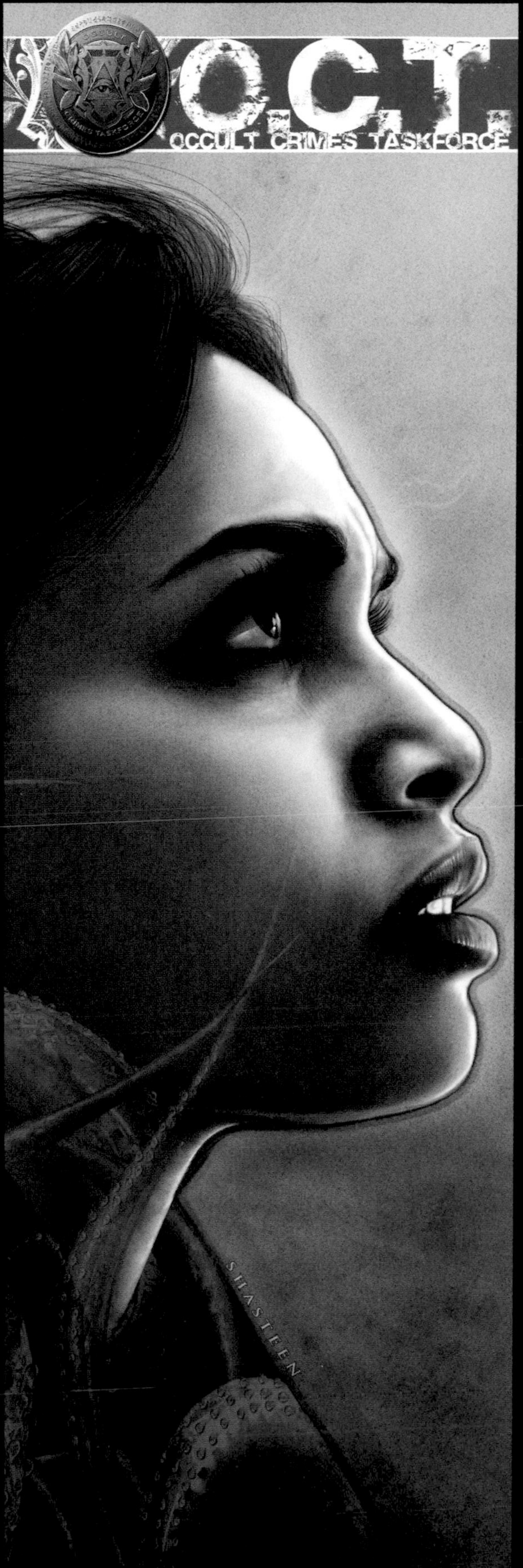
O.C.T.
OCCULT CRIMES TASKFORCE
SHASTEEN

PAUL JENKINS'
SIDEKICK

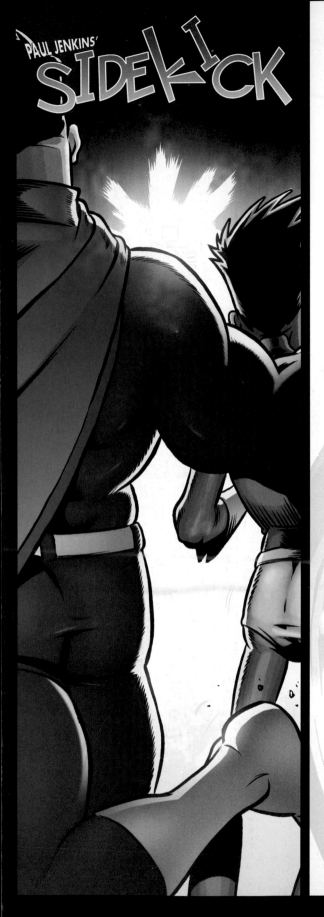

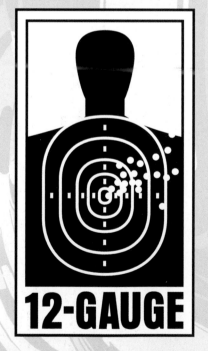